Tomorrow's Office

Creating effective and humane interiors

Santa Raymond and Roger Cunliffe

E & FN SPON
Taylor & Francis Group

London and New York

Publised by E & FN Spon, an imprint of
the Taylor & Francis Group

Design by Stephen Cary
Typeset in 9.5/11pt Gill Sans Light
Printed in Hong Kong by Dah Hua Press Co. Ltd

First edition 1997

First published in paperback 2000

© 1997 Santa Raymond and Roger Cunliffe

ISBN 0 419 21240 X (Hbk)
ISBN 0 419 24400 X (Pbk)

A catalogue record for this book is available from the British Library

Dedication

For our respective children:
Jemima, Joshua and Tabitha; and Rachel, Harry and Luke.
They are tomorrow's gold collar workers:
tomorrow's offices are for them.

Contents

Foreword by Professor Charles Hampden-Turner iv
Preface vi
Acknowledgements vi

1 Introduction 1
   *Workplace: British Telecom Westside,
   Hemel Hempstead* 4

Part I Background

2 Context 11
   Workplace: VIA International, London 18
3 Purposes and concepts 21
   *Workplace: Digital Equipment Company,
   Stockholm* 29

Part II Needs

4 Activities 33
   *Workplace: Defence Research Agency
   Haslar, Gosport* 44
5 Communications 47
   *Workplace: British Airways Compass
   Centre, Heathrow* 54
6 Spaces 59
   Workplace: Sol Cleaning Service, Helsinki 66
   Workplace: Barr and Stroud, Glasgow 78
7 Ambience 81
   Workplace: Chiat/Day, New York 94

Part III Technics

8 Process 98
   Workplace: Andersen Consulting, London 114
9 Space planning 118
   *Workplace: The Automobile Association,
   Basingstoke* 130
10 Settings 132
   Workplace: Ernst & Young, Chicago 148
11 Building services 150
   Workplace: Western Morning News, Plymouth 166
12 Furniture 170
   Workplace: PowerGen, Coventry 184

Appendices

A Procurement routes 188
B Selection criteria for consultants 189
C Data collection 190
D Space-planning benchmarks 190
E Assessment checklist for system furniture 192
F PowerGen – Coventry: arrangements for
   building occupation 193

Glossary 195
References 196
Index 197

Foreword

Professor Charles
Hampden-Turner

The patterns which connect

The late anthropologist and epistemologist Gregory Bateson used to hold up before his class a collection of sea shells. How could you tell, he asked, that a living creature once made and inhabited this? It is now a dead object, found upon a beach.

The clues to life, suggested Bateson, lie in 'the patterns which connect': the wondrous, intricate organization of the whole. It is from such aesthetic patterning that we know that shells are of life and for life: fitting habitats for living organisms.

I got the same feeling reading this book. If offices can take on the patterns of living, working and knowledge generating, then they can accommodate that life, channel its growth, celebrate all its myriad connections. For in a very real sense office design challenges our potential. There are spaces, crannies, connections, arenas into which our creative capacities can flow. Unused space is like unused human potential – sealed compartments suggesting sealed minds. It is estimated that we actually only use 10% of a computer's total functions. Are offices to become similar temples to unused opportunity?

Not if these authors can help it. They have an uncanny grasp of the dilemma-resolving capacities of good design. 'Change has engulfed humanity,' they say; 'We must dig ourselves out.' Their metaphorical solution? A friendly St Bernard, amid a growing complementarity of shared viewpoints. New regulations for the stereotyped worker must somehow be broadened to accommodate human beings in their genuine varieties. How are we to reconcile the fact that employees are hired to do our bidding, yet with their 'gold collars' have so much more to contribute than their compliance? The answers lie somewhere in the designed environments which both limit and augment the directions of enquiry.

Equally impressive is the authors' grasp of the ongoing tensions of questions and answers. Often the client does not know into what constellations the enterprise may grow, has not thought through the permutations and the possibilities. Yet the well-placed question models the challenges which the future may hold.

When people assemble they are always individuals. They also share on-going relationships, which can retrieve and retain far more than the sum of those individuals themselves. The secrets of the 'learning organization' lie in this 'more', the living whole that transcends the sum of its parts. The authors set out boldly on their elusive quest for this integrity.

To be flexible without fragmentation, to combine home styles with work styles, to be stimulated to excitement without straying into boredom on the one side or chronic stress on the other – these are the balancing acts the authors seek. They seek to combine function with feeling, inspiration with workability, space with the possibilities for filling it.

I find myself wishing in these days of fad and fashion in management theory, that clients could be as wise as these designers and could see as many possibilities and pitfalls. The way current management theory is going we need only warehouses for the storage of temporary workers, each with his locker and lapel badge that turns red at the end of the week when his assignment runs out. In the present fashion of downsizing and re-engineering, the corporation is conceived of as a machine and needs hangars or garages to house it, permitting access by consultant plumbers to 'fix the machine'.

But all these are issues for corporate clients of office interiors, not for the designers themselves. It remains to hope that this volume will be an inspiration, not simply to fellow designers, but to those who use design services to create habitats not for machinery but for humanity. In the present atmosphere of massive downsizing in which money is being redistributed from wealth creators to shareholders, office interiors which facilitate creativity and communication may have too few takers.

My favourite metaphor of current business fashion comes from *Alice in Wonderland*. Alice is trying to use a live flamingo as a mallet, a hedgehog as a ball and a stooping man as a hoop. All three 'misbehave' as only living creatures can. Tenniel's picture is a lot funnier than the current business reality but no less absurd. We have a business scene of imaginary implements run amok, a business-in-legoland of bits and pieces contracted out. Books of this quality remind us of the role of design and vision, of the pattern which connects, and its testimony to life.

Charles Hampden-Turner

Chiat/Day, New York: View through a project room door. Architects: Pesce Ltd

Preface

ROLF GIBBS

Santa Raymond

PAUL MELLOR

Roger Cunliffe

Opposite: IBM, Bedfont Lakes, London: IBM was one of the first companies to use free-address working. Places for informal meetings are a central element of this approach. The atrium restaurant in this building provides an effective setting.
Architects: Michael Hopkins and Partners
Reproduced with the permission of IBM UK Ltd

'Meet the only other architect at the party,' said our host. Small talk revealed that we both had an interest in writing about offices. Casual exchanges of ideas led eventually to collaboration. Developing the ideas and finding the right publisher took further time. Since then the pace has increased – if only to keep up with the stream of changes which are affecting workplaces and the communications between them. But it has been a long gestation.

Architect turned interior designer and architect turned management consultant; woman and man; experience in large organizations and of home working; designers of offices, homes and places to learn; work in Britain and around the world; poet and writer of government reports; Apple Macintosh and IBM-compatible: we are a dissimilar pair, yet with much in common.

In particular, we believe that our complementary experiences fuse into a shared viewpoint. Change has engulfed the humanity of the workplace in an avalanche of management theories and IT systems. It needs to be dug out. We hope that our book will be a useful spade – or at least a friendly St Bernard.

For all our experiences, writing a book has been something new. Researching such a fast-changing field has been challenging. We could not have done either without the help of a wide network of advisers, both old friends and new acquaintances. To all those mentioned below, and to any we may have inadvertently forgotten, our warm thanks for your advice, stimulation and encouragement. We have valued all three. This is especially true of those who showed us around your workplaces and took time to explain the intricacies of their workings – the practical, the technical, the humane and the strategic. Your contributions have grounded this book in reality.

Charles Hampden-Turner's foreword has provided another kind of grounding – relating what we say about the workplace to his clear views on where organizations need to go. This book is our attempt to reach out and close the gap between the two; so we greatly appreciate his hand stretched out in return.

We owe a debt to Alexander Fyjis-Walker for tutoring us in the basics of book publishing; and our warmest thanks go to our editor, Caroline Mallinder, and all her team at E & FN Spon, for guiding us through its intricacies, as well as for her encouragement throughout the project. It was her idea that Stephen Cary should design the book in close collaboration with us: he has given it clarity and integrity. This has been enhanced by the generosity of those organizations and individuals who provided photographs free of charge.

Nevertheless, the appearance – and content – of the book would not have been the same without the sponsorship of Herman Miller Limited, and the enthusiastic support of its Communications Director for Europe, David Taylor. It has enabled us to produce a visually much richer book; and time spent with Herman Miller's researchers in Michigan opened our eyes to much that is going on in office design not only in the United States but worldwide. The company's breadth of vision – which goes far beyond just office furniture – stimulated our thinking at a critical stage of the book's development.

The home office may have its advantages, but obsessive authors are not the most comfortable house-mates. Throughout our labours our families have been wonderful, patient and supportive – during what must have seemed like the pregnancy of a brontosaurus.

SR + RC, September 1996

Acknowledgements

So many people have helped us, in so many ways: technical information and judgement, putting us in touch with the right person, venturing ideas, time-consuming tours of buildings. Our sincere thanks go to: Jan Ackermans, Alastair Alexander, Suzi Allison, Bill Anderson, Lorenzo Apicella, Tim Arnold, Waltraud Beckman, Alan Black, Bill Bordass, Chris Brandon, Douglas Brennan, Donatella Brun, Joshua Burrill, Hugh Cade, Martin Callingham, Sam Cassels, Dinah Casson, Charlotte Chambers, Tchaik Chassay, Bill Church, Oliver Colman, Malcolm Davidson, Damon de Laszlo, Wiebke and Gerard Eckle, Peter and Joanna Eley, Stephen Embley, Adam Fergusson, Graham Firth, David Fish, Max Fordham, Mary Fox-Linton, Lynne Franks, Robert Fry, Michael Gilmour, Mike Gray, Gary Griffiths, Shelley Hampden-Turner, Barry Hannaford, Andrew Harrison, Judy Hillman, Robert Hinds, David Hinton, Noel Hodson, Arne Hoggren, Geoff Hollington, Chris Hood, Paul Humdeman, Brian Humphreys, Ahmet Huseyen, Sarah Hutchinson, Jim Hutton, Tony Ingrams, Kristian Isager, Alan Jerome, Jonny Johansson, Mike Johnson, Liisa Joronen, Stephen Jupp, Stephen Kalman, Alan Kell, Ben Kelly, David King, Francis Kinsman, Andrew Laing, Sarah Langton-Lockton, Judie Lannon, Richard Lee, John Leonard, David Levy, David Lindsey, Clive Loveless, Peter Lyon, Tom McAulay, Penny McGuire, Regina McNulty,

Kate Macintosh, Lynne Maddock, John Mills, John Miller, Sue Mims, Kathleen Molnar-Sinritch, Alan Moses, Christopher Nash, David Norman, Wally Olins, John Outram, Clive Pallot, Richard Pedler, Gaetano Pesce, Martin Petersen, Graham Phoenix, Martin Pickard, Keith Priest, Jerry Ramsden, Chris Ridgewell, Phil Roberts, Richard Rogers, Lynton Ross,

Phillip Ross, Philip Sadler, Jane Scruton, Antony Snow, Denise Stacey, Marilyn Standley, Bob Steedman, Ian Sternfeldt, Elinor Stewart, Christine Stratton, Derek Sugden, Colin Sully, André Tammes, Karen Teague, Alan Tye, Ken Upham, Ray Watts, Ben and Cindy Weese, Alan White, Jane Wiggins, Tony Wills, Peter Wilson, Peter Wingrave, Gary Withers,

Marcia Witte, Robin Worthington and Harvey Young.

Photographs

We should like to thank the following individuals and organizations for providing photographs:
Arup Associates, Ove Arup and Partners, Austin-Smith

Lord, Crispin Boyle, British Telecom, Designers Guild, Digital Equipment Company, Ernst & Young, Dennis Gilbert, Herman Miller Ltd, IBM, Imagination, Jestico + Whiles, Nic Kane, Murray Symonds Associates, Pilkington Optronics, PowerGen, Bill Pye, Tim Soar, Sol Cleaning Service, Standard Life, and Western Morning News.

Chapter 1
Introduction

■ **New ways of working**

■ **New workplaces**

■ **The nature of the book – and of its readers**

Too many offices disappoint: if not when brand new, then soon afterwards.

Why?

Looking at the average office interior objectively, it is a strange place: a great barrack, with bright lights shining down on the heads of workers regimented at groups of desks and with bits of screen sticking up around the place. At the far end, perhaps, are rooms where people sit in isolation – for no very apparent reason, except that they are paid more. Windows are distant and sealed tightly shut. The air is mildly stuffy, the lights are on all day, and mid-morning coffee is luke-warm and tasteless, out of one of those machines.

What kind of place is this to be in seven hours a day, 240 days a year; when back home you have fresh air, daylight, comfortable furniture and an ambience that makes you feel good? Not all homes are wonderful, but the trend towards home working confirms that offices are not good enough.

New regulations by the barrowload complicate workplace design. Desks and chairs must now fit the worker – but an idealized worker: they do not have to be adjustable to accommodate the wide variations in real human beings. Workplace ailments are public issues, but their prevention is not just a physical matter. Management attitudes are as important as clean air and an adjustable chair.

New ways of working

Business is changing worldwide. Information technology alters what we do and how. People too are changing. The worker no longer obediently does what she is told, but follows her own inclination and asks: 'Why?'

'Why do we do it this way, rather than that way which is much quicker? Why am I imprisoned in my own little office, rather than being out on the floor exchanging ideas with the others? Why do we travel two hours every morning, to work in places much less good than home? Why – when electronics will transport my thoughts to your place, and yours to mine?'

Businesses, faced with competition to deliver the goods faster and cheaper to market, also face com-

Figure 1.1 BT Westside, Hemel Hempstead: A meeting room looks out into one of the atria, which divide each of the four floors of this 16 500m² building into four sections.
Architects: Aukett Associates

petition to attract and retain talented staff – their 'gold collar workers'. Swiftness and smartness are combining to revolutionize corporate culture. Departments and processes are no longer kept separate, but all talk to each other right from the word go – sales to design, production to marketing.

GOLD COLLAR WORKERS

In our post-industrial society the key to business success lies with 'gold collar' workers: those who deploy their knowledge, skills and personal qualities creatively and decisively, and are dedicated to adding value. Such people are highly motivated, whether as independent spirits or effective teamworkers.

At the same time they have high standards, not only of business efficiency, but of quality of life. In the past it might have been enough for offices to be efficient, and homes stylish and comfortable. But as the activities in the workplace and the home become less distinct from each other, so characteristics of both must come together. That is now the expectation.

For communication is central to new work practices. The team lean over each others' desks to discuss the new product in all its intricacies. A casual word – by the photocopier or kettle – may start a train of thought leading to a major innovation. The computer operator, isolated in her virtual world, breaks and chats and feels refreshed. And in communications the young have the edge, outstripping the precomputer generation through their virtuosity on the networks, and seizing that golden resource – knowledge.

Seizing knowledge on its own is not enough. It must be understood and assimilated to be useful. And old knowledge must be judiciously discarded, so as not to clutter up our thinking. Acquisition may be a solitary affair, but understanding and judgement often come best through debate or joint exploration. Offices should be places where people can learn together, where the 'learning organization' is more than just the sum of the individuals in it.

Flexibility is essential for this: flexibility to respond to new influences, amend old practices, follow the tradewinds when they shift; flexibility to form teams, to bring in consultants, or to go away into a corner for a quiet think. But flexible working needs flexible settings, places that can change to accommodate whatever is happening now or tomorrow.

New workplaces

New ways of working: but by and large we are stuck with the old workplaces. Better light and air, more comfortable chairs, far better communications – but still mostly the large office block in the city centre or on the edge of town, with ever-expanding floorplates in the former and car parks for the latter. Inside, the lush reception area, the intelligent lifts, the long walk to the person you want to see, the open plan with its rectilinear ordering of rounded bodies. Evolution – yes; revolution – not yet.

Advances in electronics have given workers a new freedom, and a new meaning to workplace flexibility. People are now free to move about, to find the best place to work – perhaps near a colleague relevant at that time, or at some special machine. A flexible workplace can encourage flexible thinking, so workers can be more creative. The flexible environment, fitting loosely like an old sweater, gives business processes the freedom to change, while still protecting them from a hostile climate.

Flexibility can include working anywhere around the world; but extreme flexibility can frighten people. Comfort can alleviate this – comfort not just of body, but of mind. Flexibility and communication are not enough on their own; humanity is what makes change tolerable – and even enjoyable.

In the comfort and security of a humane environment the worker feels safe to take risks, and strong enough to win the fiercest battle. Coming into the office in the morning, he is stimulated yet serene, ready to work like a beaver, but laugh like a kookaburra. He feels himself at home, ready to work effectively for the company's profit – and his own.

MEASUREMENTS

The British construction industry measures buildings in metres and millimetres only. We have chosen here to use 'humane' measures – ones that relate to the body, and which can be used for rough measurement without recourse to a tape measure. They are:

the metre	the stride of a tall man
the centimetre	the width of a little finger nail
(ten centimetres	the width of a man's hand: hence the equine measure of a 'hand').

But what is this humane climate, and how can it be achieved? We believe that beyond the provision of adequate physical conditions there are aspects which can lift the work environment to become a positive creative force. If quality of life and productivity are interlinked, then workplaces designed not just to house but to uplift, will pay back fast.

The nature of the book – and of its readers

It takes a real expert to answer the difficult questions – But who is going to ask them?

Professor Reg Revans

This book is about office interiors: fitting out new ones and refurbishing the old. It is not a 'how to do' book – there are several of those on the subject. It is about 'how to ask' – questions, both strategic and detailed. We have written it for all who want to make new office workspaces that are new benchmarks. It is for the users of offices, from the chairman of the board to the newly recruited graduate; for those who create the interiors, from architects to furniture designers; and for the ones who have to wrestle with the whole thing – before, during and after: the facilities managers. It is for creators in large organizations and for those who work with just a handful of like-minded people.

It is a book for reading straight through, or for dipping into – and for coming back to. We hope that it will help you put the right questions to your experts – and judge their answers.

Our viewpoint combines function and feeling: what works, and what inspires. We identify trends and innovations rather than providing rules – not prescribing what to choose, but suggesting what needs to be considered when choosing. We contend that beauty of place enlivens and invigorates all who have contact with it.

We show examples of excellence, their influence, and how they have been achieved. Our choice is subjective: we have chosen what we believe to be good, innovative, human. Our selection is catholic: different uses, scales, styles and countries.

While this is a practical book, it is not a technical manual. There are plenty of those, and we have drawn gratefully on them. We offer handy 'rules of thumb'; but our main purpose is to focus on the human and qualitative issues that can change a functional 'paper factory' into a 'wonderful place to work'.

The book's structure

The book flows from the strategic to the tactical, although we have shaped it so that it can be read from either end. Policy makers will find that the first two parts give them an insight into the trends in office use, a better understanding of what the workforce needs, and hence an ability to conceptualize what is wanted from the new workspace. Those charged with making things happen will look to the second and third parts to help them with their practical needs. Yet others may just browse; there is 'signposting' to guide them along the way.

The first part of the book sets offices in the context of new patterns of work. It shows how the concept of the office has developed over the centuries, and what fresh ideas are emerging now. We then move on to look at what the office and its workers need in order to function well, and what makes the workspace stimulating yet comfortable. The last part is about making things happen: the process of creating an office interior, and the technical aspects that can make or mar the result. Between each chapter we give examples of workspaces that show what can be achieved.

From the first yearnings for more effective working conditions, to looking back to judge the level of success, dilemmas abound: should we open up the space or cut it into tiny bits; can you be creative with a clean desk; will open windows lead to happiness or fights about draughts; can people really share desks or does their high worth to the company justify dedicated space? At the end of each chapter we list the dilemmas that strike us: and certainly there are more which you will add.

We hope that you – building users, decision makers, designers – will take a fresh look at your own workplaces. Set aside your preconceptions about 'offices', and look instead at 'communicating, learning, humane workspaces'. See the workplace as a means to an end: a setting in which good people can produce outstanding results. Value it as a shrewd investment, not as a tiresome cost. For then you will create places where all who use them feel the better for being there, to their own benefit and that of the whole enterprise.

British Telecom Westside
Hemel Hempstead

workplace

The office of the future... should be a social stock exchange of propositions, projects and proposals...

Survey report on BT Workstyle 2000 for Westside

British Telecom moved 1250 sales, marketing and customer centre personnel from several offices in central London to Hemel Hempstead, near both the M1 and M25 motorways. Its aims were to encourage new ways of working and provide a show place for BT technology and products. In addition, the move vacated expensive premises and brought dispersed workers under one roof.

Each of the four floors of the 16,500m^2 Westside building is divided by atria into four sections, with meeting rooms and paper processing centres on the inside of each section. The ratio of open plan workstations to cellular offices is 19:1. Offices are positioned around the perimeter, with fritted glass panels providing views through. Coffee points house vending machines (other appliances are banned).

Furniture is fixed. People move. Workstations are minimal – 180 × 150cm. Two pedestals per person are augmented by two central storage lockers and central filing (paperlessness is high on the agenda). Everyone has heavy-duty 486 PCs using Microsoft Office and standard telephones (cordless ones are used in reception only).

BT uses the expression 'hot desk' to describe desks shared by team members, and 'touch down' for casual use by anyone coming by. Hot desks belong to

E-mail use	94% of people regularly
Voice mail use	77% of people every day
Video-conferencing	30% of people regularly

WORKING OFF SITE

Staff work from a menu of different workplaces: at a hot desk, in a meeting, at home, on the move, in another BT office, with customers, at a hotel, in an airport departure lounge or in the café.

APT^2 (adaptable place and technology for people and teams) encourages home working. Perhaps 10% of people at Westside work at home some of the time, and 89% say they will. Only 17% are concerned about isolation at home, and 7% about distractions. However lack of workspace rated 24%, and lack of storage 27%.

Furniture for home working can be provided by the facilities department, but equipment is the responsibility of the particular business unit.

---

the departments; touch-down desks and meeting, conference and video rooms are run (and booked) by the facilities department.

Meetings for small numbers of people tend to happen in the office or café, so of the 52 meeting rooms, it is the large ones which are in demand (for noisy meetings). The four conference rooms can be thrown together to make two larger rooms. The eight quiet rooms each provide a single workstation but no telephone.

The café, with a shop alongside, is open from 8am to 4pm. Tables spill into the atria on either side and are used day long for informal meetings. The much larger restaurant is only open from noon until 2pm and is used less (due perhaps to a combination of dull lighting and even duller furniture). There is a

Figure 1.2 Typical workstation cluster in open office areas.

Figure 1.3 The café, which spills out into the central atrium, is used all day for informal meetings.

Figure 1.4 The restaurant is more enclosed than the café, and used extensively at lunch time only. Recessed spotlights add sparkle to the space.

CHRIS GASCOIGNE

Figure 1.5 Part layout.
Key
1 atrium
2 void
3 lifts
4 toilets
5 core
6 copiers/printers/filing
7 meeting/project room/s
8 smoking room
9 cellular offices
10 open offices
11 hot desks

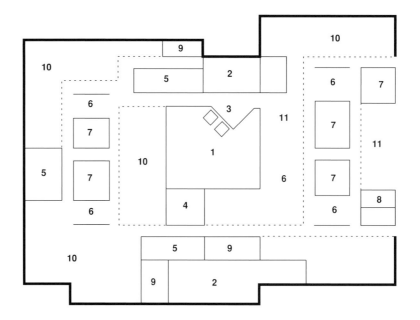

CHRIS GASCOIGNE

■ The competitive edge will be gained by companies that utilize the new technology to combine workstyle and lifestyle (conclusions of Workstyle 2000 survey).

Figure 1.6 A project room, one of the very few cellular offices in this open plan building.

rest room and two smoking rooms, but the former is under-used, and the latter need lobbying from office areas to isolate the smell.

Power, voice and data run in the floor void and rise through grommets directly into the furniture system. Patching (one room per section) is used for relocation, or to activate the ISDN cabling – allowing video-telephoning or video-conferencing at any workstation. The two video-conference rooms have six ISDN cables, making it possible to link six independent locations.

Fluorescent downlighters provide 500 lux on the work surface (there are no task lights), with low-voltage spots only used in areas such as the café. Lighting for video-conferencing is increased to about 600 lux. Infrared sensors turn lights out when cellular spaces are not in use. Otherwise lighting is centrally controlled, but can be overridden locally.

Air is supplied and returned through the ceiling, with the atria as return air stacks to roof level coolers. Heating is provided by hot-water panels set into the ceiling perimeters and into the atria floor, and is

CHRIS GASCOIGNE

Figure 1.7 An open plan area, where people move and the furniture stays put. On the left is a paper processing area, with photocopier and printer.

needed for only three hours at the most, even on winter mornings. Otherwise people and machines provide the heat.

For security, the CCTV system records internal and external movement and is monitored in the lodge at the entrance to the car park. The fire alarm system is single stage, with sprinklers throughout the building.

A 3m floor to ceiling height, low screens (45cm above worktop height) and an effective acoustic ceiling create workspaces which are serene, with low noise levels and a feeling of enough, but not too much, space.

The move was carried out in stages, with about 50 people being relocated over a weekend. Preparation included briefing discussions, visiting the site, introduction packs and training on new systems as necessary.

Outsourcing is used widely: for security (including receptionists and help desk personnel), catering and photocopying; for general cleaning, window cleaning and waste management; and for the maintenance of heating, ventilating and air-conditioning (HVAC), internal and external plant, and lifts. In the future child care and leisure facilities may also be provided, possibly in partnership with a local company.

BT believes that effective team working will have a positive effect upon productivity. The philosophy behind the layout and the design of Westside was to promote greater communication and interaction.

(conclusions of Workstyle 2000 survey)

Architects: Aukett Associates
Contractor: Interior PLC

background

Diversified Agency
Services,
Marylebone,
London: A meeting
room at ground level
for one of the sub-
sidiary companies of
the marketing and
advertising holding
company.
*Architects: Pringle
Brandon*

Chapter 2
Context

- ■ Change
- ■ People and organizations
- ■ Time
- ■ Technology
- ■ Property
- ■ Pressures and threats
- ■ Scenarios

When the wind of change blows, some build shelters: others build windmills.

Anon

The wind shows no signs of abating. There is the temptation to shelter from it: in the status quo, in the hope of a 'return to normal', in rigid dogma. But there is also the opportunity to use it: to blow away the clinging cobweb of tradition, and to energize the windfarms of new ideas. 'Constant change is here to stay': how should we use it? In particular, how should we use it to improve the workplace?

Change

Change – from the moral to the technical – influences the context of work. In each kind of change we see a contrast between the industrial age and the information age: yesterday and tomorrow. Often it is a matter of polarities: either giving up the old and embracing the new, or adding the new to the old.

Not every change is desirable – even the moral ones. But most seem inevitable. So how will they affect the workplace? For instance, constant change is now bringing on change fatigue. People can only cope with so much. We need to devise physical environments that can remain unchanged and familiar in the midst of organizational upheaval.

In the workplace, the employee is relating to the organization in a quite new way. Telecommunications and information technology are separating work from place. In parallel but interlinked, attitudes towards property are changing, with the office now seen as an asset rather than simply an expense.

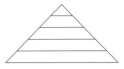

Yesterday : HIERARCHY

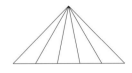

Today : TEAMS

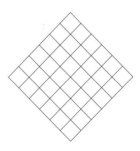

Tomorrow : NETWORKS

Figure 2.2 Organizational scenarios.

People and organizations

People are changing too. There is no longer a belief in a secure future – even with a good education. So they cannot expect, or rely upon, a continuing standard of living. If the employer is not going to give them a job for life, then the young have to take responsibility for themselves: 'I will work for you and give of my best, but only if the conditions are right.'

Figure 2.1 VIA International, London: Cellular spaces at the rear include meeting rooms, a paper processing area and a library – where a lounger offers a comfortable read and a degree of peace.
Architects: Sir Norman Foster and Partners

Figure 2.3 Polarities of change as they affect business. From Yesterday to Tomorrow change may be both/and (shown as +) or from/to (shown as →).

MORAL

corporate ethos + self-interest
formal hierarchy (West) + intimate hierarchy (East)
exploiting natural resources → conserving natural resources
exploiting the workforce → nurturing the workforce
personal responsibilities → personal rights

ECONOMIC

competition + collaboration
maximum profit → sustainable success
growth (quantitative) → growth (qualitative)
protectionism + global sourcing

outputs → outcomes
work = place → work = person
cost reduction → revenue generation
competence → excellence
stockpiles → just-in-time

confrontation → partnership
military model → jazz ensemble
line management + project management
permanent hierarchy + project team
doubting people → trusting people

BUSINESS

inner cities → suburban centres
producer orientation → consumer orientation
local general markets → global niche markets
regional competition → global competition

status → equality
vertical structure → horizontal structure
nose to the grindstone + eyes on the horizon
corporate paternalism → individualism
controlling → leading

job security → outsourcing
who you know (old boy net) → who you know who knows (networking)
doing things right (efficiency) → doing the right things (effectiveness)

SOCIO-POLITICAL

male ethos → gender spectrum
half a century of peace → terrorism and civil war
unions of nations (Europe) + tribal loyalties (Bosnia)
change for change sake + change fatigue
'stiff upper lip' → litigiousness and protest

KNOWLEDGE AND EDUCATION

know-all + know-nots
left brain (logical thought) + right brain (intuitive thought)
learning curve (acquisition) + forgetting curve (letting go)
growth of knowledge + knowledge obsolescence
college education + continuing education

TECHNOLOGY

private office → mobile working
city centre skyscraper + home office
commuting (person to workplace) + telecommuting (information to person)
face-to-face meetings + video-conferencing

The computer-literate young have easier access to the power of knowledge than do more senior staff. The result is youthful, self-monitoring teams and a structure, no longer vertical, that is made up of overlapping – and shifting – groups. Loyalties and responsibilities lie largely within the team, and the image of the team may be more potent than that of the company.

Corporate loyalty may be outmoded, but in some ways a caring culture is replacing it. Thoughtful managers see the benefits of caring for their workforce; the ecologists focus on caring for the environment; people in horizontal organizations feel the need to support each other. Sometimes at odds with short-term profit, it provides a balancing force. This culture comes the easier because of the growing importance of women – and feminine values – in the workplace.

MEASURES OF GROWTH

'My! How she's grown.' Said about a nine-year-old girl, it means an increase in height. Said about a 39-year-old manager, it means she has grown in experience and skills. The one quantitative, the other qualitative. The business concept of growth is usually the childish one; but tomorrow's sustainable growth must be the mature interpretation. In parallel, workspace will not need to grow in size, but in quality. Quality will also come from a closer relation with the customer. And, as providers and customers move in and out of each others' workplaces, so will workplace image become even more important.

DENNIS GILBERT

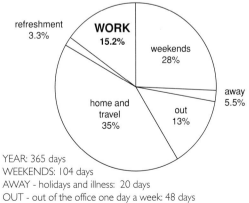

YEAR: 365 days
WEEKENDS: 104 days
AWAY - holidays and illness: 20 days
OUT - out of the office one day a week: 48 days
TOTAL DAYS IN THE OFFICE: 193 days

HOME and TRAVEL - 2/3 of each day: 128 days
REFRESHMENT - lunch, coffee etc: 12 days

WORK: 53 days (average time desk is fully occupied)

Time

Time was once a fixed measure, a linear progression from Monday morning to Friday evening, with night-time for rest. Now time is global, parallel and overlapping: Moscow time, London time, New York time. But it is also flexi-time: workers coming and going as suits their tasks – and their domestic needs. Used wisely, time gives an added dimension to office space – an extended use of a fixed asset. Neglected in space planning, however, it can cause chaos. It has become a major factor in the planning and use of the workplace.

Technology

Information technology is changing the way we all work. Technology enables us not only to process and

Figure 2.4 Energis, Reading: The telecommunications arm of the National Grid Company is a 24 hour a day, 365 day a year operation. Telesales operators use specially developed workstations arranged in small groups. Designed to comply with the most stringent legislation, the height of the separate worktops can be adjusted hydraulically.
Design Consultants: Murray Symonds Associates

Figure 2.5 Net annual use of workspace.

store information far more efficiently, but to make it readily accessible. Telecommunications allow us to move this information round the world, and communicate with anyone, anywhere, any time. Libraries and archives as the repositories of knowledge are being replaced by browsing the corporate database and the Internet: active rather than passive storage. To move information is now swift, compact and cheap; so large agglomerations of workers, huddled around equally large concentrations of paper, are no longer necessary or economic.

The jobs of the farmer and the dockworker will always be place dependent; but office work can now, in theory, be done anywhere. Concentrated tasks and long-distance communication can happen where it suits: at base office, the customer's office, at home or in a telecentre. Interaction, however, whether formal or informal, still needs a physical setting – the office.

Property

Space is being used in new ways. Mobile working discourages personalization, so territoriality moves from the individual to the team space. Spaces are now provided for activities rather than individuals. Privacy is seen as fulfilling a specific need – for confidentiality, for concentration – and not as a right of seniority. Cellular offices signify function, not status.

Office space used to be seen by most organizations as a cost. While such costs were low, or not fully identified in a company's accounts, it seemed handy to 'have a little slack'. Soaring rents have made firms look at space costs more comprehensively.

'Churn' – the moving of staff and rearrangement of office space – costs £1000 or more for each person moved, with up to 70% of staff moving each year. Higher construction standards have raised the real costs of building by one-sixth over 15 years. Workstations may be unused more than half the time in businesses such as accountancy and management consultancy – even in banks the figure can be as high as 20%.

Yet office space is a major asset, and workspace design and its management a serious business. Off-the-cuff decisions by the managing director (or his personal assistant), partition changes by the maintenance engineer, and decorations by the MD's wife is no longer a sensible formula – if ever it was. Hence the activity – and profession – of facilities management has emerged.

Facilities management

Facilities management, like project management and design, is about the co-ordination of complexity; but unlike the others it is also about dealing with people at work. The complexity is compounded by the fact

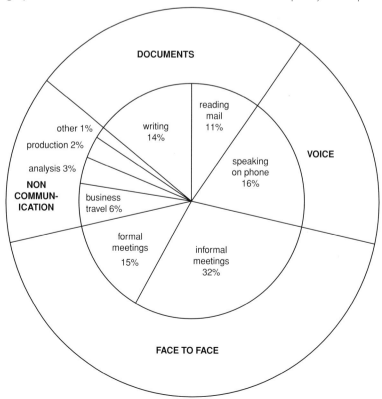

Figure 2.6 Executive communications: how managers spend a typical day.

THE FACILITIES MANAGEMENT PORTFOLIO

Facilities management can include a wide range of responsibilities, even if some activities are commonly outsourced (+).

Premises
Leases	+
Design and construction	+
Lifts, escalators and conveyors	+
Artworks	+
Mains supplies	
Energy conservation	
Building management systems	+
Maintenance	+
Landscape maintenance	+
Redecoration/refurbishment	+

Business operations
Space planning	+
Furniture	
Equipment	
Telecommunications	+
Office consumables	
Furniture and equipment maintenance	+

Security
Receptionists	
Guards and porters	+
Electronic systems	+

Janitorial
General cleaning	+
Window cleaning	+
General consumables	

Catering
Restaurant	+
Executive dining	+
Shop/delicatessen	+
Vending machines	+
Tea kitchens	

Management
Liaison with staff and management	
Supervision	
Procurement	
Data collection and analysis	
Records and inventories	
Insurances	

■ Facilities management is the practice of co-ordinating the physical workplace with the people and work of the organization.
British Institute of Facilities Management

that managing facilities does not have a foreseeable end.

The challenges of facilities management are immense: the reality of bricks and mortar set against the elusive needs of the 'virtual team'; the need to create an image of stability and calm in a world of 'churn'; the reconciliation of human needs with those of electronics; the need to balance the cost of high quality office space with the cost of sickness caused by poor working conditions.

To be creatively resolved, the dilemmas of facilities management need to be grasped by everyone: by the main board, by department heads, by staff representatives and by design consultants of all kinds. Each

worker too must understand the key issues that affect him and his immediate work group, so that in 'owning the problem' he can help to shape the solution.

Will we ever have 'virtual facilities management'? Perhaps not. But a 'management of virtual facilities' – most probably. The company will have to set – and monitor – workplace standards for a variety of environments, many of which are not under its direct control. The base office, whatever size it may still be, will demonstrate these and the company's ethos in a distilled but potent way. The main task of facilities management will be to knit all this together, in a framework of operating policies, information technology and company values.

PCs VERSUS PCs

A two month test carried out in the USA of regular communication by conventional mail and E-mail produced these results:

	Average transmission time	Reliability
Postcard	Three days	All arrived
Personal computer (E-mail)	Twelve minutes	Five lost without trace

Figure 2.7 Dynamics in the workplace.

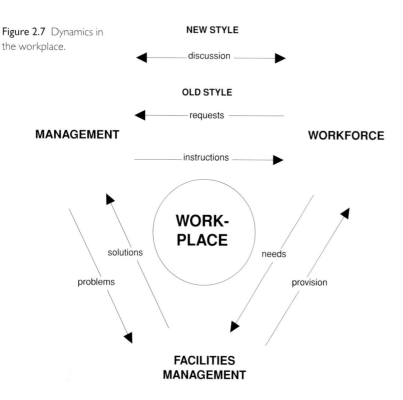

NEW STYLE

← discussion →

OLD STYLE

← requests

MANAGEMENT   WORKFORCE

instructions →

WORK-PLACE

solutions   needs

problems   provision

FACILITIES MANAGEMENT

Pressures and threats

The workplace is under pressure from powerful forces:

– rapid changes in markets and thus in businesses' objectives;
– a continuing flow of new concepts and products in telecommunications and information technology;
– a stream of ideas on how companies should be organized and run.

The first sets the challenge, and the others respond. With all three, the pace is faster than ever before: far faster than many organizations or individuals can handle. So the first problem is the rate of change. Markets and business structures are now changing faster than buildings can. Too tailor-made a workplace will soon burst at the seams or hang like a dieter's suit.

Information technology will keep up, however. You do not need the town planning committee's approval to bring in a new microchip. So the solutions being offered are technological ones, built around the personal computer. However, on the

Figure 2.8 Heathrow Airports Ltd, London: A team 'cul-de-sac' in this new headquarters building. A total of 240 people work in principally open plan space, designed to encourage communication.
Architects: DEGW

whole these solutions are dehumanizing, and distance people from each other. The 'virtual team', the 'virtual office' and the 'virtual organization' are feasible, exciting – and exist. But they lack humanity. People need environments with a feeling of well-being. 'Virtual' concepts also lead on to tactical questions, such as how important physical adjacency then becomes, and how much demand there may still be for the individual office.

Beyond their functional needs, organizations also need an appropriate image. This is not keeping pace either. Many firms are working in quite different ways from before, but their offices still look like conventional offices – even inside. The profound organizational changes need new physical symbols.

The management consultants and the IT experts offer businesses a range of new solutions: value-added strategies, learning organizations, tele-conferencing, business process re-engineering, wide-area networks. The designer is then called in to house them – fast. But design moves more slowly, and estate agents slower still. Their concepts are still for the most part those of the last decade: either heroic neo-Edwardian halls of splendour, or lightweight sheds in business parks.

So other advisers are emerging. Computer suppliers are now offering space-planning services; furniture manufacturers suggest organizational strategies. But for all their good intentions, these experts are not skilled in the creation of integrated and satisfying environments. The result is that organizations are not getting the workplaces that they need and deserve.

Scenarios

The spectrum of offices is widening. At one end is the 'mega-office' – the large city centre operation: an expensive building on an expensive site. It is a citadel: secure, with an armoury of technology, an imposing presence, and surroundings that contain the ancillary activities which support it. Workers travel long journeys to reach it but, once inside, are served and supported by everything – and everybody – they need. But is it affordable; and is it flexible enough?

At the other end of the spectrum is the 'virtual office': a medley of semipermanent and transient workplaces, from home and car to hotel and aeroplane. Its workers are guerrillas, linked by a common purpose and a network of IT. It is highly flexible – but how can new workers become part of the human team, and how can they be given a sense of belonging? It is heavily dependent on its communications – but how robust and secure are they?

Between these extremes are 'families' of modestly sized offices, where everyone knows everyone else, and the drive to work takes only 15 minutes. The workspace is human in scale, and set in attractive surroundings. IT networks connect each office with its sisters in other towns and countries. Perhaps, however, people will identify too much with the individual unit, and 'sibling rivalry' between offices will weaken the organization.

These models already co-exist, and will probably continue to do so. But which will be the norm?

Figure 2.9 Lexington Post, Soho, London: In the offices of this post-production video-editing company, 10 staff work in teams, mainly for advertising companies. Between intense sessions people meet and talk around the table, with the administrator sitting nearby.
Architects: Bissett Adams

VIA International
London

workplace

The art of life lies in a constant readjustment to our surroundings.

Kakuzo Okakura

When change management consultants Vision Into Action celebrated their metamorphosis from Dent Lee Witte, the poster that decorated the office displayed the above quotation. Being in the business of helping organizations to change, they 'hold themselves accountable to the same beliefs and values' that they encourage in their clients.

In 1991 the office was conceived as a 'club', with the 30 consultants working around great tables 'reminiscent of a farmhouse kitchen'. No one had her own desk, not even the directors. ('It would be suicidal to say I'm boss and that's my place by the window.') Four years later the mobile 'puppies' are still used, but the tables have been dispersed into smaller, more fluid units, and people tend to have their set work positions.

And it is now more than just a club: relationships between people are more enduring and supportive. With a complex system of performance bonuses to which all are entitled, they feel responsibility for and ownership of the office as a resource. The club was like a hotel for similar sorts of people, whereas the VIA concept is perhaps more like that of an extended Oriental family.

Papers on a desk (desks are not as clean as they used to be) are moved without question if the space is needed, but there is no sense of territorial infringement. The fluidity of this office underwrites the flexibility so essential in today's workplace.

The 300m² space occupies the ground floor of architects Sir Norman Foster and Partners' own offices. The glass and steel building provides 'a useful statement of corporate culture. Its minimalism, beautiful clarity and unfussy design reflect the way we work and serve our clients'. Sliding glass doors open onto a Thames-side walkway, with a degree of privacy and daylight control provided by special glass patterned with tiny dots, backed by venetian blinds. Artificial lighting is by fluorescent downlighters and task lights fixed to the desks.

'Relay' desks, puppies, bollards and tear-drop tables can be positioned in different configurations, and illustrate the versatility of freestanding furniture – including here the high-level desk for the back pain sufferer. Added to these in the recent rearrangement

■ Herman Miller's Relay allowed us to move and gather moss – unlike the rolling stone.

Jenny Aynsley – administrator, VIA

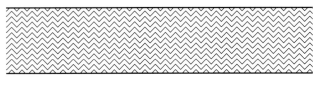

9

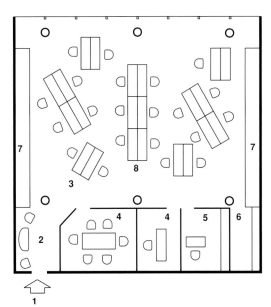

1

N

Figure 2.10 Layout.

Key
1 entrance
2 waiting
3 reception
4 meeting room
5 library
6 machines/coffee
7 storage
8 open work area
9 riverside walk

GRAHAM CHALLIFOUR

■ More than half of the staff are women. They have motivation and the sensitivity to people so critical in the change business. The juggling act – the pragmatism and flexibility needed to balance work and family – makes for high productivity.

Richard Lee

Figure 2.11 This change management consultancy, situated on the ground floor of architect Norman Foster's own office building, looks out through a fully glazed wall onto the river Thames. The original layout arranged the work surfaces as 'farmhouse tables' for group working (but these have since been moved into less formal groupings, which change as the need arises).

is a relaxed meeting area by the window to augment the two meeting rooms, library and reception seating at the rear of the space. Storage remains in the two end walls, running from floor to ceiling.

In this fully networked office the whiteboard photocopier has now been joined by a lap-top powered projection system. However, there is no space for the much needed carrels for periods of quiet working or intense telephone interviewing.

In the early days flashes of colour counteracted the predominant grey of the furniture – cut flowers, bowls of oranges and green apples, artworks. Today there are plants too, standing by the windows and giving a more human and relaxed feel – 'though you might call it naff'.

As the new company brochure states: 'The creation and support of an environment in which change is the norm requires a different set of skills from that which protects the status quo.' To see a workplace that is changing in step with its users' evolution is uncommon. To see it done so well is rare indeed.

Architects: Sir Norman Foster and Partners
Project evolution: 1991–94

Chapter 3
Purposes and concepts

Why do we still need offices?

The reasons for having offices

■ **Concepts of the office**

Situation

Historical models

Tomorrow's offices

■ **Business functions**

Direct functions

Indirect functions

■ **Dilemmas**

office – of'is – n. – from Latin officium – a favour, duty, service.

Chambers Twentieth Century Dictionary

What is an office? The word has many meanings, just like the French 'bureau' or the Arabic 'maktab'. Its first meaning is a service. From this follows the post or organization that performs that service, and only last the room or building in which the service is performed. So we have got it back to front when we assume that an office is primarily a place.

Nevertheless, in most climates, performing such a service calls for protection from the elements, somewhere to sit, and storage space: a workplace.

Why do we still need offices?

Until quite recently the reason for having offices, and the form they should take, seemed self-evident. During the course of the nineteenth century office work expanded and, with the advent of the typewriter and the telegraph, became more mechanized. Growing numbers of managers and clerks had to be housed and supervised.

Between the wars management consultants began to apply to office work the same organization and methods principles that they were using in factories. The office become a white collar 'paper factory': rows of desks along which papers and files travelled, with managers overseeing the process from their glass-walled offices. Enlightened organizations and sophisticated architects developed this concept in a series of elegant examples, such as the Seagram building in New York, the UNESCO headquarters in Paris and the Economist building in London.

However the mechanistic aridity and lack of humanity of this model led to behavioural scientists looking at how people worked best. Forward-thinking management consultants such as the Schnelle brothers in Germany, and architects such as Herman Hertzberger in The Netherlands, applied these findings to new concepts of the organization and its workplace. The emphasis was on informality, individuality and trust.

Meanwhile the computer was shrinking from a mainframe to a desk-top, and no longer needed a special environment. Its uses and power had developed so that 'the Bible on the head of a pin' could be sent across the world in a split second. Dispersed working became a real possibility.

■ Walker's outer office was impressive…Walker had two secretaries, one chosen for looks, apparently, and one for utility. A pale-yellow carpet lay on the floor, and there was a yellow leather armchair for callers. Walker himself was closeted in an inner office which was separated from the rest of the room by a partition of …glass brick.

Sloan Wilson: The Man in the Grey Flannel Suit

Figure 3.1 Leo Burnett, Chelsea, London: In the atrium of this advertising agency visitors are greeted by a club-like waiting and meeting area. It has comfortable and colourful furniture, and views to the world outside.
Architects: Stanton Williams and Fletcher Priest

Figure 3.2 Human aspirations (after AH Maslow and D McGregor).

If you could trust the workforce, and if technology allowed people to work in a variety of locations, then the centralized and regimented office was no longer essential. Now, as we come to the end of the century, there is a new freedom to experiment.

What kind of office we need now depends on what we do. There are many kinds of office work, and many kinds of office workers. Some face an exciting future, and some a rough one. Both futures are unpredictable.

— Routine tasks are being taken over by the computer and, thanks to telecommunications, they are being done in countries with low labour costs. The airline ticket you buy in London or Frankfurt has probably been keyed in by someone in Bombay or Bangalore.
— More people are working in self-managing teams, so there is less need for middle managers.
— With the customers' needs paramount, more people are working close to them, or travelling in between. Such journeys may be down the street, or global.
— In an age of discontinuity, the career path has become a series of stepping stones, with sometimes perilous leaps between them.

WHAT COLOUR IS YOUR COLLAR?	
blue collar	traditional manual workers
white collar	traditional office workers
ultra-white collar	top executives
open collar	academics, writers
no collar	virtual office workers (at home in their T-shirts)
gold collar	thinkers and creators – the ones who add real value

A job for life, nine to five, the daily commute, a neat office with hatstand, desk and pictures of wife, kids and cat: such concepts of work and workplace have been blown apart.

This chapter sets out to explore where the workplace is going: what concepts are being discarded, and what new – or borrowed – ideas have relevance. If managers are to create appropriate workspaces for the future, then a framework for understanding and a menu of possibilities are helpful tools. More than that, they can excite managers to imagine new models to suit their own particular businesses.

Clearly there is no one model any more: soon the word 'office' will no longer conjure up an image of orderly rows of desks, arrays of filing cabinets and the boss behind a huge desk in his corner office. Once again the word will denote a duty or service; and the physical embodiment will relate to the way that particular firm (or person) sees the job being done.

Nevertheless we believe that the office building has a future: that it is not an obsolete building type like a castle or a cave. There are practical reasons: hotel rooms and people's homes are often inadequate. There are powerful psychological ones too. People still need to work together: to sniff the same air and drink the same coffee while bandying ideas or battling tight deadlines. And people need a symbol of what they belong to, perhaps all the more so when that belonging is no longer for life. What does my workplace say to others about my company's values and attitudes; what does it say to me?

The reasons for having offices

People still need to come together for work – for business and personal reasons. For the sake of the business they need to exchange ideas, instructions and information; and they need to stimulate each other to be creative and energetic. For themselves they need to bond with their colleagues, and to be valued by them.

Information technology works well for remote transactions that need formal recording. But informal and sophisticated exchanges benefit from personal contact. Body language speaks far more clearly than words; so when dealing with the nuances of ideas, group discussions achieve far more than conference calls.

The office is also the repository of information, with incoming mail, file archives and reference books. For intensive use the worker needs direct access to this wealth. Electronic filing, while allowing access from anywhere, has limitations. Though hard copy may diminish, many businesses will remain paper based for some time to come.

This data may simply provide information; but it may also be a source of stimulation, a spur to creativity. In the office, stimulation can come from enthusiastic juniors or wise elders, from a structured focus group or a casual chat in the corridor. The office should be a place both of study and of serendipity.

Abraham Maslow talked about people having a psychological 'hierarchy of needs', a mounting scale of motivators. According to him, once a need is reasonably well satisfied it ceases to motivate; the drive then comes from higher up the ladder. On this basis the lower level needs of office workers can be met by their salary – which could be credited to their bank account without them coming near the office. But they still need to belong, and they still need the esteem of their peers and their leaders. Both of these call for personal contact.

Historically the office has been valued as a physical asset – although today the reverse may sometimes be true. For while businesses can be very flexible and mobile, office buildings cannot. The office is, however, still showcase, symbol and theatre. It reflects the company's wealth, its values and its attitudes; for visitors and workers it is the company's tangible image; and it provides the stage on which the more static elements of the company perform for their customers, staff and community.

Concepts of the office

Situation

Where an office is located is fundamental to its nature. It may be:

Centralized
All operations are together, under the direct guidance of top management. The centralized office gives customers access to all services in one place – a 'one-stop shop'; and it can present a powerful corporate image. It makes face-to-face communication easy for staff. But journeys to work may be long and costly and, if in a city centre, rents and operating costs may be high.

Decentralized
This may simply be a split between a head office and its 'back office', or it may be full decentralization by department or by profit centre. Provided the decentralized units have a critical mass, and that customer access remains easy, it may allow at least parts of the business to be in low-cost locations.

Mobile
Salesmen have always worked on the move, their bulging briefcases now giving way to slim lap-tops. Improved mobile communications, and the growing desire to be near to customers, now makes this way of working common in other parts of the business.

'Third-party site'
This can range from home through hotels to customers' offices. There is a similarity with mobile working, although sites such as home may be regularly used.

Historical models

Concepts of the office in history are in many cases remarkably up to date:

FLOWER
Centralized

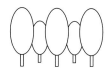

FOREST
Decentralized

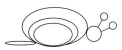

SNAIL
Mobile

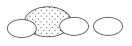

CUCKOO
'Third Party Sites'

Figure 3.3 Concepts of the office.

Figure 3.4 Home office, Camden, London: Architect Dale Loth works in the basement of his house. Although on a different floor, his office is purposely not separated from the domestic activities taking place upstairs. *Architect: Dale Loth*

Figure 3.5 Harper Mackay, London: Climbing two sets of stairs from street level in an old warehouse building, visitors wait overlooking this architects' studio, where daylight floods in.
Architects: Harper Mackay

Figure 3.6 Ernst & Young, Sears Tower, Chicago: 'Name menu' which can be scrolled backwards and forwards. Touching the name shows the person's location on screen.
Architects: Sverdrup Facilities Inc.

Monastery

The monasteries were the first pan-European businesses: with a common culture, common procedures and, in Latin, a common language. The organization was enclosed and secretive, yet at the same time wealthy and powerful. Its communications were effective, and the monasteries provided a network of workplaces through which the monks could move: an early form of 'touch-down desks'.

Palace

In contrast the royal palaces made great show of their wealth and power. 'Corporate image' was an important part of retaining both. Unlike the monasteries, however, where individual workers moved between static buildings, with the palaces the whole organization – the Court – moved from place to place.

Palazzo

The Italian Renaissance palazzo was different yet again. Impressive homes were also places of business – banking, trading and land-owning – and provided an image that has predominated in banking ever since.

Market

Meanwhile, outside in the street lesser traders conducted their business. The sheltered arcade and galleria developed over the centuries into the Victorian coal and corn exchanges, and then into stock exchanges. But here, unlike in banking, information

technology has broken the mould, and the trading floor has become a virtual one.

Confessional

Town houses also provided the model for the professional office. The professional firm was small: a doctor, or a lawyer and his clerks. It needed modest space, an image of knowledge, integrity and stability, and privacy.

Tent

Napoleon had his tent, General Montgomery his caravan. These were mobile, lightly staffed and lightly furnished offices, always close to the 'customer' – the enemy. They had the best communications of their time, whether carrier pigeon or short-wave radio.

Factory

And so to the office as factory. We described this earlier: highly rational, tailored closely to then current theories of the organization and of human behaviour. It worked well for a long time; and in some cultures it still does.

Landscape

The office as landscape – Bürolandschaft – was an attempt to supersede the factory model. Its arrival from Germany in the 1960s presented the first modern alternative to the then ubiquitous American pattern. Wide, open spaces, informally arranged furniture, plants and screens defining modestly sized work groups: these were its components. Its significance was that it stemmed from a fresh management approach; the architecture was a consequence of this.

Tomorrow's offices

Bürolandschaft re-established the interdependence of management thinking and office design. It showed that a new vision of the organization could be reflected in – and enhanced by – its environment. It not only did away with partitions, it also removed the barriers to experiment. People could think about the real needs of office workers, and find other models for the office.

Continuing powerful strides in IT and telecommunications have led to a host of new concepts. Some of these models, such as 'office as college' are complex and embracing; others, such as 'office as laboratory', may form components of them.

Laboratory

This model reflects the move towards project teams in office work. It is expensive to reconfigure the office

every time a new team is formed. It may be better to have well-serviced workspaces that are large enough to give some flexibility of use, but small enough to provide the intimacy that a committed workgroup needs. If these are arranged around circulation routes and common areas, then informal cross-fertilization between groups is more likely to happen.

College

The college is the archetype of the 'learning organization'. But for centuries it has also been an 'earning organization'. It provides a wide variety of workspaces: lecture and seminar rooms, laboratories and workshops, libraries and places for quiet study. It also has common rooms, dining halls and bars for social interaction; squash courts and running tracks for physical recreation; and shady trees under which to read a book quietly or to argue passionately. The college is a place focused on pushing outward the boundaries of knowledge – both for the individual, and for society at large. Its products are not only trained graduates, but marketable research.

Club

The 'office as club' has many similarities with the collegiate model; but with more of an emphasis on interaction and on transience, and less on solitary learning. It also has a more domestic aura. Transience is balanced by a feeling of belonging; the member is among friends, however infrequently she may visit. By the same token, she can feel at ease in welcoming guests

to 'her' club. For the virtual organization this model is attractive; the stability and strong image of the place countering the intangibility of the organization.

Hotel

A hotel is a less personal but more highly organized and serviced variant of a club. Whereas a hotel rents out personal sleeping spaces and function rooms, in the 'office as hotel' these become personal workspaces and meeting rooms. There are two office versions: the company office run on these lines, and the business centre, with its independent users. Like its namesake, 'the office as hotel' depends on a high quality of facilities and service, and on efficient running at high occupancy levels.

Shopping centre

This is a place for transients: a safe and comfortable environment where the businessman on the move can buy a variety of services, or have a one-off meeting. Airports are an obvious location; but business centres may also offer this service – particularly if they are part of a chain. The 'telecottage' is a more modest version – a 'village shop' where the local home worker can buy small quantities of office services, or offer his own on an electronic bulletin board.

Control centre

This is the tangible part of the 'virtual office'. It is the centre of the communications web, responding to customers and co-ordinating far-flung staff. Like air

Figure 3.7 CDP, Soho, London: Advertising agent Collett Dickenson Pearce aims to provide 'a sense of people working together to achieve the same end'. Open plan working and stylish circulation encourage communication.
Architects: Harper Mackay

■ *The office as*
McDonalds
Consistent image
    with high visibility
International
Nourishing
Outlets where you
    need them
Reliable quality
Simplicity
Value for money
Well-trained staff

traffic controllers its operators must be faultless and resourceful; in addition, they must personify the image of the company.

Oasis
The nomadic worker needs a place of refreshment and rest. He needs to cross the paths of his colleagues, to trade information and ideas, and to provision himself for his next journey.

Village street
This is a physical manifestation as well as an organizational concept. The SAS Headquarters in Stockholm is a well-known example. It contrasts the street as a place of casual encounter and café conviviality with the privacy of adjoining homes or shops. It may be no more than a spacious main route linking focal points. But beware! It uses up a lot of space, and has a powerful architectural image which may be imposed unsuitably.

These models help to open up our thinking about the workplace; and they can be used to test ideas about the relationship between ways of working and places of work. Each model contains elements that may suit a particular organization, depending not only on its culture, but on what it produces in terms of product or service. There is scope for lateral thinking in exploring other concepts.

Business functions

The business functions that occur in offices are both direct and indirect. The former are those which are the prime – and usually profit-making – ones. Some kinds of organization are dedicated to one; others combine several. The indirect functions are those that enable the organization itself to perform well; they normally all exist to some degree.

Direct functions

Trading
Trading may be an ancillary activity, but often it is central, as with multinational trading companies, stockbrokers or estate agents. In financial dealing rooms it can be very intense and active; with diamond merchants, discreet. It can be done by information technology, mail or face to face – over the telephone

or over a meal. Each setting is different, but each is highly focused.

Advising
The banker has similar needs to the diamond merchant: confidentiality, an image of reliability and an aura of wealth. The lawyer has the same, although the wealth that she displays is intellectual rather than material. Groupings tend to be small, although as matters grow more and more complex, the supporting back office becomes a more dominant feature.

Negotiating
The lawyer is a negotiator too, as is the politician. 'Smoke-filled rooms' may be a thing of the past, but again a confidential and focused environment is called for.

Controlling
Government is about regulating as well as managing and negotiating. An orderly way of working is necessary if other things are to be kept in order. At the same time, regulators are often the public face of government, so their workplaces should not be forbidding.

Creating
Film directors are creative; so are sewerage engineers. But they work in different ways, and project different images. Creativity takes place in a variety of surroundings. What is common to most creative enterprises is the combined need for solitude, and for intense collective brainstorming.

Communicating
Creation and communication often go together: the academic and the publisher; the advertising agency and the broadcasting studio; the journalist and the newspaper. Communication is a funnel: ideas – and idealists – in at one end; budgets and timetables in the middle; and precise messages flowing out. It thus embraces a variety of spatial activities and moods.

Indirect functions

Managing
All businesses save the very smallest have a discrete managing element. In many cases it is ancillary, as in manufacturing or retailing businesses: a minor part of a large building or complex. Management is a continuous struggle to combine strategic forethought with swift reactions to events. It ranges from solitary brooding through routine monitoring to crisis meetings. Because of this, it needs a variety of work settings.

Learning

In a fast-changing world, businesses need to learn the new – and forget the old. It is not enough for individuals to learn. There must be collective learning: an intellectual and social experience which adds understanding and power to the corporate effort. Spaces for group training and debate, as well as for solitary study and reflection, support the learning ethos.

Research

Research and development are profit-oriented forms of organizational learning. Market research, and the development of new 'products' (anything from chairs to pension plans), are as much a part of this function as conventional laboratory work.

Resourcing

Successful businesses are the ones that continually use their resources – people, know-how, money and plant – to best effect. Knowledge is now the key resource, but money and plant still count. But how many buildings help, rather than hinder, the activities inside them?

Each function has its strategic pattern of needs: the kinds of spaces and how they fit together; the way they are shaped and fitted out; the atmosphere that they have and the image they project. The good workplace is the response to these strategic patterns.

On a larger scale, different kinds of business will not only have their own particular space needs, but also their own kinds of image. The banker and the lawyer need to project stability and reliability; the advertising agency and the theatrical impresario wish to appear creative. The bridge engineer wants both. Businesses also have different rhythms. Some remain constant in market, purpose and size year in and year out. Some – such as the construction industry – have a history of fickle markets and definite cycles. Others, for instance financial services, may have an unprecedented surge of growth, but then be caught off balance by an equally dramatic falling back.

All these factors are indicators to those charged with meeting a company's workspace needs. It takes skill to interpret them and to make predictions, and courage to then invest for an uncertain future.

This first part of the book has looked at the changing environment in which organizations, their people and their workplaces exist; at the new attitudes beginning to affect how they operate; and at how the idea of what 'office' means is under radical review. But what are the practical and psychological needs of the office workplace, and of the activities that happen there?

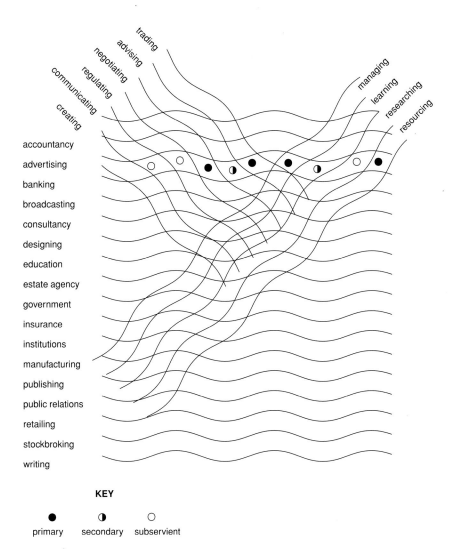

KEY

● primary   ◑ secondary   ○ subservient

Figure 3.8 Businesses and their functions.

Dilemmas

■ How much is territoriality inhibiting mobile working and the introduction of shared workstations?

■ How soon will senior executives accept that they too can be mobile, and can retain status without the trappings?

■ To what extent will offices become communications centres and meeting points, with most solo activities being carried out off site?

■ How will the demands of logical 'intelligent buildings' be balanced with the increasingly informal and intuitive organizations inside them?

Figure 3.9 Imagination, Bloomsbury, London: The atrium of this design and communications company is the roofed-over space between two Edwardian buildings. Bridges fly across at each level, and encourage people to stop and talk – as does the café, with its tables spilling out into the atrium at ground level.
Architects: Herron Associates

Digital Equipment Company
Stockholm

Industrial efficiency has improved some 1400% since the Second World War in most western countries. Office efficiency has increased by only 200%.

Jonny Johansson – Digital

Digital Equipment not only manufactures and sells electronic equipment worldwide but also, through its flexible work practice consultancy, encourages customers to use it effectively. The 'virtual office' is an integral part of Digital's own style, with employees working in local offices, small work centres, at home and with the customer.

Increasingly new work practices are mirrored by new-look offices, usually designed with a heavy user input. In Digital's Stockholm office it was decided that bad communications between sales, customer services and the design and management department (DecSite) were largely caused by the isolation of enclosed offices, as well as by being on two sites. The move into a single building was used to completely redesign the way people worked and the place in which they worked.

Consultancy sessions clarified objectives, and personal effectiveness programmes questioned ways of working and then considered solutions. A project team of four users was delegated to design the new workspace. A 3000m² open area now accommodates 450 people, with 20 meeting rooms. Of the staff, 230 are home based, but there is room for over half of these in the office at any one time.

Users' comments led the team to create an envi-

ronment considered stimulating and encouraging creativity. It was based on four themes: the archipelago, the beach, the garden and the golf course. Since all these are outdoors the result is known as 'The Natural Office'. In the centre of the office is an artificial tree, with fruit hanging down. Pressing a fruit causes a fully connected computer to descend from the leaves to any height. The user can then wheel up his personal workdesk (with bookcase and drawers) and set to work – sitting, standing or reclining as he finds most comfortable.

The administrative support staff operate on 'the bridge of the ship', sitting on a dais to see eye to eye with the customers. The floor around is decorated to resemble water and a beach. A glazed meeting room with reclining chairs looks out onto a mini golf course. Another raised area is a café, used for informal discussions.

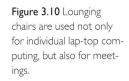

Figure 3.10 Lounging chairs are used not only for individual lap-top computing, but also for meetings.

Figure 3.11 The computer pulls down from the ceiling to whatever height suits the individual, and the trolley (seen in the background) is wheeled alongside. When not in use, the computers are stored among the branches of a great artificial tree.

Figure 3.12 'The Natural Office' is designed to simulate environments that encourage creativity. Elements of four concepts – beach, garden, golf course and archipelago – form backdrops in this innovative office. Because of Digital's flexible mode of working, the 3000m² space provides a base for 450 workers.

Slatted wood panelling, a standard domestic finish in Sweden, is used extensively, and this and an absorbent ceiling give reasonable acoustics. The remaining sound is masked by piped music. Artificial lighting adjusts to balance with the natural light coming in through the windows. Telephones are cordless, operating both in the office, and also off site. Paper has already been reduced by 70%; the target is 90%.

The success of this project has not only influenced developments in Digital's offices in other countries, but also its advice to clients.

Design: In house
Project completed: 1993

Figure 3.13 The café is domestic in scale and uses traditional Swedish materials and detailing. In crossing the bridge and changing level a different setting is created, for relaxation and informal meetings.

needs

London Underground Limited, Canary Wharf, London: These 26000m² open plan offices for the Engineering Directorate of LUL were designed to provide maximum flexibility for the 2300 technical and administrative staff. *Architects: Pringle Brandon*

Chapter 4
Activities

■ **The character of activities**

■ **Types of activities**

■ **Looking at activities**

Physical needs

Psychosocial needs

■ **Dilemmas**

Activities are at the centre of any decision-making about the workplace. Before anyone can decide what workspace an organization needs, even whether to move to new offices or to refurbish existing ones, they need to think through what should really go on in the new place.

Not what has always gone on, nor what everyone assumes may go on but, as near as possible, what should happen in the fresh context if the change is to make commercial sense. What will each person do – on their own, with others, sitting still or moving about, being quiet or noisily developing next year's brightest slogan? Pinning down what each task requires helps to define the workspace needs of each person and each group.

In the past everyone had their own desk, and did a variety of things at it: it was a general-purpose workstation. Now there is a tendency towards shared special-purpose workstations and a parallel tendency – thanks to mobile telephones and computers – to work wherever one chooses: in the cafeteria, the corridor or on the terrace.

Spaces reflecting the status of the person occupying them no longer make sense. The assumption that the chief executive gets the biggest chair, in the largest office with the corner view, is changing. It is not just that it may be more effective for the company if he works out on the floor among the staff: the bright creative team may take over that corner office, or it may disappear altogether.

This chapter is about questioning assumptions. It is about looking at the component activities of business functions, so that the pieces can be fitted together to form the complete workplace.

All activities have both physical and psychosocial needs. Some have similar needs, and can therefore go on in the same space – either side by side, or at different times. Others may need to be close to each other, but have incompatible requirements. Yet others are best kept well apart. Only by thoroughly analysing these needs can space planning become effective.

The character of activities

Business activities can be defined by their character, which may be:

– *Creative*. Brainstorming, designing, strategic planning, report writing.

■ …Man himself and what he wants to do… represents the yardstick by which design solutions must be measured.

Robert Sommer: Personal Space

Figure 4.1 Defence Research Agency Haslar, Gosport, Hampshire: Windows now pierce the brick walls, and skylights are set between the trusses. Staff work in groups of about two dozen, in spaces delineated by meeting rooms.
Architects: Percy Thomas Partnership

■ In a design office of 80 staff a delicious free lunch is available for everyone – provided that they eat it together. People are not allowed to take it back to their workstations. The directors believe strongly in the positive human and creative benefits of socializing.

–   *Persuasive.* Negotiating, presenting, training, selling.
–   *Absorbing.* Reading, researching, computing.
–   *Reflective.* Thinking, philosophizing.
–   *Humdrum.* Word processing, filing, photocopying, checking.
–   *Refreshing.* Greeting, eating, exercising.
–   *Informative.* Actively telling or passively overhearing.
–   *Compassionate.* Counselling, helping.

The activities may involve members of the firm only, or also include customers and suppliers, and even the general public. Activities can involve one person or many, and be wholly work oriented or not.

Types of activities

People work by themselves, by themselves but alongside other people, in groups relating to each other or as teams interacting closely. The divisions are not sharp: it is a spectrum along which different ways of working are ranged.

Solo activities

Solo activities, although usually done alone, may include moments of shared activity – such as discussing the exact wording of a draft or exchanging information with a neighbour.

Many solo activities take place collectively, in shared space, but with limited working contact between individuals. For instance, telephone operators and sales people may sit side by side, but work independently. When they communicate with each other it is not about work, but to make life more fun.

Group activities

Group activities are those in which the participants share a common purpose. Such groupings may be permanent or just temporary – like a group of disparate people meeting together to learn, to analyse or to decide. In group activities such as presentations, the focus may be on one person or a few. In others, such as meetings and seminars, everyone may interact with each other.

A team is a particularly potent group, where interaction between its members is the essence. It may have a long-term role, but is more likely to be focused on a specific project. By working sometimes alone and sometimes together a good team can produce more valuable results than the individuals on their own.

The dynamics of groups vary at different sizes,

with teams ceasing to operate effectively over about 15 people. Groups may be classified as:

–   pairs and trios
–   small groups   up to one dozen
–   medium groups   up to two dozen
–   large groups   up to four dozen
–   gatherings   over four dozen.

Traditionally, the large majority of group activities has taken place in pairs and trios.

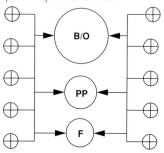

CO-ACTIVE GROUP
INDEPENDENT
dealers, telemarketers

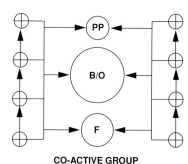

CO-ACTIVE GROUP
SEQUENTIAL
magazine production

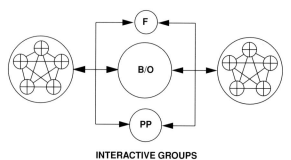

INTERACTIVE GROUPS
TEAMS
advertising, designing

Figure 4.2 Groups and teams: work linkages.
B/O – break-out space including coffee point
PP – paper processing: fax, printers, copiers
F – group filing

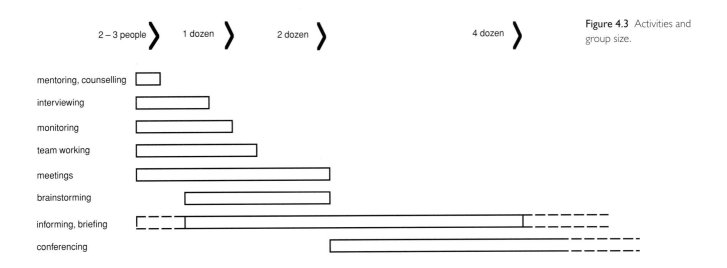

2 – 3 people > 1 dozen > 2 dozen > 4 dozen >

Figure 4.3 Activities and group size.

mentoring, counselling

interviewing

monitoring

team working

meetings

brainstorming

informing, briefing

conferencing

CRISPIN BOYLE

Figure 4.4 Designer's Studio, Hertfordshire: The studio of Alan Tye, Royal Designer for Industry, is attached to his house, illustrating his belief that home and work should not be separate. For easy cleaning the adjustable workstations have no legs. Daylight, heating and materials are all used to create a pleasing and comfortable workplace. A movable system provides storage, and also a place to conceal mess.
Architect: Alan Tye

Figure 4.5 The vectors of an activity.

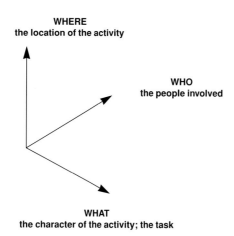

WHERE
the location of the activity

WHO
the people involved

WHAT
the character of the activity; the task

Congenial activities

We use the word congenial to describe those work activities that have a distinct social element; where it is possible to socialize while carrying out the task. The task itself may be a solo activity such as photocopying, or a group activity such as a working lunch. Or it may be a routine personal activity during working hours, like going to the toilet, making coffee or just circulating (especially waiting for lifts). Conversations may be work or socially oriented, often depending on the tempo of the moment or the ambience.

Social activities

Socializing is a major element in modern work processes, and designing for it to be effective is critical to business success. Social activities not only keep the customer and the worker happy, but encourage the invaluable exchange of ideas. The activities may be very casual – a quick word as you pass in the corridor; or formal – ten people sitting down for lunch.

Some activities can be done in more than one mode, as shown in Figure 4.10. None of the activities listed there is in the least unusual. We all think we know everything about them. But this book aims to look at work with new eyes, and face old issues as well as new ones, freshly. Work and home used to be kept quite separate (and many still like it that way); but now activities from both overlap, with babies being brought to the crèche and work being done on the dining-room table. Activities now need to be defined by the three vectors of 'what', 'who' and 'where'.

Figure 4.6 Aspects of activities.

Looking at activities

It used to be simple: writing was done with a pen on paper. Now it is also done with a keyboard and a computer. Soon it will be spoken to the computer and converted into text that way. If so fundamental an office activity can now be done in such very different ways, what are the physical design criteria for the activity of 'writing'?

Defining the needs of an activity involves discovering:

Operational aspects
What happens
Who makes it happen
When and how often it happens
What its characteristics are
In what different ways it can happen
What results from it
What other activities it needs to be near to, or separated from, and how important these relationships are
How valuable it is to the organization
Whether it still needs to happen

Physical aspects
What space it takes up
What environmental conditions it needs
What support and enclosure it needs
What mains services it needs
What furniture and equipment it needs
What are its physical effects

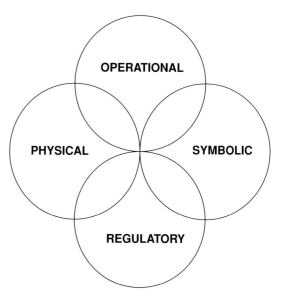

OPERATIONAL

PHYSICAL

SYMBOLIC

REGULATORY

Regulatory aspects
What laws and codes of good practice govern it
What procedures of the organization affect it
What customs of the workforce influence it

Symbolic aspects
What its symbolic significance in the organization is
How it should contribute to the organization's
    external image
What status it should confer on the worker

The operational aspects may be clearly defined, well established and unlikely to change. Or they may not. Business process re-engineering, abetted by IT, is re-examining many ways of doing things – and is questioning whether some things need to be done at all.

The physical requirements of 'writing' vary with the way it is done. So do the physical results. Pen on paper is a quiet activity: talking to a computer is not. And in a reconfiguration or refurbishment the physical capabilities of the premises may well affect the way in which the task can be carried out.

Regulations include not just law but the policies, procedures and cultures specific to an organization. While re-engineering may change the way an organization intends to do things, cultural change may be slower. Taking this into account avoids costly and demoralizing mismatches between organizational intentions and what is actually happening.

The prominence and quality of the group co-ordinators' workstations in a free-address office makes it quite clear how important their job is. All activities have an element of symbolism; and how this is treated says much about a company's aspirations and culture.

Physical needs

The needs of an activity are dictated partly by its nature, partly by the equipment used for it, but largely by the human requirements of those performing it. The needs are both physical and psychosocial (that is, needs related to a person's own feelings, and to his relationships with others). Although we start by isolating the physical ones, in reality the two are intertwined.

Space

Activities are just that: active. So space means not only room for furniture and equipment, but also room to open drawers, come round the desk to greet a visitor, or lean back in a chair without banging the wall. It means allowing face-to-face distances that are comfortable for conversation, and shelves that maximize storage close at hand while staying within a short secretary's reach. It means room to accommodate that extra chair, or the new (and slightly bulkier) piece of equipment, without having to shift everything.

In larger spaces such as meeting rooms it means providing space just inside the door for newcomers to pause while glancing around for an unoccupied chair, and for the presenter to move freely from whiteboard to flip-chart.

A degree of 'loose-fit' – if affordable – gives elbow room for change. To be really effective it should be carefully designed to relate to the way that the particular organization uses space.

Light and view

People prefer to work in daylight; but for part of the day it is usually insufficient, and for parts of the year it is too bright and hot. So artificial light is necessary, and also sun-shading. Different tasks call for different amounts – and kinds – of light.

Aspects to consider are listed below.

- *Illumination.* Enough light, but not too much.
- *Contrast.* The work more brightly lit than the background, but not glaringly so.
- *Direction.* Enough directional light to define the shape and location of objects, but not so much as to throw heavy shadows.
- *Colour.* Light that renders colours accurately, and that creates the right atmosphere.
- *Concealment.* Bright sources, whether windows or luminaires (light fittings) and reflections kept out of the main field of view.
- *Control.* The ability to adjust the light to suit the task and the worker.

Figure 4.7 Ernst & Young, Chicago: Reception area outside the main conference room. *Architects: Sverdrup Facilities Inc.*

Figure 4.8 Leo Burnett, Chelsea, London: Coffee area with venderette, comfortable seating and views.
Architects: Stanton Williams and Fletcher Priest

A view through a window provides respite from concentration, a change of focus for the eyes, and renewed contact with the 'real world' outside (whether scurrying passers by or wheeling swallows).

Air and temperature

Some workspaces may be small or crowded; some activities may use machinery or materials that give off fumes or smells. Good ventilation keeps people refreshed, machinery cool and odours away. Draughts, on the other hand, can disrupt paper handling and chill the sedentary worker. And where is the ambience of a cafeteria without its delicious aroma?

There is no such thing as a 'right' temperature for a particular activity. There is only a 'right' one for a particular worker at a particular moment. Factors that affect people's thermal comfort include: air temperature, air humidity, radiant heat from or to adjacent surfaces and sources (including the sun), the energy they are expending on the activity, the amount of clothing they are wearing, their tiredness and their perceptions.

Temperature and ventilation are closely connected. They both need variable controls, and in many cases these controls will be the same.

Sound

'How sweet the sound…' – but how awful the noise! The acoustic challenge in offices is to enhance the former and eliminate the latter. But this is complicated by one man's sound – say a telephone conversation – being his neighbour's noise – an unwelcome distraction.

Sounds need to be loud enough and clear enough. People need to be able to communicate, whether in pairs, groups or over the telephone. Calm and quiet may be needed for the conversation that must not be overheard, serenity for developing wide-ranging thoughts, and silence for carrying out complex calculations. At the same time, however, there is the psychological need to feel 'connected' to the workplace and to the world outside. The murmur of voices and the distant hum of traffic can be subconsciously reassuring to the solitary worker.

Furniture and equipment

Furniture and equipment are essential tools; but they also strongly convey the image of the organization – and maybe the status of its workers.

Robustness, ease of movement and versatility

ALISTAIR HUNTER

Figure 4.9 Standard Life Assurance, Tanfield, Edinburgh: The lower level of this two-storey building has an exposed coffered ceiling lit by uplighters, which also include emergency lighting. They are supported on service 'bollards' positioned in the centre of workstation clusters. Air is supplied from the deep floor void and extracted through the three atria.
Architects: Michael Laird Partnership

enable furniture and equipment to meet the varying demands put upon them. Ergonomic requirements, for comfortable and safe use, are becoming ever more demanding.

Ergonomics

Ergonomics relates to the whole way the body moves at work, but for the individual worker the chief issue is his workstation and chair. Well designed, these can help him avoid bodily damage. Repetitive strain injury (RSI), and upper limb or cumulative trauma disorders (ULD and CTD), are all names for

conditions in which the upper body has been damaged through forceful or awkward movements repeated over a long period of time. They are on the increase, RSI being most commonly caused through intensive use of a computer keyboard.

The operator who uses a keyboard intensively requires a workstation and chair tailored to his physical specifics – right height, depth, slant and so on. These operators tend to stay in one place, so it is not unreasonable for the workstation to be designed to fit them.

However, free-address working puts ease of adjustment at a premium. An approach may be the

---

RULES OF THUMB: ANTHROPOMETRICS

Anthropometrics provide measurements of people. The figures show dimensional ranges for desk workers, from the smallest woman to the tallest man.

	Centimetres
Keyboard/mouse/paperwork height (seated elbow height)	50–80
Near reach range (elbow to knuckle length)	30–40
Seat (pan) height (height to back of knee) – if this is less than 40cm, use a footrest	30–50
Centre of VDT or document display (seated eye height) – at 60cm viewing distance	100–140

■ One organization with a highly mobile workforce insists that everyone spends time in the office on one particular afternoon a fortnight. Despite shared desking, there are just enough seats for everyone to work or get together.

■ You are sitting at the airport drafting a complicated report, with people milling all round you. There are frequent loud announcements and two small children are fighting on the next seat. No problem: but then you catch the eye of a friend passing by, and though he doesn't stop to talk, concentration is never quite the same again.

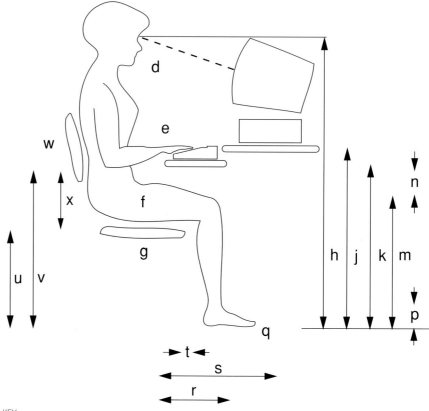

Figure 4.10 Workstation ergonomics. Dimensions cover male and female averages, but not extremes (nor individual preferences).

KEY

		centimetres
a	arm reach	40 - 60
b	distance to screen (more for large screens) + document holder	50 - 75
c	elbow to keyboard reach	30 - 40
d	working angle from horizontal eye level to centre of screen	20 - 30°
e	neutral forearm and wrist angle	5 - 30°
f	open trunk to thigh angle	90 - 100°
g	adjustable seat (+ / -5° from horizontal forwards and backwards)	40w x 36 - 40d
h	eye height to top of screen	1.0 - 1.40m
j	general worktop height	65 - 76
k	keyboard height (rounded edges and wrist supports)	58 - 70
m	under desk knee clearance	50
n	clearance between thigh and worksurface	20
p	under desk foot clearance	25
q	feet in firm contact with floor or footrest	
r	clearance for knees beneath desk	40 - 45
s	clearance for feet beneath desk	60
t	clearance between calf and front of seat	4 - 8
u	seat (pan) height	35 - 50
v	relaxed elbow height	55 - 75
w	seat back adjustable in height and angle (+ position of lumbar support)	
x	armrest height above seat (adjustable & set back from seat edge 10cm)	20 - 25

mobile mini-workpoint: personal chair, work surface and storage unit which the worker takes wherever she goes. An alternative is that the critical dimensions for her ergonomic comfort would be measured at the beginning of her workplace life and, as she changed jobs, she would take this prescription with her.

On the other hand, with the advent of voice- or stylus-operated computers, workers are being freed from the keyboard, and workstation fit becomes less critical. Chairs no longer need to be super-adjustable; and sofas and loungers can take over from the formal workstation.

Despite the extreme variation between individuals, adjustable desk height is still a rarity. Likewise, tilting work surfaces. Under European Union regulations such adjustability is not obligatory. Even in designers' own offices almost without exception desks are fixed – often being simply a flat panel resting on two filing cabinets.

Nor is chair design wholly satisfactory. The regulations call for task chairs to have both adjustable seats and backs, but certain chairs – with integral seat and back which adjust as one – are seen to comply.

Psychosocial needs

The psychosocial needs of the worker, like physical needs, vary from one activity to another, and between different people.

Interaction

Interaction between individuals and groups is becoming more important all the time. At an operational level, activities are integrated with each other; at a creative level, interaction breeds innovation; at an organizational level it compensates for dispersed working; and informally it provides the medium for that vital system of business communications – office gossip. The coming together of team members is critical to the underpinning of corporate culture and loyalties in a world in which everything is changing. There is therefore a need to see how each activity can be shaped to relate well to other activities and people. At the same time, unnecessary interaction can be expensive and time consuming.

Proximity

Proximity and interaction are two sides of a coin. Although telephone, E-mail and video-conferencing are reducing the need to meet face to face, spending time together is still the foundation of working rela-

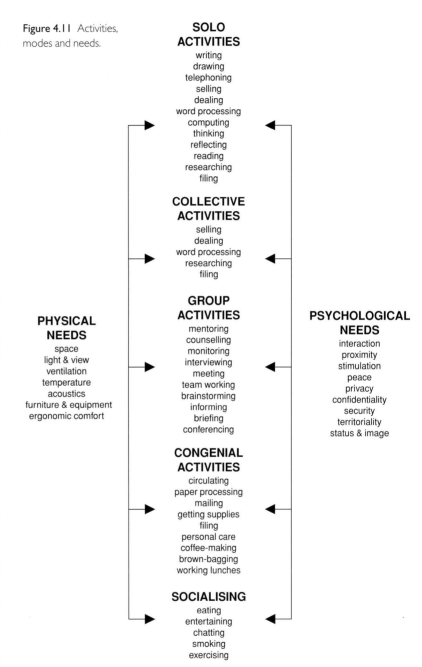

Figure 4.11 Activities, modes and needs.

SOLO ACTIVITIES
writing
drawing
telephoning
selling
dealing
word processing
computing
thinking
reflecting
reading
researching
filing

COLLECTIVE ACTIVITIES
selling
dealing
word processing
researching
filing

GROUP ACTIVITIES
mentoring
counselling
monitoring
interviewing
meeting
team working
brainstorming
informing
briefing
conferencing

CONGENIAL ACTIVITIES
circulating
paper processing
mailing
getting supplies
filing
personal care
coffee-making
brown-bagging
working lunches

SOCIALISING
eating
entertaining
chatting
smoking
exercising

PHYSICAL NEEDS
space
light & view
ventilation
temperature
acoustics
furniture & equipment
ergonomic comfort

PSYCHOLOGICAL NEEDS
interaction
proximity
stimulation
peace
privacy
confidentiality
security
territoriality
status & image

■ We observed a banker and a management consultant discussing confidentiality. In the bank everything was kept confidential, the directors always working behind closed doors. In the specialist consultancy, all client files were accessible to all staff. Both probably served the same blue-chip companies!

Figure 4.12 Ernst & Young, Chicago: Administrative area for 'hoteling'. *Architects: Sverdrup Facilities Inc.*

Figure 4.13 Ernst & Young, Chicago: Permanent offices for partners are on the external walls. *Architects: Sverdrup Facilities Inc.*

tionships. Proximity makes this easier; so each activity needs to be near the other activities with which human links are important.

Line-of-sight proximity scores in that what is said with the voice is often less important than what is communicated by the eyes, gestures and the whole body. The telephone filters out these subtle messages; chatting in someone's office doorway does not.

The design implications of proximity include space allocation and distribution, circulation routes, security and control, and the image such relationships can convey to staff and customers.

Stimulation, distraction and peace

Interaction can stimulate or distract. Repetitive activities benefit from visual or aural stimuli. Most people, on the other hand, need undisturbed solitude for reflective tasks. Although some can keep working through an earthquake, others' minds will wander

when someone in the distance crosses their line of vision. People react individually to sights, sounds or physical discomfort, and respond differently on different days and in different circumstances. It also depends on the activity, with reflective thought and brainstorming at opposite ends of the spectrum.

Some people need true peace for activities like creative writing: the totally non-intrusive environment, cocooning the body so that the mind can soar. Peace is found working at home, or being at the office early or late; but is such peace a reasonable demand during the working day?

Privacy and confidentiality

Privacy is personal, and generally to do with visual shielding. You may feel a need for privacy to weep when you have been sacked. Confidentiality, on the other hand, relates to communication, or rather to blocking it. It may be aural – preventing conversations, meetings or telephone calls from being overheard; or it may be visual – concealing documents, VDU screens and even theatrical but telling gestures from the wrong eyes. It may give protection from staff, customers or even the world outside.

Confidentiality has more to do with the work function (such as senior management, accounting, personnel) than with the specific activity. It also has a great deal to do with business culture.

Security

Security in part relates to confidentiality. There is good-housekeeping security, such as the backup of all IT systems and having sensible filing arrangements, and there is security against the intruder – whether man or mouse. There is also security against such hazards as fire. This can be two way: protecting things from fire, as with a filing archive; and stopping fire from occurring, as with a kitchen. Like confidentiality, it is often whole functions – such as research and development – that are security focused, rather than individual activities. Nevertheless, it is at the activity level that thinking about security needs to start.

There is also the human need to feel secure. This may include all approaches to the workstation being clearly visible, or safety from electric shocks from equipment.

Territoriality

Territoriality occurs at different levels, from the corporation putting its stamp on the reception area and the boardroom, and the team putting up posters in its workspace, to the individual workstation with family photographs and mementos. Where the activity area is not the preserve of one person, 'territorial markers' must relate to a higher level: the team or the organization. Locationless working is accelerating

ALISTAIR HUNTER

Figure 4.14 Standard Life Assurance, Tanfield, Edinburgh: Piercing the floor-plate of 18 300m², the three domed atria provide daylight, air extraction and automatic ventilation in case of fire. Each atrium is enhanced by themed planting, and is used for shared activities: meetings, group sessions, parties and the occasional performance.
Architects: Michael Laird Partnership

this trend, and affects workers' feelings of personal security and comfort.

Status and image

Status symbols can demonstrate how valuable an activity is – to the team, organization or customers. Physical manifestations continue (antique furniture, and a corner office) and, although contrary to the trend in work practices, may still be necessary for the corporate image. But in the long run image only operates effectively when it is an outward reflection of an inner corporate truth.

Dilemmas

■ To what extent will lightweight and mobile devices take over from desk-top equipment, and how will this affect the physical needs of the related activities?

■ How compatible are individual needs for privacy and personalization with open and informal work patterns?

■ To provide future flexibility, should space be 'loosely fitted' around each individual activity, or around teams or departments? Or is it too expensive to be loosely fitted at all?

■ Can the 'psychic synergy' of the vast dealing room justify its high cost?

Defence Research Agency Haslar
Gosport

workplace

Figure 4.15 The finance department of this new government agency is housed in a refurbished linear building only 6m wide. Careful layout and lighting creates a humane environment.

The DRA is one of four subsidiaries of the Defence Evaluation and Research Agency (DERA), the amalgam of a number of former government laboratories for defence research. Given agency status in 1992, DERA employs some 12 000 people nationwide. Although its main client is still the Ministry of Defence, increasingly it services the private sector – for instance it is providing simulation conditions for an attempt on the world land speed record.

To become commercially aware and viable called for a major rationalization. This has involved bringing specialists together into 'business sectors' focused on air, land and sea systems. It has also meant reducing over 40 sites around Britain to nearer 20. This is in train, with eight refurbishment or new-build projects completed or under way (for laboratories – a major

element – new build is generally more cost-effective). By the end of 1996 some 3500 people will have been moved.

Open plan working was seen as essential for encouraging effective team working, creativity and coherence, and for providing flexibility. It has therefore been adopted for all DRA's new offices. Cellular spaces are provided if needed for security and confidentiality, but not generally for status.

This building at DRA Haslar houses the financial services department, handling not only accounts for DERA but for other bodies such as the Meteorological Office. Here the Director of Finance sits out on the floor with the rest of his department.

The building was constructed in 1887 to house the first Froude ship tank (designed to test model

Figure 4.16 Part layout.
Key
1 meeting room
2 computer room
3 open office
4 coats/filing/copier

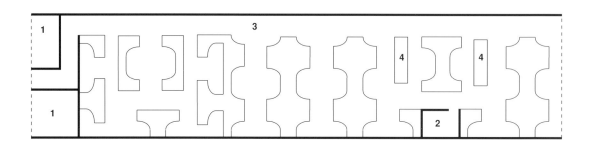

ship hulls for their hydrodynamic capabilities). Now this long thin brick building (6m by 160m) has been converted to house 120 people, almost exclusively at open plan workstations. Beneath a new concrete floor the tank itself is now used for paper storage – including seven years' worth of DERA timesheets!

The length of the building is divided by clusters of cellular offices and meeting rooms into open areas each housing about 24 workstations (one space has 66). Overhead are black timber trusses at 3m centres, each still with its number stencilled large as a marker for the original testing. Good natural light and ventilation is provided by windows which pierce the previously blank walls, and there are new rooflights above. With the trusses 2.85m above the floor and the ridge of the roof about the same height again, this creates a series of humane and well-proportioned spaces.

Workstations are normally 10m² gross (including storage and all circulation), but in some confined situations furniture dimensions have been reduced to provide workstations of around 7.5m². Each one has a basic 180cm by 150cm L-shaped worktop with a curved inner edge; additional straight or curved surfaces can be added according to need.

Generally the workstations are in paired clusters of four (known as the 'dogbone'), with circulation down one side of the building. Pedestal storage underneath is augmented by centralized lateral or drawer filing; but tall cupboards are located against cross walls only, so as to ensure a visually clear space.

Walls are white with grey-finished furniture and beech worktops ('look great but need treating with respect'). Timber doors throughout the building provide warmth; otherwise colours are shades of blue: carpet, chairs (star and sled based) and low screens (only 40cm above worktops). All storage is painted to match. Existing units were generally repainted, although in some cases it proved more economical to buy new.

Fluorescent lights hang between the trusses, and although basically downlighters, just enough light is directed upwards to illuminate the sloping ceiling. Heating is by hot-water radiators, and cabling generally runs in a perimeter skirting and from there it is distributed through the furniture. Patched telephones allow for easy workstation changes. Staff may share a printer with three others, but conversely may have two or more terminals each. Optical filing is gradually being adopted wherever possible.

The architects for the space planning, and the furniture suppliers for both the workstations and chairs were selected through a staged competitive process. An advertisement in the *EC Journal* called for expres-

GRAHAM CHALLIFOUR

Figure 4.17 At night downlighters over the windows accentuate the rhythm of their spacing, and counteract the blackness of the glass.

sions of interest, and these were then evaluated. Up to half a dozen firms in each case were asked to tender. Interviews confirmed not only the suitability of the product, price, competence and delivery, but any necessary understanding of the particular workings of this sort of organization.

The main problem with the move was persuading people that it was actually going to happen, and then getting sensible details of their needs (creative scientists may be a little impractical, but have a strong liking for shelf space for books and whiteboards for diagrams). 'If people are given enough time to get used to the idea and are helped with preparations (like disposing of 20 years' worth of papers – which may need to go to a museum or the Public Records Office), they can be moved with another dozen or three people over a weekend.'

Experts working for the DRA are a resource of high value – true gold collar workers. Though many still enjoy relatively high job security, a new environment such as this at Gosport not only helps them get over the cultural shock of moving into open plan; it should also discourage the asset from wandering.

Architects: Sawyer Architects
Space Planners: Percy Thomas Partnership
Project programme: Continuing

■ Creative thinking can happen anywhere, provided you can adjust. In my first job, 60 of us carried out complex technical tasks 50m from a runway and with everyone smoking away.
David Norman

■ Herman Miller and the space planners from Percy Thomas Partnership gave us first-rate professional support and excellent value for money.
David Norman – DRA Rationalization Team

■ The trouble with having senior managers out on the floor is that the space they need for spreading and confidentiality might cost less if provided by cellular offices.
David Norman

Chapter 5
Communications

■ **Kinds of communication**

Movement of people

Movement of objects

Movement of information

Choice

■ **Aspects of movement**

Patterns of movement

Circulation

Mobility

Orientation

Safety and security

Entering and leaving

Encounters

■ **Dilemmas**

Communication is the activity that links all the other ones. It may be physical – people, paper or things – or it may be electronic. Information may pass between people standing face to face, or between two pieces of equipment ten thousand miles apart. Now that business communications are more and more about information and ideas, what real advantages are there in being in a room together that justify the cost and time spent in getting there? Moving information electronically is far cheaper and quicker.

At the same time, the new technology also gives people more freedom to move if they so wish. Cordless equipment allows them not only to work anywhere outside the office – home, car or up a mountain – but anywhere within it.

So what is the right balance? Should people move around and the furniture stay put? Or should people stay put and talk to each other via the screen?

This chapter considers the kinds of communications in an office, and how they are being affected by information technology. It looks at the physical and psychological aspects, and how movement patterns can provide the armatures for physical layouts.

■ Jetting round the world makes the executive spend his energy on travel rather than real work. Virtuality allows the mind to travel, but the body to stay put, avoiding those 'junk-trips'.

COMMUNICATING

Talking. The words that are used, tone of voice and what is left unsaid are all a part of the communication.

Conversing. Casually, formally, privately or publicly have different characteristics.

Listening. Active listening means really identifying with the speaker: very different from allowing the sound to wash over you.

Looking. The eyes can deny a statement, colour it, or even change it completely.

Signals. Smiling, waving or gesturing can send messages of friendliness or antipathy, or with the precise: 'Let's go for coffee now'.

Body movement. Hands, arms and the whole body can tell much about what someone is feeling and thinking.

Touching. The meaning of a harsh statement can be subtly changed by a gentle touch on the arm.

Figure 5.1 British Airways Compass Centre, Heathrow, London: Escalators in the central atrium carry personnel up to the first floor, where flight and cabin crew check in automatically on a bank of computers.
Architects: Nicholas Grimshaw and Partners Interior Designers: Aukett Associates and Davies Baron

■ A manager, video-conferencing for the first time, was surprised to find herself feeling closer to the distant colleague on the screen – with whom she had eye contact – than to her other colleague sitting in the next chair.

■ Hundreds of years on the Bible is still accessible to all. Would it be if it had been written in Fortran?

Kinds of communication

Communication in and out of the office, and communication within it are different. Given the scope of this book, our overview of the first is limited – but important. For points of entry and exit usually have complex needs, as well as symbolic significance.

People, paper and other objects, and electronic information are what move around within an office. Historically, offices were designed around the movement patterns of the first two. With the rapid increase in information technology the pattern is changing.

Movement of people

People arriving at the workplace include staff and visitors – mostly customers or suppliers. They may include people who are handicapped, or even people who should not be there at all.

Once inside, a range of movement patterns emerges. There are mass movements at either end of the day – or when a major event takes place. There are movements of staff, who know their way around and have free access to most parts; and of visitors who may be unfamiliar with the office and, in any event, may need to be restricted for security reasons. People may move alone, or in groups. They may be sprinting to catch someone, carrying or wheeling bulky objects or be handicapped in various ways.

Movement of objects

The objects that are taken in or out of an office, and move around within it, include:

– *Paper.* Mail in, post out, files and folders all about: a myriad of small, individual items. Although the increase in office paper flow is diminishing, it is not until the next century that the total flow is forecast to reduce. Files and reports are still the most important objects moving around an office. Specialist items related to the business activity may include rolls of drawings, display panels or sets of product documentation.
– *Office supplies.* Most relate to paperwork: stationery, photocopier and fax consumables, pens and pencils, envelopes and file covers, brochures.
– *Office equipment.* Furniture and machines. Much is bulky, heavy or fragile. It may need to be trolleyed. New items arrive, and others go away to be serviced or repaired.
– *Special supplies and equipment.* Items for catering, housekeeping and maintenance. They may be perishable, bulky or unwieldy – and need trolleying.
– *Waste.* Moving out of the building – probably through a temporary holding area – is waste of all kinds: paper, kitchen refuse, housekeeping and maintenance waste, and discarded furniture and equipment.

Movement of information

Electronic communications can handle voice, text, data and images.

– *Voice and text.* These two forms, which are largely person to person, may take place by telephone, fax, telex, or computer (networks, E-mail, voice mail), or by a public address system, or closed-circuit television (CCTV). Video-conferencing has a growing attraction, but the technology still has limitations: reduced eye contact, less ability to see body movement (and an inability to keep up with rapid movements).
– *Data.* Large amounts of data can be handled by local (or wide-area) networks within the organization, and packet switched elsewhere. Advances in cordless technology are giving data greater mobility within the office, and with it, greater freedom from reliance on paper files. Whether data is kept on paper or electronically is now, except for certain professionals such as lawyers, more a question of the legal requirements than of

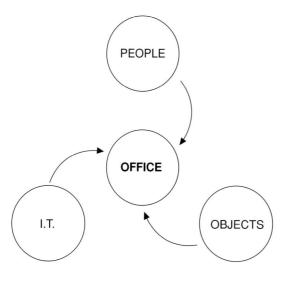

Figure 5.2 Kinds of communication.

the technology (although flicking through pages – and seeing them side by side – is still quicker than scrolling the computer).

Not only does electronic filing have the advantage of reduced storage space, but it can be retrieved from anywhere in the world. This allows a dispersed team to use joint information and, in allowing easy access, reduces the imbalance between those who have information and those who do not.

On the other hand there are drawbacks: controlling access can be difficult; it may be hard to get at old data when the technology on which it is stored becomes obsolete: and the ease and compactness of storage encourages keeping every scrap of information. How then to find what you want?

– *Images.* The transmission of images ranges from those that are linked to voice (video-phone and video-conferencing), through simple video images (e.g. security cameras) and faxes, to desk-top publishing (DTP) and computer-aided design (CAD). The last two bring enormous commercial benefits in terms of efficiency and speed, but continue to call for wired technology.

Choice

The growth of knowledge-based work and the paral-lel developments in information technology combine to give office workers greater mobility than ever before. They do not need to go to the office, or to stay at their desk if they do go there. 'Work is where the worker is'.

This new flexibility gives a company greater freedom in deciding how to run its business. The strategic decisions it takes about its communications can fundamentally affect the location, size and configuration of its offices. But – on the assumption that it still does want office space – the way movement is handled within that space can have a significant impact on operations, staff and the economics of the space.

Figure 5.3 Association of British Insurers, City of London: The reception desk with its three security monitors lies on the axis of the entrance bridge and controls access to the four lifts behind it. Revolving entrance doors keep it draught-free in winter, and it is cooled in summer by the stack effect of the atrium. The 4m diameter semicircular desk is 110cm high, with a visitors' bag shelf at desk-top height. *Architects: GMW Partnership*

Figure 5.4 Ernst & Young, Chicago: 'Swipe card' reader, which analyses the holder's access rating before opening the door. *Architects: Sverdrup Facilities Inc.*

tantly, to what links are not needed – for circulation is usually seen as a waste of space. These relationships may be considered from the viewpoint of the individual, or from that of the team, department or organization as a whole. They can be illustrated by bubble diagrams.

Whatever the basic circulation pattern, the system is ultimately hierarchical. The primary routes of the star, grid or ring are usually also the fire escape routes. Along these main routes are the group work areas and support facilities – 'magnet' areas (paper processing centres, kitchenettes and toilets), restaurant and library. The smaller branches serve teams, and twigs each individual workplace.

Clarity of circulation demands not too many

Aspects of movement

The functional and psychological needs of movement are interwoven, and are best looked at together, as are the needs of the individual and of the organization.

Patterns of movement

The star, the grid and the ring are the principal patterns of physical movement in an office. The first two can be three dimensional, but the last only relates to single floors. Their characteristics are:

–   *Star.* Centralized / orientation good / access good at the centre, but poor at the periphery / only one choice of route / easy to control and make secure / major meeting point at the centre / isolating (the linear building with a spine corridor is a simplified 'star').
–   *Grid.* Decentralized / orientation poor / access equally good everywhere / multiplicity of routes / hard to control and secure / variety of meeting points / integrating.
–   *Ring.* Peripheral / orientation reasonable / access moderately good everywhere / choice of two ways round / relatively easy to control and secure / ring itself is a linear 'meeting zone' / semi-integrating / if combined with several links between floors, takes on some of the characteristics of the grid pattern.

Circulation

The circulation routes in a particular workplace are related to who needs to be near what and, as impor-

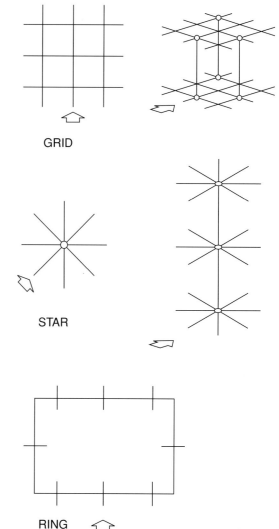

Figure 5.6 Patterns of movement.

PETER COOK

Figure 5.7 Glaxo Holdings, Mayfair, London: The headquarters of this pharmaceuticals company has detailing and finishes of the highest quality, including those in the circulation spaces. Double metal pilasters and domed plaster ceilings (uplit to give the impression of rooflights) define junctions in corridors.
Design Consultants: Murray Symonds Associates

changes of direction. Maximum movement should be channelled along the primary routes, with major facilities and 'magnets' relating clearly to them. Space for stopping and talking without blocking the way is desirable, and the ambience should sometimes encourage dawdling. Secondary routes, as within a department, should allow casual interchange, but not disruption. Tertiary routes are for the briefest movements – as within a team.

Mobility

Mobility is about freedom to move, and hindrances. People have always been able to move to new posi-

tions, but physical moves of their workstations have been costly. Because much of their electronic equipment is now portable and cordless, it can move about with them. Workspaces with a multiplicity of hard-wiring (such as dealing rooms) can use electronic patching, so that flicking a switch reroutes data to a new position without moving anything physically. Workstations can be rapidly 'repersonalized' – and this 'electronic churn' costs a few pounds, and takes only a few minutes.

Older workers, however, may have neither the physique nor the mindset to emulate the 30-year-old executive striding down the corridor barking into his mobile phone, and there are some for whom mobility is difficult: those with physical handicaps. The workplace should be designed to allow mobility – but not to exclude the immobile.

Orientation

For both practical and psychological reasons people need to know where they are. For new members of staff and visitors, offices can be confusing places. The floorplates may be large, and an orienting view to the outside far away or non-existent. Often the partitioning and desking systems, the lighting and the carpets are identical throughout the building.

Movement needs clear indicators. A distinctive view out, a clear sight of the building's core, the way the space is organized, or lowered ceilings are all

Figure 5.8 IBM, Bedfont Lakes, London: Reception area – 'meet and greet' stand-up reception modules enable receptionist and visitor to be both physically and psychologically 'on the same level'. *Architects: Michael Hopkins and Partners*

'structural' indicators. Or there are 'surface' indicators such as wall and carpet colours, and lighting. All these can guide and reassure people in a pleasing and subliminal way.

More direct are signs. Some offices are full of signs, from names and numbers on doors to arrows pointing in all directions. Others, even quite large places, have none, presuming that if you work there you know your way round; and if you do not, you should be accompanied. Signage often presumes that people can, and do, read. But many people take no notice of written signs, so the most effective communication is often with visual indicators.

Safety and security

The movement needs of safety and security are largely conflicting. Safety is principally to do with escaping from the building in an emergency. The statutory requirements for means of escape in case of fire are a major influence on the layout of any workplace. The essence is quick escape for the able bodied, staged 'places of refuge' for the disabled, and

protected routes inwards for the firefighters. Some buildings with very large open floorplates or open atria require additional measures to contain the spread of smoke and flame, and to enable the building to be evacuated swiftly.

Bomb threats are often treated similarly to fire, with the building being evacuated. However this may place the occupants in equal danger: from flying glass and debris, or even from a second bomb. The alternative is to create 'places of refuge' (for all staff, not just the disabled) within the building.

Security on the other hand is to do with restricting movement: controlling the entry of people and goods, and monitoring them once they are inside, using human or electronic systems.

– *People*. There are many control systems, and the aim should be to select a system – or combination – that is secure enough; but which is not unfriendly, intrusive or hampering to communication and flexibility. Easy ways out of the building make the occupants feel in touch with the world outside, but too many are hard to monitor, so that fire exits tend to be a weak link – especially when used for other purposes (such as smoking) during the working day.

– *Telecommunications*. Installations (e.g. telephone and cable intake points, PBX and computers) need to be protected from damage such as vandalism, fire or water. An uninterrupted power supply may be needed, and secure storage for back-up tapes and disks. The possibility of 'electronic eavesdropping', may call for electronically shielded areas for machines where the risk is high.

Entering and leaving

How people enter and leave a building, or an office suite, has a strong impact on their perception of the occupier. The first real point of contact with the company workplace is – literally – the door handle. Is it comfortable to grip? Is it clear whether you push or pull? Once inside, is the reception point visible, or else clearly signed? In parallel with the feeling of welcome, however, is the practical need for security: one monitored route, with a point for issuing passes (and possibly bag inspection).

Sometimes everyone comes in through the front door, including deliveries. However, separating people from goods allows for a tidy reception area, and may often be necessary for practical reasons. In some blue collar operations, workers and deliveries may be separated from executives and visitors, but this is now much less common. A more likely split is between

DENNIS GILBERT

Figure 5.9 BHP Petroleum Ltd, Piccadilly, London: These award-winning offices are a refurbishment of a 1920s building. 5300m² on four floors accommodates 180 people. Wavy walls not only turn corridors into exciting places to be in or pass through, but conceal columns or storage. *Design Consultants: Murray Symonds Associates*

those who arrive on foot at the front door, and those who come in by a side door from the car park.

As well as dealing with visitors singly or in small groups, the entrance has to handle crowds of arriving and departing staff. Although with 'smart' cards and badges much security control can now be self-service, the space needs of the daily staff fluxes are greater than those for visitors.

Even in the most open of offices there are still doors, and the fact that they are fewer and more deliberately placed gives them added significance as barriers. How they are approached, how generously sized they are, whether they open to screen or to reveal the room: these design aspects affect their functional and symbolic performance.

Encounters

Casual encounters can take place in cafeterias and toilets, or just passing by. Conversations in a corridor are visible to all, but so are potential eavesdroppers: a good place for brief but confidential exchanges.

Innovation comes from intragroup communication; but team members who casually see each other in the course of their movement around the office can be in different rooms or even on different floors without damaging their group effectiveness.

However, the way the building is planned can facilitate or discourage such random interaction. The individual at her workstation is generally presumed to be 'engaged' and therefore not to be disturbed; but once she moves around she is seen as 'free' to contact.

SPATIAL INTEGRATION

Professor William Hillier and Alan Penn of University College London have carried out research on 'spatial integration' as a key factor in determining communication networks that develop within a workplace. They believe these networks foster an innovative and entrepreneurial atmosphere. Computer programs predict whether a building will be easily understood and intelligible to move around in, whether it will be welcoming to staff and visitors and how lively it will be. Other checks include how interactive a particular space will be, the clarity of the circulation routes and whether facilities are correctly placed.

Dilemmas

■ How can concerns for disability, security and free and civilized movement patterns be combined?

■ Can the office notice board continue as a congenial meeting point, or will notices on people's personal computer screens take over?

■ With people now chatting on computers, will they bother to chat face to face?

■ Is the keyboard on the way out, and how soon will alternative methods of computer control come into normal use?

■ If the office becomes a meeting place for groups, rather than a fixed workplace for individuals, how will this affect internal circulation spaces?

■ If flexi-time and virtual working between them eliminate the morning and evening surges of workers, what will be the effect on the design of main circulation routes, and entrances in particular?

■ The directors of a small creative firm decided to have no internal telephones in their new offices. This has forced people to move about and talk face to face.

British Airways Compass Centre
Heathrow

The objective of the Centre for Combined Operations was to bring together flight and cabin crew reporting with operations, planning and delivery; the aim being 'to promote synergy and ensure that the business of flying passengers is conducted in the most successful way possible'.

This is not just an office building, but rather a highly complex focus for a round the clock operation. It was designed to be a physical reflection of BA's business strategy, with the smallest number of elements necessary to provide an effective and flexible infrastructure.

This called for a sophisticated approach. Specialist consultants were appointed to prepare the strategic brief, which was based primarily on comfort, operational criteria and the human perspective. The process included off-site brainstorming sessions for the whole team – sponsor, designers and contractor.

The 20 000m² building caters for a 24-hour operation, with 900 office workers and around 3000 crew members passing through each day. It is the base for 12 000 employees worldwide. Flight and cabin crew use the building on their way to and from their flights, for briefing (both electronic and face to face), personal administration and security checks. The operations function covers long-, medium- and short-term planning, and provides immediate worldwide cover every hour of the year. For emergencies there is a crisis centre – shared by BA with 60 other carriers – equipped with the most sophisticated and extensive technology for handling the internal and external aspects of any emergency.

A measurable result of bringing together personnel from 20 different sites around the airport is that flight and cabin crews – who previously would have met only on the aircraft – now meet in the Centre and then spend at least 20 minutes together driving out in the bus.

The Compass Centre consists of three buildings each three storeys high with an atrium. Glazed streets run through at each level dividing each block in half, with various facilities and places to sit, or stop and talk, along the way.

The main reception in the west atrium combines dignity with humanity, buzz with calm, hi-tech components with upholstered chairs and decorative place settings in the restaurant alongside. The atrium swoops up grandly, and contains shops and a bank, a crew baggage store and seating areas. Skeins of hostesses in patterned dresses, blazers and school-girl hats stream through constantly.

Automatic crew briefing is central to the system. Computers triggered by identity cards display or print out the relevant information. This equipment is on the first floor of the central block, and crew are swiftly lifted to it by escalator. Briefing rooms, help and welfare desks, and notice boards are round about. Operations and operations control are on the top floor. Crew, fleet and cabin services management offices are on other floors. Crew members and their baggage undergo full security checks at ground level before boarding sealed buses to take them out to their flights.

On all floors, single-person cellular offices with glazed fronts surround the open plan offices. Lack of

■ Changing lamps, cleaning luminaires, rewiring – maintenance of all sorts – for an around-the-clock place is a facilities manager's nightmare.

Figure 5.10 Automated reporting allows staff to obtain instructions by the insertion of ID cards. Computer consoles provide flight crew with full printed itineraries.

Figure 5.11 The crisis centre is designed to deal with internal and external aspects of an emergency, ranging from aircraft malfunction to a terrorist operation. Information technology includes land lines and duplicated receivers, fibre-optic and copper backbones and stringent security. The 'media wall' permits projected displays and the simultaneous viewing of several broadcasts. The centre is available to other airlines as needed; it is used normally as a training centre.

individual air-conditioning encourages doors to be left open, which is helped by double doors. Ceiling heights vary from 2.4m to 3.0m in the centre of each floorplate, reflecting the fall-off in depth required for services. The greater height allows ceilings to be lit by collars of uplighters around the columns.

System furniture is used throughout, with few screens except in certain areas. Work surfaces are wood, with chair upholstery, screen coverings and carpeting in either red or blue: red to pep up the executive east and west blocks, blue to calm operations in the central one.

Staff facilities include restaurants (open from 7am to 10pm), a bar, shops, a hairdresser, vending and coffee areas and sitting spaces of all flavours – including the totally domestic, with sofas and low lighting from table lamps. Meeting and conference rooms occur throughout the building.

The walls are largely glazed, with solar control provided by horizontal glass louvres and internal blinds. Even the north facade has the latter, due to strong reflections off an adjacent white building.

The offices are generally lit by fluorescent downlighters providing 350–400 lux at desk height (with task lights in some places). Lamps throughout the building are mostly high-frequency fluorescents. White SON, metal halide, and low-voltage spots augment these in atria, streets, vending and restaurant areas. Controls are designed to default to off, with presence and daylight sensors, and local switching.

Power, voice and data cabling run in the floor, with junction boxes for each desk position. In office areas the electrical supply is interleaved to provide a 50% supply in case of local distribution board failure.

HVAC (with fan-powered VAV boxes) is separate for each block, which provides a measure of back-up. Up to 45% of the air is fresh, and though there is no humidification, it could be added later. Plant rooms were delivered to site ready assembled and commissioned – time and space benefits overriding cost.

■ BA expects its flight and cabin crew to perform consistently at a high level; but if the crew aren't happy on the ground, then BA can hardly expect them to perform well in the air.

Sam Cassels – briefing consultant

CHRIS GASCOIGNE

Figure 5.12 Operations Control – a space for intense concentration, furnished and decorated in calming blues (conversely, red is used to liven up the administration areas). Even minor maintenance is difficult where such focused activities are continuous around the clock.

Figure 5.13 Layout.
Key
1   main entrance
2   secondary entrance
3   staff exit to aircraft
4   reception
5   restaurant
6   offices etc.
7   escalators to upper floors
8   security

Figure 5.14 Reception at the west end of the building is in an atrium with walkways running around at two upper levels. High-tech steel and glass mix comfortably with the timber reception desk to create a friendly place. Behind it, a tall blue glass panel is emblazoned with the airline's logo. Upstairs are a café, a bar, a hairdresser and a variety of spaces to sit and talk or just be quiet.

A single-stage fire system includes dry rising mains, separate firefighting stairs and sprinklers in some offices; but there are neither sprinklers nor smoke detectors in the atria. Fire doors separate the three blocks. The crisis centre is provided with total isolation, and the computer room has double-trigger sprinklers with dry pipework.

The Compass Centre is effectively a pre-let speculative building. This allowed a tailor-made fit-out, while keeping the basic building attractive to other tenants should BA ever outgrow it. Both shell and core and fit-out work were procured through construction management and competitive tendering for all packages.

BA expects the building to save £1m a year through improved safety, efficiency, customer service and operational excellence. The outsider can see that it also reflects the airline's avowed management belief that team working, interaction and staff contentment are central to a successful operation.

Architects/Interior Designers: Aukett Associates/ Davies Baron
Architects (for the building): Nicholas Grimshaw and Partners
Management Contractor: Bovis Construction Ltd
Project completed: 1994

Chapter 6
Spaces

■ Primary spaces
   Spaces for solitary work
   Spaces for collective work
   Group spaces
■ Ancillary spaces
   Paper processing centres
   Filing centres
   Refreshment points
   Toilets
■ Support spaces
   Reception areas
   Libraries
   Training suites
   Auditoria
   Mail rooms
   Reprographic units
   Archives
   Medical centres
■ Social spaces
   Restaurants and cafés
   Shops
   Clubrooms and bars
   Health centres
   Retreats
   Crèches
■ Service spaces
   Workshops
   Staff rooms
   Stores
   Plant rooms
■ Circulation spaces
   Lifts and lift lobbies
   Escalators
   Staircases
   Refuges
   Corridors
   Passages
   Delivery areas and goods lifts
■ Home spaces
■ Dilemmas

We define a space as an activity area with a boundary. It may contain several different activities, either simultaneous or sequential; and its boundary may be more or less substantial, varying from a solid wall to a line in the carpet.

Ease and speed of response to change is now a central design criterion. Businesses must change in order to survive; processes must change and with them workers' roles and relationships. So too must spaces, in order to accommodate the new ways of working.

New patterns reverse the old. Workstations are becoming single purpose, and fitted to the task: booths for solo activities, small rooms for quiet discussions, and tele-conferencing rooms. Libraries, conference rooms and cafeterias, on the other hand, are now used for a wide range of activities. It comes back to economy: workstations must be tailored to support excellent performance; and large spaces cannot sit idle for long parts of the day.

This chapter aims to illustrate how the needs of activities and communication may be best accommodated. Spaces form the 'building blocks' that must be fitted together to create an effective office layout. At the same time they are the 'boxes' in which activities take place.

We divide spaces needed by an organization into:

- *Primary.* The principal workspaces (housing the core activities).
- *Ancillary.* Spaces containing functions which support an individual work group or department.
- *Support.* Spaces containing functions that support the work of the whole organization.
- *Social.* Spaces containing functions to do with the non-work activities of the occupants.
- *Service.* Spaces containing functions to do with the operation and maintenance of the building.
- *Circulation.* Spaces to do with movement around the office.

Figure 6.1 Leo Burnett, Chelsea, London: General workspace, with cellular offices on either side, their glazed partitions providing borrowed light and a feeling of openness in the building.
Architects: Stanton Williams and Fletcher Priest

Figure 6.2 Types of spaces in an office.

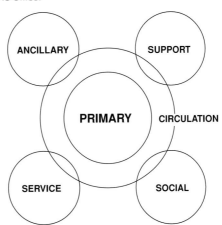

■ If the business machine – typewriter and computer – had always been lap-top light, how would work surfaces be configured today?

Primary spaces

Primary spaces in the office should make it easy for individuals to concentrate and groups to interact. A balance of different spaces helps to create the conditions in which skills and talents can develop.

The work carried out in primary spaces may be done alone, collectively, in teams or in groups. Each kind of space has its specific needs; and many spaces are being given fresh names to free them from historical preconceptions – though perhaps attaching them to other ones.

Spaces for solitary work

The places people need when working alone have particular characteristics. Reflective tasks want no distractions: people nearby can be a disadvantage. The solitary worker is more aware of physical comfort. So good environmental conditions, and the right equipment and furniture, are particularly important, especially for repetitive work.

Confidentiality may be necessary; from overlooking but more particularly from overhearing. Conditions for confidential telephoning may be relatively easy to create, but with voice-activated computers the level of sound insulation may need to be higher still.

Workstations

Activities and functions vary, but each individual needs somewhere to carry them out. The setting of desk and chair has remained remarkably unchanged for the last 150 years; but the individual may well prefer to stand up to work, to lie in a hammock or to walk back and forth with her voice-activated computer hanging round her neck.

Workstations need space for the worker, furniture and equipment. Space means room to carry out tasks, convenient access to storage and freedom to move without bumping into things – 'room to swing a cat'. It is a matter of both ergonomics and ambience.

For the conventionally seated worker, the most basic furniture element is the human support: chair, stool, sofa, bench – whatever it is that holds us up once we are off our feet. Chairs should be comfortable for everybody, whatever their shape or size; so to provide a single type of seat for everyone, as most employers do, looks pretty silly.

The work surface – desk in old language – is usually more or less horizontal, and with a number of functions. Paper pushing is still a main office activity,

THE JARGON OF SPACE NAMES	
Individual spaces for concentration	*Teamworking area*
	Commons
Booth	Combi(nation) space
Box	
Carrel	*Congenial area*
Cave	Break-out area
Cell	Village pump
Cockpit	
Cubby-hole	
Den	*Shared facility*
Hoffice (= home office)	Hot desk
	Touch-down area
Personal harbour	
	Parking place for storage trolleys
Team workstation area	
Cove	Garage
Cluster	Kennels

and the desk supports paper, to be read or written on. With the computer, screen and keyboard can be mounted to suit the individual and the processor tucked neatly down below.

Despite talk of the paperless office, quantities of paper still need to be stored. Current work files, reference material and stationery, and office tools (pencils, staplers, scissors and sticky tape) all need their proper place.

Personal possessions, both practical and iconographic, need their places too. The practical often relate to bodily needs: tissues, medicines, biscuits or bottled water. Iconographic items are usually decorative: photographs, souvenirs, things which bring the outside world to the office and illustrate your place in that world to your mates or visitors. They may also confer status, like diplomas or a shelf of learned books.

On – or built into – this furniture is the equipment: telephone, computer, and specialist items ranging from arrays of dealing screens to PBX switchboards. Around and about are accessories such as filing trays, bookshelves and wastepaper baskets, and maybe a freestanding task light. The well-planned workstation provides enough space for all these.

Transient space

'Hoteling' and 'touch-down desks' have created a new form of workstation. These shared desks are used by shift workers (like telesales), those dropping by the office for a short while (such as the sales force) and free-range workers who are probably part of a team.

The physical requirements for telephoning, computing and paperwork may be the same as for a permanent workstation, but the social nature of the space is entirely different. People have no personal territory, their neighbours change and may even be strangers from other branches of the organization; and any storage is movable in some form. In such space, orientation and arrangements need to be clear and simple, so that they can be quickly grasped by the occasional user.

Shared desks make good sense economically, but their impersonality may not be much liked. The answer could be some kind of 'work pod' – the private parts of the workstation separated off from the more general parts. The mobile storage trolley ('caddie' or 'puppy') or tote bag used in several organizations does this to an extent; but perhaps seating, task lighting and the PC should also be included. The work pod could move to different settings, its owner fully equipped to work anywhere, with all her tools and personal belongings to hand, and ready to plug in.

Booths

Like the monk's cell for peace and contemplation, the booth can provide a useful antidote to normal workplace bustle. As it is for general and transient use, it can be minimal in size and without permanent storage. It may not even contain a PC or telephone. It is either fully enclosed, or well screened and acoustically treated. Lighting, heating and ventilation should be excellent, and preferably directly controllable. It can do without the distraction of views to the outside world.

Private offices

At one level the office is a workstation with walls round it; at another it is the imposing throne room of the chief executive. Historically, personal offices have occurred at all levels of the management hierarchy, providing private places to work, but also underwriting the status of their occupants. This scenario is changing, and private offices are now more to do with function than rank. The office as perk is giving way to the office as tool.

The symbolic aspect of the private office continues, but not as unquestioned right. It may now be the lair of the executive team, rather than one person's domain. The gap between workstation function and

JON MILLER – HEDRICH-BLESSING

Figure 6.3 Ernst & Young, Chicago: Concierge at his workstation in the main document control centre. *Architects: Sverdrup Facilities Inc.*

the traditional office function is closing too, with almost everyone from chairman to clerk using a computer. Now each needs the same kit.

Executives spend most of their time talking to people, sometimes walking about but frequently – and perhaps confidentially – in their offices. Given the pressures on their working day, strategic thinking is more often done 'off site' – at home. Their offices may only have a minimal workstation, with an elegant table for paperwork or meetings. Often there is relaxed seating for more informal discussions.

Their office space may be a multiple of the workstation module, with standard furniture; or it may be quite different in both size and furnishings. Paintings, photographs and souvenirs on display shelves may all be used to stamp identity on the space. Because executives are now so mobile, personalization is likely to lie in the small accessories rather than the furniture. But conversely, the style and quality of the general furnishings may confer status on whoever is occupying the 'throne room' that day.

Spaces for collective work

The typing pool is now consigned to history, but much individual work in offices is done in shared spaces: accounting, telephone selling, technical draughting or share dealing. The book-keeper may be a quiet introvert intent on his ledger or screen, but the dealer is more likely to be noisy and hyperactive. Thus pool spaces can have very different requirements in terms of furniture, IT, lighting and acoustics. A common need, however, is to provide nearly identical working conditions throughout the space, even if far from a window or wall. In contrast with this uniformity, the aim should be to give everyone a sense

■ At Flemings Bank in London the partners have always shared a single office. Situated at the top of their building, they work at large 'partners' desks' in three groups of four, separated by slim screens, but able to share and discuss anything that comes across their desks.

Figure 6.4 CDP, Soho, London: The reception area of Collett Dickenson Pearce, with its colourful furniture, and a television and coffee to hand, aims to set the tone and display the company ethos. *Architects: Harper Mackay*

Figure 6.5 Glaxo Holdings, Mayfair, London: This oval meeting room is set between two cores, with an uplit fibrous plaster ceiling making up for the lack of natural daylight. Eames aluminium chairs surround a specially designed table. Veneered panelling of polished pear-wood faces the core wall, with a carpeted floor changing to concentric rings of marble in the reception area beyond. *Design Consultants: Murray Symonds Associates*

of place and orientation – a chain of pools rather than a vast sea.

Many pool areas are private to an organization, but others, such as a secretarial area outside a group of executive offices, have a public face. This raises conflicting issues: the area should be welcoming, but the secretaries should be able to do confidential work without being overlooked or overheard by visitors.

Group spaces

Group spaces are the heart of any business. They are where people meet to talk, listen and together create and implement solutions to the job in hand. They may be in the open – at a workstation or the whole team space – or in a dedicated and enclosed room.

Meeting points

The simplest are just meeting points: a spare chair or two at the workstation, and perhaps some extra worktop. Separating off the table and chairs may be more space efficient and flexible, with a cluster of workstations sharing one meeting point. It is important, however, to ensure that these discussions do not unreasonably disturb nearby workers.

Team spaces

Today team spaces are the focal point of many offices, particularly those of creative organizations. Most of

the time teams work in a common space, where all members can get together without moving far. Much of the interaction is in pairs and trios; but at times a small group may go off to a meeting room, and at others the whole team may get together in a special room for formal presentations.

The size of the space depends on how big the team is and what it does. The location should enhance access for the team members, and minimize cross-circulation by other staff. Depending on the team's activities, physical comfort may be less important than good environmental conditions and access to IT. Often team spaces have furniture that can be moved about to meet temporary working needs.

Furniture may be unconventional and aimed at encouraging a high level of relaxed discussion. Indeed, if team members reckon they work best up a mountain or in a conservatory, then the space may be designed and decorated to put them in mind of those places. This can work well for long-term teams, but short-term teams will have less opportunity for such idiosyncrasies.

Even if personal territory is harder to come by in today's workplace, team territory is likely to be clearly staked out. Boundaries may be formed by screens, tall cabinets or planting, and the 'market place' can happen around the team notice board or coffee machine. The team may have its own grouped filing and storage, and its own paper processing equipment.

0830: group area

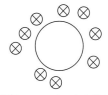

1000: personal workstations

1030: coffee area

1315: restaurant

1400: meeting room

⊗

1700: study cell

Figure 6.6 Settings for daily activities showing how different settings may be required in the course of the day.

Studios and drawing offices

These spaces are hybrids: sometimes team spaces and sometimes collective ones. The studio tends towards the former and the drawing office to the latter, but much of the time both spaces contain collectives of small teams. Where the work is paper based, space demands are considerable: drawing boards, lay-out and pin-up areas, and drawing storage (horizontal, or vertical – which, like lateral filing, is more space efficient). High-level, even and shadow-free lighting is needed, with good colour rendering where artwork is involved.

Studios often need sinks; and sprays, producing unpleasant fumes, demand open working areas and extra ventilation.

CAD workstations, while larger than those for word processing, are smaller than traditional draughting stations, but they still need spreading and storage space for drawings. Lighting levels are lower, and designed to be glare-free. Colour rendition is probably less critical.

Boxes

Booths keep noise out, boxes keep it in. Sound-proofed rooms are useful for noisy creative activities – either people arguing vigorously, or loud music to get them stimulated. To be acoustically effective all elements must do their job: partitions, doors, ceilings and ducting, and even the windows. Glass partitions provide the exciting spectacle of the antics in the box seen as in a silent movie, although they can be expensive to get right.

Meeting rooms

As space becomes more flexible, enclosed space is increasingly valued. Meeting rooms are not only used for meetings, but as telephone booths, cells for concentrated work or even places for a quiet nap.

However, the chief purpose of meeting rooms is to help people communicate well. Just as activities take place in different-sized groups, so too meeting rooms need to vary: from a den where two or three people can huddle together, to a boardroom where a couple of dozen executives can concentrate in comfort.

The smaller rooms may be used for very personal activities such as mentoring, counselling or interviewing. Furnishing can be simple, and people may want to sit side by side rather than facing each other.

Often meetings do not take place sitting round a table, and certainly smaller ones can be effective in the more informal atmosphere created by comfortable living room furniture. Brisk decision-making can be encouraged by people remaining standing.

A round, oval or even square table is better at encouraging participation than a conventional rectangular one. However some organizations still cling to the status of the head of the table (conversely, at Cabinet meetings the British Prime Minister sits in the centre of the long side). Chairs need to be comfort-

■ At award-winning public relations company HHCL, architects Harper Mackay designed a Chinese yellow meeting room to discourage long meetings: no chairs and just a counter to lean against or jot notes on.

able, easy to move and suitable for a variety of physiques. Meetings can be long, and there are not the same opportunities to get up and stretch as there are at a workstation.

Monitors, videos, screens, PCs, whiteboard photocopiers – even a video-conferencing facility – may all be found in meeting rooms, as well as the more basic flip-charts, display surfaces and telephones. The most sophisticated meeting rooms have such equipment built in, and often concealed behind panelling. Other rooms adopt an alternative approach, with modular tables and freestanding equipment that can be configured in a variety of ways, or removed altogether to an adjacent cupboard.

Meetings often happen over lunch. This can be sandwiches and coffee on trays, cordon-bleu salads wheeled in on a trolley or a hot meal from an adjacent pantry. Between meals fresh coffee from the sideboard and cool drinks from the fridge make the room self-sufficient.

Meeting rooms tend to be rectangular, with comfortable proportions of around 3:2. Even if the table is square or round, some milling space at one end makes the room more convenient to use. Acoustics need to be considered; in larger rooms people at one end of the table need to be heard clearly at the other – even over other muttered conversations. This calls for a rather less absorbent ceiling than in normal office space.

Lighting too needs to be effective without being tiringly harsh, illuminating not only documents on the table and displays on the walls, but also the participants' faces. Body language and expression form the largest component of face-to-face communication, and give meetings one of their main advantages over other means of communication. The daylit meeting

room may need light from other sources so that people with their backs to windows do not become faceless silhouettes. Meeting rooms are often shut tight for confidentiality, so good ventilation is essential.

Electronic meeting rooms

Video-conferencing technology is moving ahead rapidly. Before long it will not be people talking to others on a video monitor, but a virtual meeting. Video-conferencing facilities vary enormously in scope and sophistication, but a dedicated room is similar to a small studio, where small groups face the monitors and video camera (or cameras). Faces need to be lit well and sympathetically, and slightly dead acoustics are helpful.

Computer conferencing is now being used in the USA. In this case the participants are all in the same room, but communicate with each other – and the group as a whole – through their own computers and screens. The arrangements have more in common with a small dealing room than with a video-conferencing room.

Presentation rooms

Presentations and lectures may be given in meeting rooms, but differ from meetings in that participants face towards one or more presenters (often backed by projection screens, whiteboards or monitors). Furniture must be flexible, and the technology may be sophisticated. In the simpler rooms the monitors, videos, projectors and loudspeakers may always be visible. Alternatively they can be concealed behind panels when not in use. Sophisticated installations have a projection room and sometimes a translation booth. Control may be from a lectern, or from other single or multiple positions.

The complexity of this technology (as with video-conferencing) may well require a specialist installation, and a design that brings together the needs of the participants, the technology and environmental considerations such as acoustics, lighting and ventilation. The whole installation should be capable of accommodating frequent technological advances.

Seating may be in straight rows or arcs, although fire regulations in some instances require that it is fixed, or in semipermanent sections. If fixed, then seats can be provided with their own microphones in the larger installations. It is unlikely that there will be a raked floor: to achieve good sight lines a permanent or modular dais is more common. Eating and drinking are normally discouraged, so no special provisions are needed.

Figure 6.7 Talk Radio, Soho, London: Conference room with audiovisual screens that can receive transmissions from three other locations. *Architects: Harper Mackay*

PETER COOK

Ancillary spaces

Ancillary spaces – those which support departments or floors of the office – mostly involve paper handling or personal care.

Paper processing centres

These are the focal points throughout the office area where equipment used by a number of people is grouped together: photocopiers, binders, printers, fax machines and shredders – as well as stationery stores and mail points. These centres need to be efficient, with good lighting and ample layout space and storage; but there is also the opportunity to encourage interaction, both by people in the same work group and by a wider mix. It is desirable to keep them separate from eating and drinking areas, to avoid spillages on the work or the machines.

Filing centres

Paper filing continues, but it is more efficient to file centrally than at each desk. People coming and taking files away to their workstations may linger for a chat if the place is congenial. Providing stand-up work counters in the filing centre where people can work briefly on files without taking them away can generate more purposeful interactions if adjacent working is made possible.

The filing may be traditional, with file folders in drawers or lateral racks. The latter take up less floor space, but are significantly heavier. This may affect location. Many offices have overdesigned floors that can take heavy loads anywhere, but the more economical ones have only limited areas where such loadings are possible – such as around the core.

Where mobile workers use their own 'puppies' (mobile pedestals or trolleys, tote bags, or brief cases) there needs to be a central 'kennels' or locker area (which may also have space for outdoor clothing).

Refreshment points

Today's self-service office has a range of facilities, from water fountains to small local cafés. The most common are the kitchenette (which may contain a microwave for heating up snacks, a fridge, sink, storage and waste provision) and what we call the 'venderette': an area for vending machines of greater or lesser sophistication.

Where a vending machine is within a kitchenette it is easier to control it all. The area can also be made attractive, with good light and ventilation, and tables and chairs, creating small informal meeting places. These larger refreshment points can, like paper processing centres, be positioned to encourage interaction between groups and teams that would normally have little contact.

Toilets

Girls cry in the loo, and fellows brag. Toilets can be a significant element in the informal communications of an organization, provided that their social, as well as their functional, aspect is recognized in the design. Their quality (and management) can also tell much about company culture, and its concern for the individual. Being offered a choice of towels or warm air indicates that individual preferences matter; and a thoughtfully placed seat will help the momentarily unwell, the milk-expressing mother, or the pair who need a moment to clinch a deal.

Entrances to toilets are often cramped and unfriendly; WC cubicles may be more like equine loose-boxes than private compartments; basins, mirrors and hand-dryers may be so positioned that using one blocks use of the others; and unisex toilets for the disabled may be limited in design or location.

Men and women need good mirrors, including at least one full-length one, lighting which, though diffused, is bright enough for shaving or making up, and hooks and shelves for hanging up a coat or putting down a file. If showers exist nowhere else in the building, one for each group of toilets becomes essential in these times of bicycling workers and lunch-hour joggers.

Easy cleaning is obviously a high priority, but this should not lead to sterile finishes. Toilets can be fun. As areas used for short periods only, the designer may legitimately stretch his imagination.

Figure 6.8 Cable and Wireless, Mercury House, London: Even the toilets are carefully detailed to be elegant yet practical. *Architects: Austin-Smith Lord*

■ In Scotland there is a trend for unisex self-contained WC cubicles, similar to small disabled toilets. While this is highly civilized, it is also space hungry, and eliminates the social aspect of toilets.

Sol Cleaning Service
Helsinki

workplace

Sol Cleaning Service is one of Finland's most respected enterprises – winning the quality prize in the large company category in 1991. Employing 2700 staff and with a turnover of over $50m and growing, it is the main cleaning and waste management company in the country.

Its 20 offices around the country are described as 'studios' – which signals a unique attitude. The innovative culture almost eliminates hierarchy. Everyone does their own clerical chores and makes coffee for guests (note – not 'visitors' or 'clients'). Supervisors are seen as being there to facilitate employee success, or to act as 'peer counsellors'. The firm's strict quality control system works both ways, with customers as well as staff making suggestions on how to improve service.

Five years before moving to the new office, Liisa Joronsen, the president of Sol, started planning the workplace. Together with the 'Sol people' she asked: 'Why must an office look like an office? Why can't it be colourful and as nice as a home? Why must we have our own rooms and desks and use office furniture chosen by someone else?'

'What are office hours for? Why not just work when it suits you best – even evenings and weekends?'

'Why can't we work anywhere that suits us?'

Over a thousand ideas came out of the discussions, which made for a difficult but exciting time for the architect – Jari Inkinen. However, this interaction generated such staff commitment that the change to the new premises and work methods was accomplished with ease.

Here shared facilities really work. The new head office has 26 workstations for 75 people – a space reduction of 70%. The 600m² single-storey building, once a film studio, has a ceiling height of 8m, and walls decorated with naive paintings. It is described as chaotic – with occupant numbers and noise levels fluctuating wildly.

Everyone works in the open plan space, learning to concentrate surrounded by noise. For confidential calls or meetings with clients or friends, they just go to a quiet corner, taking their mobile phone. Joronsen says: 'The freedom is a joy. None of us would ever like to work in a "normal" office again.'

Using domestic furniture reduced fit-out costs by 40%, despite technical sophistication, which included advanced data processing equipment and mobile phones for everyone. Brightly coloured tote bags are used for personal storage, rather than the more common 'caddie', and are stored on a high central rack. Cleaning materials for the company's business operations take up 200m², but office paper storage is down to the minimum – Sol had a good spring clean before moving and now uses electronic filing almost exclusively.

When asked what practical advice she would give to others creating new offices Liisa Joronsen says: 'Choose materials which are easy to clean, and provide good places for cleaning equipment – of course! But the main thing is that the space must arouse positive feelings and happiness. The happier people are, the better they work. Don't prevent your people from doing good work – let them enjoy it.'

Architect: Jari Inkinen
Project completed: 1991

JUHA RAHKONEN

Figure 6.9 Workstations for free-address workers. Belongings are kept in tote bags, stored in high (and decorative) racking when not in use. Mobile phones allow calls to be taken in the most convenient spot.

MANAGEMENT PHILOSOPHY

No rooms – no desks – no specific hours of work. A lot of creativity.
Freedom to work how you like – where you like – when you like.
What is good for the individual is good for the company.

JUHA RAHKONEN

■ Our corporate culture has been created in co-operation with our people. We thought carefully and decided you shouldn't differentiate between work and leisure. Why should people who act totally independently during their free time need rules and regulations at work – just switch off their brains and take orders?

Liisa Joronsen

Figure 6.10 'Why must an office look like an office?' An old film studio now contains 26 workstations serving 75 people, but looks anything but an office, with its meeting space equipped with domestic furniture.

Figure 6.11 Layout.
Key
1   reception
2   billiard table
3   television corner
4   archive
5   forest (with mice and
    birds)
6   7 person workstation
7   kitchen table
8   kitchen for baking
9   living room/library
10 drinking fountain
11 bag rack

■ At the offices of Leo Burnett in London and Cellnet in Slough there are two facets to reception – welcoming and security. On entering, visitors are greeted by the receptionist behind the desk. She provides badges and alerts the person who is being visited. Beyond this point lies the 'security threshold', although the guards only come forward if necessary.

Figure 6.12 The British Council, Prague: The Palac Dunal – a 1920s building – has a traditional 'doughnut' plan. It has been substantially restored and now provides a reception area in the atrium. The original glazed ceiling has been renovated, as has the glass block floor which allows daylight to penetrate into the library below. The space is lit by uplighting through the glass floor, indirect light through the ceiling and some accent lighting. *Architects: Jestico + Whiles*

Support spaces

Support spaces serve the operation of the whole office, and may also present a public face. They frequently have complex functional requirements, and even defining their design criteria (as with an auditorium) may call for specialist advice.

Reception areas

Reception is where the company greets the world. It is the first part of the company that most people see. So its design – how it works, how it looks and how welcome the visitor feels – can set the tone for what may be a long business relationship. But welcome may be at odds with security, and how this is handled is a challenge both to the company's philosophy and to the designer's skill.

Except in the small office, where there may be an entry-phone, the security threshold normally lies beyond the reception point. Main entrance doors are free-opening (though sometimes draught-lobbied), and usually within clear sight of the reception desk. Additional control may be simply by a security man walking around or at a desk (where random bag checks may take place). Stricter security may involve gates, turnstiles, light beams or doors – usually operated by some type of card. However the physical security barrier, as well as being slow, does send out a message of mistrust that is at variance with many a corporation's culture.

The reception desk is one area where designers are encouraged to go to town, even in the staidest of companies. Nevertheless it does have to accommodate a variety of functions. Visitors must be greeted, and may be asked to write their names in a book, positioned to be comfortable for those standing (or in wheelchairs). Couriers deliver or collect small packages, which have to be stored temporarily. But the reception desk is also the receptionist's workstation, so it usually has a word processor and sometimes a telephone switchboard. It may also have CCTV monitors if there is no separate security point.

The design issues needing particular consideration are:

– *Tidiness*. How to conceal incoming and outgoing packages, and the shaggy back of the wordprocessor.
– *Eye contact*. Whether to raise the seated receptionist to be nearer the standing visitor's eye level.
– *Disabled*. How to make part of the desk low enough for wheelchair users to have eye contact and to sign in.

RADOVAN BOLEK

Waiting visitors are often deterred from sitting down by chairs that are so deep that they feel at a disadvantage when rising to greet their hosts. Seating areas to the side of the main circulation (situated so that legs are kept out of the way) allow visitors to converse discreetly – and even to have a brief meeting with their host. Comfortable seats send out welcoming messages, as does easy access to coat storage, toilets, hot and cold drinks, and reading material (all of which should be outside the security threshold).

Information in reception – whether the company logo, brochures or products – should be displayed with elegance and practicality. The computer terminal too, for staff to log in and for finding out where people are (or what 'hot space' is available), should be placed prominently, but not in such a way as to cause a bottleneck.

Libraries

Libraries have traditionally been places where people worked alone or talked in whispers. However the resource centre provides a different paradigm. Collaborative study is encouraged, and more than ever librarians are information advisers. Both these activities call for small spaces where quiet discussions can take place without disturbing other users.

The design of the library should reflect the material that it contains – books, magazines, papers, catalogues, samples, slides, photographs, drawings, microfiche – and may require expert design input (beyond even that of an experienced librarian). Shelving, drawers, cabinets and cupboards may all be specialist items. The librarians need horizontal work surfaces for processing books and documents, and each needs an extended workstation (often with two VDTs) from which the whole library or at least the exit may be viewed.

Users need comfortable seating and work surfaces, power points for their computers, even, shadowless light, acoustics that mop up excessive sound – and no telephones. Increased use of computers demands careful attention to lighting and ventilation.

Training suites

For the learning organization, training is a continuous activity, and in larger offices it may have its own dedicated space. A feature of modern training methods is their great fluidity. One moment the group may be sitting in rows watching an audio-visual presentation, and half an hour later they may be working in small teams, role playing or video-recording each other.

Training space has therefore to be flexible and well equipped, with mobile furniture and equipment (and storage for it), blackout, and acoustic isolation (team competitions can turn noisy!). The training officers need office space as well: a place for administration, preparation of training material and occasional escape from the stress.

Auditoria

Few organizations need a full auditorium. Its basic function is very similar to that of a presentation room, but an auditorium tends to be less flexible and more impressive. Clearly directional in plan, with fixed seating and often a raked floor, and with sophisticated acoustics and lighting, the space is restricted in its use. Sometimes it is positioned below ground, where lack of daylighting reduces its adaptability still further. Nevertheless, where there is an auditorium its interior design is functionally and symbolically important. It needs to combine the functional efficiency of a presentation room with the elegance of a boardroom.

Mail rooms

For many organizations the mail room is a key element in their work process. It is a 'paper factory' handling inward and outward flows of letters and packets and, even with offices, a certain number of parcels. The need is for a space with two arrays of benches or tables, for inward and outward flows. Letters and parcels flow separately. Peak times can be hectic, so the layout needs to be rational and spacious enough to minimize the chances of confusion and error.

Stages in the inward flow for which separate workstations are needed include: rough sorting of letters from bulky items, opening, extracting and date stamping, sorting and pigeonholing or placing in internal carriers, and possibly a scanning machine for suspicious items.

■ Entering the offices of an electronic giant, blobs of Blu-Tack stare one in the face. Stuck to the inside of the glazed doors are two notices – different sizes, heights and typefaces – telling the departing visitor to return his badge to reception, and to press the button if the door is locked.

```
RULES OF THUMB: LIBRARIES

Space allowances
2.5–3.0m² per user, of which
  1/2 materials
  1/3 users
  1/6 administration

Performance criteria
floor loadings (bookstacks)      6.5kN/m²
lighting levels                  250–350 lux
```

Figure 6.13 Cable and Wireless, Mercury House, London: Conference and lecture theatre seating 100 people.
Architects: Austin-Smith Lord

■ A London firm of solicitors keeps its paper archive in cheap storage 30 miles away, and employs a full-time dispatch rider to ferry files back and forth.

The outward flow needs workstations for: sorting, weighing, franking and bagging. If the organization is involved in direct mailing, the outward flow may also include workspace for printing, collating, addressing, folding and inserting, and plastic sleeving. Where bulky publications have to be sent out, packaging and strapping need space, as does storage for stationery and wrappings.

Reprographic units

DTP now enables organizations to produce their own literature. For short runs (and confidential items) the whole process may be carried out in the office. Longer runs, and those involving complex artwork or binding, may be designed in house, and have the production contracted out. As a result, a large part of a reprographic unit may be a studio, with the in-house processing element relatively small. The creative disorder of the studio may require separating from the tidiness of paper processing.

Archives

Even though bulky paper files are often stored off site in special repositories or low-rent premises, much archiving remains on site (as disks or microfiches) and needs to be secure.

Where files are stored densely, floor loading may be an issue; in all cases light, temperature, humidity and vermin need careful control if documents are not to deteriorate. Archives may seem safe in a fireproof room in the basement; but water from a burst pipe or a backed-up drain can cause as much damage as fire and, if the archive is used only intermittently, may not be discovered for some time. Few organizations will need a strong room; even those that handle cash will normally find freestanding safes sufficient.

Medical centres

Apart from normal first aid requirements, large organizations in remote locations (which may include inner city development areas as well as rural sites) may find it practical to provide a medical centre (even if it is only staffed part time). It may be used for health checks, travel inoculations and even routine dental treatment or physiotherapy. The suite is likely to consist of a waiting area, one or two treatment rooms and its own toilet. Particular design considerations will be hygiene (including hazardous waste disposal), and the security of valuable equipment and medicines.

Social spaces

Social spaces are the ones in the office that people use for activities largely unconnected with work: the cafeteria, the gym, the club room or the crèche.

Restaurants and cafés

In offices the most common formalized social activity is eating. Although it may range from 'brown bagging' at the desk to formal entertainment of customers, the main eating space is likely to be the restaurant. The utilitarian canteen is disappearing and more attractive restaurants and cafés are taking its place. For companies out in the wilds a restaurant is essential; but those in city centres are seeing the business advantages of having one – and a good one – even if it costs money and space to do so. Good subsidized food can promote healthier eating habits and encourage staff to relax and socialize with their colleagues. It expresses management's attitude to its staff. It also usually leads to shorter lunch breaks.

Single-status restaurants are increasingly the norm, with the chief executive eating alongside the workforce except when entertaining or having working lunches. But single status does not necessarily mean a single space; imaginative variation can give great flexibility of use.

Staff canteens used to be buried in the basement using up cheap space, with the directors' dining room in the penthouse. But the modern single-status café now takes pride of place: on an upper floor with wonderful views; enjoying the extra dimension of the atrium or an outdoor terrace; and increasingly, close to reception. Sunny atria or jazzy caves can be a powerful antidote to the business environment, and encourage a relaxing change of pace. However, this should not prevent the use of the restaurant for informal discussions throughout the day. Only then can the space be used economically.

Planning restaurants often involves working with the caterer nominated to run the facility. Although this brings practical expertise into the design team, it also carries the risk that the result is purpose designed for that one firm, and will restrict the use of other caterers at a later date. Whatever the

■ Our café shows the staff that we care for them, and the client that we have high standards: a single level of excellence, and generosity without extravagance. Our food reflects our work ethic: simple ingredients, not dolled up, good looking, wholesome, creative. Our way of eating …demonstrates the sort of work we aim to do.

Jane Scruton: founder partner, Wolff Olins

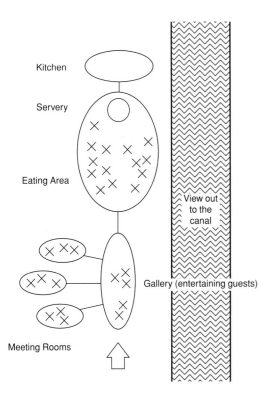

Figure 6.14 Wolff Olins, London: Staff restaurant with people eating in different settings.

Figure 6.15 Restaurant with glazed doors opening out onto a canal. *Interior Designers: Wolff Olins*

■ If we need to have a heart to heart we come here, into the restaurant. We sit out of the way over there, have a cup of coffee – the buzz of conversation drowns what we say. We are quiet and can be really hard hitting. Much better than getting people into the office.

Tom McAulay: facilities manager, Motorola, Edinburgh

RESTAURANTS: SERVICE CRITERIA

Checklist for establishing type and extent of service:

Facilities other than the restaurant that are available in the office (executive dining rooms, sandwich bar/delicatessen, venderettes);
Number of people likely to use the restaurant;
Proportions of managerial, clerical and manufacturing staff;
Proportions expected/intended to use the facility;
Hours the facility will be open (lunch only, breakfast as well, 12 or 24 hours, coffee meetings, etc.);
Use of the facility for meetings outside meal times, and how this will affect cleaning and preparation;
Times staff like to eat/need to be persuaded to eat;
Feasible number of sittings (will relate to business operations);
Types of food and service required;
What customers will pay (nothing, token payment, basic food cost, percentage of food and labour costs, full cost including cost of facility);
Worth of the facility to the organization, and in what ways.

---

approach, it is necessary to establish the service criteria.

Eating areas

Although seating can be packed in as densely as one seat to every 1.4m², this limits flexibility of use. If at least some parts of the restaurant are more generously planned, then both at and outside meal times it can be a relaxing place for reasonably private conversations. Privacy is also better if the circulation to the servery is separated from the eating areas. Round, square or rectangular tables for four to six people are generally the most popular, although banquettes and booths are economical with space and give additional privacy. They are, however, less flexible than open spaces with loose furniture.

The eating area is normally two to three times the size of the support areas (servery, kitchen, stores and staff rooms); but if space is at a premium it may be more efficient to have a separate coffee area so that a second sitting can be accommodated.

Dining rooms

Private dining rooms still exist to entertain and impress customers, but increasingly they double as board or meeting rooms. Their aesthetic varies from reflecting the dining room of a minor stately home, with antique furniture, old master paintings, curtained windows and fine silver and glass, to the more functional (though still opulent) room with communications equipment hidden behind panelling.

As the highest standard of food may be served in these rooms they either need to be close to the main kitchen or to have their own (or at least a pantry with reheating facilities).

Serveries

In office restaurants self-service is the norm (and self-clearing increasingly so). While the operating and regulatory requirements of the servery are more complex than those of the eating area, the design of both should be considered together, with harmonized materials, colours and lighting.

Serveries may be laid out with linear counters or islands. The latter take more space, but allow swifter throughput, particularly if people are not choosing the full menu. The cash desk can prove a bottleneck, and an extra position to cope with peak loads reduces diners' frustration.

Kitchens and ancillary areas

The design of the kitchen depends not only on the number of meals to be served, the number of eating areas (such as directors' dining rooms) and the length of service through the day, but also on the kind of food served and the purchasing policy. Complex meals require more preparation and cooking space; preprepared supplies need less preparation area (and refuse storage) but more food storage (much of it refrigerated). Catering consultants or equipment suppliers can give valuable advice, the former for a fee – the latter less impartially.

Shops

Delicatessen

A delicatessen provides a useful service in larger offices, and may, like the catering, be outsourced. It may be located in the catering complex or be on the 'main street' alongside hairdressers and health centres. While its overall design is part of the general interior scheme, it needs to conform to normal retail requirements, and to the specific requirements of the tenant.

Newsagent

Often a newsagent and general store is run by the catering contractor. Apart from selling sweets, stationery and toiletries it may well provide other services such as film processing, video rental and cleaning.

Hairdresser

Where this exists, it is normally a concession. Like the newsagent, it may only require a modest space, but needs plumbing as well as power.

Travel agent

Organizations with substantial international travel can find it convenient to 'implant' a branch of a travel agent within their offices. While its principal purpose is to support the business activities, it forms a staff amenity as well. Although it does not need much space, because it handles high-value items such as air tickets it needs good security arrangements.

Clubrooms and bars

These are less a feature of offices than formerly; indeed some firms have 'no alcohol' as well as 'no smoking' policies. Nevertheless, remoteness or company culture may create a demand. The clubroom may contain a lounge area with a pool table and a dartboard. The bar itself is likely to be a modest affair, operated by the members themselves. If the staff club has wider responsibilities, there may be a small meeting room/office.

MARCUS HILTON

Health centres

In major complexes there is often a health club, usually situated below ground level, and probably run as a concession. It may include a swimming pool, squash courts, gym and sauna, or be simply an exercise room for aerobics and table tennis with adjacent changing rooms and showers. Because it is likely to be used before and after work, as well as at lunch time, access to it is often controlled separately.

The more substantial elements such as a pool or squash court are likely to be part of the original building design; but even fitting out a gym or sauna can be highly technical, with specialists involved in the design as well as the installation. Particular issues are keeping the centre's noise and its ventilation separate from the rest of the office. The space does not have to be wholly utilitarian. Decorations, furnishings and especially lighting can make the place, as well as the activities, a refreshing experience.

Retreats

People in all organizations need occasional privacy – to say prayers, to be quiet, to lie down; or separation – to smoke without disturbing others, to concentrate on a game of chess. With the open office removing this freedom, the quiet room becomes of increased importance. Although such retreats do not need to take up prime space, they should not be too inaccessible. It is not only smoking rooms that may be needed during office hours.

The provision of these retreats, with natural light, good ventilation and comfortable furniture shows that a company is aware of the wide needs of its staff.

Crèches

As mothers with young children re-enter the workplace (and fathers become more involved with child rearing) the company crèche becomes a more common feature in the larger office. The actual need varies depending on type and age of staff, location and so forth. Large office complexes may house an independent crèche, available for all tenants and run by a specialist organization.

The office crèche allows parents to lunch with their young, to be apart for less time and to be available in case of crisis. Not only does this add another dimension to the humane office, but it encourages mothers back to work more quickly. Absenteeism is reduced, as the parent feels more confident in leaving the mildly ailing child nearby, rather than miles away.

The statutory requirements for crèches lay down

Figure 6.16 British Airways Compass Centre, Heathrow, London: Quiet rooms. 'We put the furniture tidy each morning and by the evening it is all over the place.' – Jane Wiggins, Facilities Manager. *Architects: Nicholas Grimshaw and Partners Interior Designers: Aukett Associates and Davies Baron*

Figure 6.17 Lloyds Bank, Canons Marsh, Bristol: This 33 500m² building houses 1400 retail banking staff. Three floors are linked by staircases which connect with the primary circulation running around the perimeter of the courtyard. Added to these views are others out of the building towards the harbour.
Architects: Arup Associates

needs for space, toilet facilities and such like; but again the atmosphere of the place is critical. Staff, infants and parents all react to light, colour and comfort. Reducing the scale of furniture, lowering glazing heights so that toddlers can see the grass outside and breaking down large spaces all help to create a friendly family environment.

Atria and terraces

Atria, terraces, courtyards and conservatories may be used as part of many of the social spaces listed above. Whether within a building, or just outside it, they provide part of its functional space; equally, they often have an outdoor character – more generous dimensions, natural materials, planting and water. They also offer another benefit: an attractive view from other parts of the office.

Atria are the lungs of a building: literally, with foul air exhaled by stack effect; and metaphorically, by revitalizing the spirit (and eye) with their longer views and flourishing greenery. Increasingly they are being used throughout the day for meetings and study, and not just for circulation and relaxation.

External green spaces – terraces, courtyards and gardens – can be designed as extensions to the office interior, and add greatly to its amenity. Not only can they act as overflow space in balmy weather, but even in winter a brisk walk can generate an equally crisp discussion.

Service spaces

Some organizations outsource their building maintenance, so need little space within the office. But others still carry it out themselves and need to accommodate it.

Workshops

The workshop is likely to be a general-purpose space, for woodwork, metalwork and electrical repairs. Although repairs may well be simple, if they include furniture, then ample space must be allowed both to work on it and to store it temporarily. Generous doorways (and the space around) help make manoeuvring bulky items easy.

Good lighting, and ventilation to remove dust and fumes are necessities. If painting is to be done this may require a separate, ventilated space. Storage of inflammable materials such as timber, glues and solvents must meet fire regulations, and health and safety requirements should be to the fore in the design of the work areas. Unless power tools are bench or floor mounted (which is unlikely) there should be no need for a three-phase electrical supply.

Staff rooms

Even in today's integrated organizations blue collar staff need some separate facilities. Maintenance

CHRIS GASCOIGNE

Figure 6.18 Leo Burnett, Chelsea, London: The escalators that connect first floor reception with street level were not part of the original design. However, early selection by the tenant allowed this major customization of the shell and core. *Architects: Stanton Williams and Fletcher Priest*

workers need somewhere to change, and drivers somewhere to make a cup of tea and read the paper before setting off again. A suite of mess room, changing room, shower and toilet meets all these needs.

Stores

All offices need to store their working supplies; and larger ones have store rooms rather than cupboards. Much of the active storage is for office consumables: stationery, and computer and photocopier supplies. There may also be brochures and other publications. More bulky is the storage of furniture (spare chairs, tables and screens). Major furniture storage is often done off site or even with the supplier. Secure storage may be needed for projectors, computer spares, telephones and other expensive equipment. Refreshment points and venderettes need back-up supplies; restaurants have their own storage.

Apart from this routine storage, there may be transitory storage associated with the delivery bay,

mail room and reprographics unit, and catering. Clean items need to be stored separately from dirty ones; and office waste may need separating for recycling, compacting or both. Catering refuse should be held in an area that can be easily washed down.

Plant rooms

Main plant rooms come with the building, but local plant, patch and control rooms may have to be incorporated at fit-out stage to deal with new technology.

Pride in the 'engine room' (showing off shiny insulated ducts and colour coded pipes) remains prevalent and is a part of humanizing the office for those 'backstage'. Engineers have to work the same hours as secretaries, so why should their workspace be any less attractive? It is also practical. The engineer at his BMS console needs to be alert; and to sit in a comfortable chair in a refreshing environment enables him to play his part in the organization all the better.

■ At Canary Wharf in London's Docklands, the seventh floor restaurant of Crédit Suisse First Boston has fabulous views on all sides. Essentially it is a daylit place, so the lighting in the internal lift lobby, from which you enter, simulates daylight with cold cathode tubes set within a glazed ceiling.

■ At the Standard Life Tanfield building in Edinburgh, a red line in the carpet on major routes indicates the limit beyond which furniture may not be placed.

Circulation spaces

Circulation routes are like rivers and their tributaries, and it is their eddies as much as their flow that are important to office life. They are not just about facilitating the movement of people; their quiet corners are essential for casual interaction.

Despite its transitory use and lack of specific function, circulation space can be a positive design element. Its character can tell more about the culture of an organization than many other spaces.

Lifts and lift lobbies

Lift lobbies are places for action, and for interaction. When the lifts are there, people need to move swiftly on and off them. While they are waiting it is good to be able to chat. This can be encouraged by using sympathetic materials, lighting and acoustics, as it can within the lift itself. But the pleasure of travelling in glass-sided lifts and admiring the outside world can mean that they become inefficient through overuse and under-occupancy (three-fifths full as against four-fifths for normal lifts). Lift lobbies are too often places set apart, as much by their design as by their location. Integrating their design with the rest of the workspace can give circulation movement a comfortable unity.

Escalators

Escalators, as an alternative to lifts, have the advantage of moving people fast and without an actual or perceived barrier. They are rarely installed within the office itself, as their great carrying capacity is seldom required (4500 people an hour or more); but they can be useful for bringing people onto an upper main floor from a lower level entrance. The feeling of movement that they create is generous, especially when they pass through atria – but they are even less conducive to casual conversations than lifts!

Staircases

The grand staircase rising through the atrium is not only a focal point, but also a place from which to look around, to wave to colleagues and to pause for a chat. But people rarely stop to talk on an enclosed staircase unless it is made comfortable – with views out, perhaps soft flooring, lighting that is domestic

rather than institutional in character and acoustics that do not resound. Escape staircases are normally too utilitarian to encourage dawdling, yet where they are designed sympathetically they become attractive and convenient routes for short journeys.

Refuges

The refuge concept is a response to the problems of the disabled, and to the hazards of terrorism. A well-protected area within a building provides a staging point for the disabled when escaping, and shelter from bombs. A refuge should provide protection from blast and structural collapse, as well as from heat and smoke; and it needs a structurally secure exit route. As well as emergency lighting it may have its own independent ventilation system.

Corridors

After reception areas, corridors can do more to set the tone of an office than any other part. Some of the most attractive corridors avoid an institutional feel by the use of curved walls, indentations, lay-bys and carefully designed ceilings. Raising the ceiling height at junction points, and uplighting or highlighting doorways can do much to relieve monotony. Glazed partitions and open doorways, providing natural light and views, can make for a civilized space at little extra cost.

Figure 6.19 CDP, Soho, London: Stairs are important communication links between the five floors of this advertising agency. Generous landings make progress pleasant.
Architects: Harper Mackay

Passages

Whereas corridors force people to follow specific routes, what we call 'passages' in open plan space are less well defined. Nevertheless they need to indicate clearly the circulation hierarchy. Otherwise not only is it difficult for strangers to find their way around, but people may short cut along secondary routes and thus impinge unnecessarily on others' privacy. There has to be a balance between encouraging contact as people pass by, and discouraging uninvited interruption. Screens of a height that shields the dropped gaze of the seated worker from that of the passer-by are an effective compromise.

Passages also need to indicate which are primary escape routes. Width is a major indicator, and this may be underwritten by higher screens, carpet colour, and plants or pictures emphasizing changes of direction.

Delivery areas and goods lifts

How to handle goods moving in and out of the building depends on the size and sophistication of the operation. Access, checking, recording, storing and issuing all need their own system, space provision and route. Trucks and trolleys may be involved, as well as service lifts or hoists. Goods handling can be noisy, and may well include outgoing waste as well as incoming clean supplies. For both these reasons, goods lift lobbies and delivery bays are best kept separate from the main office circulation.

Goods circulation comes under particular strain during a fit-out, especially if other parts of the building have to be kept working normally. At first there may be a flow outwards of dusty (and perhaps hazardous) waste from stripping out; then bulky construction materials arrive; and finally there is a flow of valuable and delicate furniture and equipment.

Home spaces

Young mothers and sales people have long combined their work and home personalities, but home working is no longer something only for them. Chief executives to the youngest recruits now work from home, at least sometimes. Home working also allows those with disabilities to enter fully into the marketplace.

Some people can write a report amidst children watching television; but others need a physical change of conditions before they can get into work mode at all. Whereas the office in the corner of the living room may be fine for some, others need a sep-

---

HOME WORKING NEEDS:

Space. To work, for equipment and tools, for storage – your space, not family space.

Place. To be uninterrupted (different from being undisturbed – the children may shout, but they don't ask for help).

Servicing. Warmth, coolth, light, power and IT connections.

Protection. From a mug of orange juice ruining the freshly printed report, the computer getting disconnected at a critical moment, or the child being electrocuted by a loose power lead.

Confidentiality. Of information – whether paper based or electronic.

---

arate place: a converted garage at the bottom of the garden, or the local telecentre.

It also depends on what work they are doing. Senior managers use home time for thinking and for report writing – which may require as little as a chair in the garden or an extra pillow on the bed. For sales people, however, home may be their main base with files, samples and considerable computer work.

Workspaces in the home may therefore vary from a corner of the kitchen table with filing beneath the stairs, to a specially built and equipped extension. The degree of sophistication can also vary enormously. If the home worker is an employee of a firm, what responsibility does the organization have for the home office (even if the employee only works there some of the time)? What statutory regulations must be observed? Should the home office be designed to the same level of sophistication as the main office?

Dilemmas

- What are the characteristics of spaces that encourage creativity? For groups? For individuals?
- If the library becomes the brain of the knowledge-based organization, how will its layout change?
- What features should a space for reflective work have?
- What is the smallest enclosed space suitable for periods of concentration, and what are its specific characteristics?
- Is the move towards dedicated telephoning spaces practical – or necessary?
- What elements of the home workspace are the most critical for effective working?

■ Joanna Foster, Director of the BT Forum on communications, does major thinking at home during a three-day weekend, but writes serious reports back in the office.

Barr and Stroud
Glasgow

workplace

RICHARD BRYANT – ARCAID

Barr and Stroud is part of Pilkington Optronics. The company designs, develops and produces opto-electronic equipment, mainly for the defence industries: periscopes for the British navy, and night-vision sights and laser rangefinders for tanks.

The company needed to move from four separate buildings. It wanted somewhere that would suit present and future operational needs; be affordable to build, operate and maintain; and make a positive statement – to customers and the community – about it being a high-technology firm. The move was seen as an opportunity to embrace information technology and organizational change, including single-status working.

The solution is a beautifully designed shed – 12m high and 166m by 108m on plan. It is laid out simply: the manufacturing processes to the south are divided from research, development, design and administration to the north by an internal 'street' running from the goods entrance at one end to the staff one at the other. This is enhanced with stained glass panels; and the street too is a civilized place for lingering in, with a shop and a hairdresser.

The white collar 'Factory North' consists of a 7000m² space with a fully glazed end wall into which the 16m diameter reception 'drum' cuts. This contains a presentation suite on the first floor, looking out over the River Clyde, and views across the office floor from the open space at the top of the stairs. Below, a porte-cochere leads to visitor reception and interview rooms.

Fire regulations required four enclosed staircases, and a wall with one and a half hour fire resistance between manufacturing and administration; but there is also an open stair to the mezzanine and windows in the wall to encourage a feeling of unity.

Unity too happens with refreshment. No eating or drinking at the work bench, no eating or drinking at the desk. Instead, throughout the building there are break-out areas – two chairs and a table by a window, lounging chairs off a main route, raised platforms that look out over the floor – where workers can take their coffee from a nearby machine, or eat their sandwiches.

The restaurant is stylish. A conservatory with timber furniture leads to a walled garden where people sit when the weather allows. Greenery cascades down from the mezzanine, and throughout the space there are silver birches (only in the restaurant is it apparent that they are artificial – complete with 'dead' brown leaves).

A mezzanine backs onto the 'street', and the glass-fronted conference rooms beneath it have soft white curtains that can be drawn when privacy is needed. There are no individual offices, but 'some

Figure 6.20 The company makes defence equipment such as periscopes. The administration area is at one end of this beautifully designed shed: manufacturing is at the other. Additional workstations are on the mezzanine, and meeting rooms are tucked underneath it.

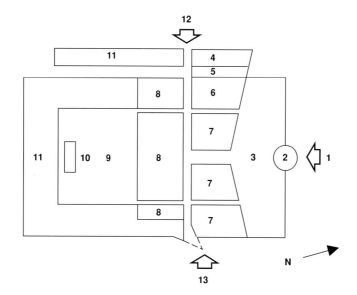

Figure 6.21 Layout.
Key
1 vistor entrance
2 reception
3 open office
4 garden
5 conservatory
6 restaurant
7 meeting rooms etc.
8 clean rooms
9 test and assembly
10 periscope tower
11 production
12 goods entrance
13 staff entrance

Figure 6.22 A drum set into the north end of the building contains visitor reception and meeting rooms at ground level, and a presentation suite above. The curved glass front of the reception desk is a reminder that glass is the basis of this firm's products.

people tend to camp in conference rooms'. Workstation furniture was chosen by normal tendering, a particular criterion being full height adjustability.

The industrial aesthetic is enhanced by the elegance of the detailing: nicely jointed portal frames; exposed stainless steel air ducts hung from the ceiling and dropping down at key points; and all pipes, valves and air-handling units carefully integrated with the structure to create orderly and rhythmical events in the large volume.

With rooflights augmenting the glazed north wall, natural daylight is excellent. Solar control, where necessary, is provided by motorized blinds regulated by the building management system. Artificial light comes from metal halide lamps in cylinder downlighters. The soft acoustics are achieved by using a 5cm PVC-faced glassfibre lining on the underside of

the roof and by the volume of the space. The 45cm floor cavity accommodates cabling and acts as an air input plenum, with neat circular grilles in the floor directing the air flow. A linked fibre-optic backbone serving internal and external IT networks throughout the company provides enough capacity for current and future needs.

At £15m (1991) this is a cheap building housing quite complicated processes. Yet within the rigorously simple envelope, a highly civilized environment has been achieved, the 'wasted' high-level volume greatly adding to the overall ambience.

Interior Designers: Design Images
Architects and Engineers: The Ryder Nicklin Partnership
Contractor: Sir Robert McAlpine and Sons

Chapter 7

Ambience

■ **The aims of ambience**

■ **Corporate aspects**

   Mobility

   Legibility

   Sustainability

   Image

   Artworks

■ **Psychosocial aspects**

   Status

   Personalization

   Privacy

   Feng-shui

   Good manners

■ **Physical aspects**

   Accessibility

   The senses

   Colour

■ **Dilemmas**

Despite the lack of direct, empirical evidence, it is diffi-cult to deny the potential importance of the physical working environment for an organization's effectiveness. The workplace apparently can influence individual satis-faction and performance; it also seems to have a role in communication and in the formation of groups. These in turn can contribute to organizational effectiveness.

Eric Sundstrom: Work Places

A Brandenburg concerto played by a fine ensemble, a magnificent sunset, a blowy day in a boat – all can make the spirits soar, the mind and body feel alive. Places too can make one feel good. The Gothic nave, the hill top chapel in Greece, Granny's flat, that tiny restaurant on an Indian beach under palm trees – the atmosphere of each affects the way we are.

Thus it is with the office interior – sometimes. But too often the workplace is the lowest common denominator, offending nobody. The office interior says as little as possible – beyond some bland corpo-rate statement of solidity, efficiency and respectability. Far too few organizations really use their workplaces as tools: tools to help people work better, and which tell everyone that better work is going on.

Atmosphere encourages better work; image shows that better work is being done. Together they constitute ambience. Looked at in another way, it is the synthesis of what our senses tell us as we move around, and how our feelings respond.

What can ambience achieve; what do the senses tell us, and how does each overlap; what physical ele-ments are the critical ones; and how can these all be brought together in spatial terms? These questions are what this chapter is about.

The aims of ambience

Part of a good corporate culture is providing a stimu-lating yet unstressful environment in which people can perform at their best. Creativity is essential for the competitive company. It can take many forms, from the Nobel prize-winning invention to the clerk devising a simpler way of filing information. But what-

Figure 7.1 Taylor Joynson Garrett, City of London: These solicitors' offices are set around an atrium, at the base of which is a café. This forms a focus to the building and encourages a shared culture through in-house eating. The atrium was designed to catch any lunchtime sun.
Architects: ORMS

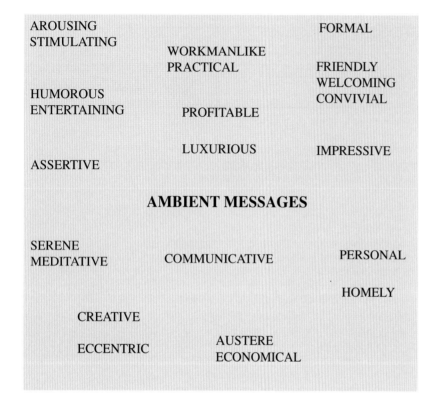

AROUSING
STIMULATING

FORMAL

WORKMANLIKE
PRACTICAL

FRIENDLY
WELCOMING
CONVIVIAL

HUMOROUS
ENTERTAINING

PROFITABLE

LUXURIOUS

IMPRESSIVE

ASSERTIVE

AMBIENT MESSAGES

SERENE
MEDITATIVE

COMMUNICATIVE

PERSONAL

HOMELY

CREATIVE

ECCENTRIC

AUSTERE
ECONOMICAL

Figure 7.2 Ambient messages.

■ When Longman, a publisher, was drawing up the brief for its new building in Harlow, it questioned its staff on preferences. Open-able windows came top by a long way.

ever the task, whatever the situation, a good environment helps.

When considering what a nourishing ambience might be, we should look at when we were at our most creative – as children. Our world then was a rich mixture of playing and learning. Add working to these and you have the lively atmosphere of the creative office.

The creative workplace should make worker and visitor alike feel:

- at home, comfortable
- confident, sure of their individual identity and of their worth as a human being
- safe, knowing that they can share without losing out, and can take risks without retribution
- in control of their destiny, and a partner in an endeavour
- responsible for the good of themselves and towards those they work with
- creative and innovative.

How can this be achieved: what messages have to be emphasized, or eliminated? At all levels – corporate, team and individual – choices should be made. Ambience should not be created by default. What characteristics fit the company? What is the essence of the team? What resonates with the individual? What messages should each space, and the whole interior, convey?

It is likely that the messages chosen will be different from those that were common a few decades ago. Ambience is being affected by the increasing voice of women in the workplace. Women, as nest builders and homemakers, bring flowers and 'tender loving care' to work. Men do too; but women in particular flatten out the difference between office and home, and so are having a powerful effect on how the workplace feels.

Corporate aspects

The ambience that a company creates will reflect the way it works, the way in which it responds to wider concerns and the way in which it wants to be perceived. For most companies the globalization of business is changing the way they work. For all companies the conservation of the globe's resources is changing the way they build.

Mobility

Mobility means working all over the world – flying there in person, or sending verbal and visual messages through ether or cable. This ability to go anywhere, to work anywhere, reduces social and organizational bonds and can leave the individual feeling insecure and disoriented.

On the other hand it encourages cultural interchange and an understanding of what others, in foreign places, are thinking – and why. It can also result in a clearer knowledge of the strengths and weaknesses of the homeland.

How, though, does mobility affect the way people feel about offices in strange places? The German's sense of private space, the American's lack of it, the Japanese valuing every inch but being less upset by sound, the British with a national sense of privacy: each culture's demands on the workplace are very different; but with mobility there is pressure for homogeneity. Offices around the world too often look alike; yet does this sameness fit everyone, or no one?

The challenge for the transnational organization is to create offices that are easily comprehensible to all,

NICHOLAS KANE

and eminently welcoming. Arriving at the office, the visiting worker should easily discover where to find everything and everybody. Clear and consistent organization and signalling in the transnational workplace is essential; but so too is a flexibility that can accommodate a variety of national work cultures.

Legibility

Mobility makes legibility essential. Users and visitors should be able to 'read' the building easily. The porch fronting the terrace house makes a strong visual marker. The entrance to business premises should be

just as obvious. Clear too should be the definition between the main entrance for staff and visitors, and the service entrance for deliveries and refuse removal.

Legibility is increasingly important for transient workers: part-timers, out-workers, contractors or simply those on the road. For them its benefits are:

- not wasting time trying to find where things or people are
- feeling immediately at home upon entering the building
- immediately intelligible circulation (and escape routes).

Sustainability

Green issues affect ambience both physically and psychologically. Openable windows, negating the need for air-conditioning, is an example of friendliness both to the environment and to the user. Daylight likewise is highly prized.

Both strike chords with the worker: the personal one of being in a 'natural' environment; and the communal one of conserving planetary resources. Building management systems, in saving energy and ensuring comfort for the user, again respond to both communal and personal concerns.

Figure 7.3 Talk Radio, Soho, London: A splayed blue wall of polished plaster marks the studios behind, with spot-lit insets for display. Main circulation is indicated by the wood block flooring, and columns, while constricting the way through, also accentuate it. Low-voltage and fluorescent lighting provide sparkle without extravagance.
Architects: Harper Mackay

NICHOLAS KANE

Figure 7.4 Ted Baker Ltd, Euston, London: The general office of this shirtmaker is in a back extension of what was originally a tannery. A post-modern shell is set within the structure, which has a largely glazed roof. Furniture is a mixture of desks brought from elsewhere, and specials – 5cm timber planks supported on chrome legs with outsize casters for total mobility.
Architect: Robert Graves
Designers: Ted Baker in-house team

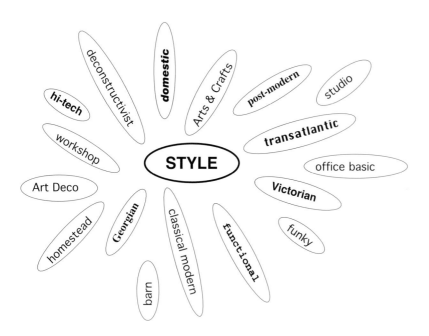

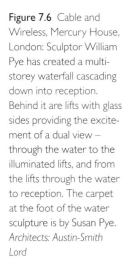

Figure 7.5 Style, taste and image. A simplistic name may help to orientate the designer but can easily become a superficial straight-jacket.

The green aspects of designing and installing the internal parts of a building include using recycled materials and those that come from sustainable sources; materials that are non-toxic in use; and production and installation methods that do not damage the environment.

Image

The aesthetic of the workplace is a potent public relations tool. It may be designed to impress with luxury, economy or efficiency, or just by making people feel comfortable. The old dichotomy of a pretentious front entrance and a scruffy service bay at the back is being replaced by 'fitness for purpose' throughout. The efficient company looks efficient, and every space is designed to function well – in psychological as well as physical terms. The friendly company makes everyone feel at home.

In the architecture, but more particularly in the furnishings, personal taste will show. Whether it expresses the chairman's passion for audacious prints, or the facilities manager's shrewd understanding of how the company is positioning itself in the eyes of its customers, it is more effective if it is consistent. A coherent image is clearer to the outsider, and reassuring to staff.

Concentrating on 'style' can lead to superficial decisions, and to stultifying the designers' energies. To create a unique solution strategic input is needed from the sponsor, whether it be first stirrings or highly developed imaginings. If these are handed over with-

Figure 7.6 Cable and Wireless, Mercury House, London: Sculptor William Pye has created a multi-storey waterfall cascading down into reception. Behind it are lifts with glass sides providing the excitement of a dual view – through the water to the illuminated lifts, and from the lifts through the water to reception. The carpet at the foot of the water sculpture is by Susan Pye. *Architects: Austin-Smith Lord*

out strings, they can form the basis for an effective dialogue between sponsor and designers. But it is often hard for the layman to think in these terms: it comes more naturally to say 'Georgian', 'hi-tech'or 'like a studio'.

The cost of creating the image has an overt as well as a private aspect: how much has it cost and should it look as if it cost that amount – or more, or less. Like pride in a dress's designer label or a flea market bargain, organizations may want to flaunt the price tag.

Artworks

Many organizations own fine collections of paintings, ranging from portraits of the founders to important contemporary works. Others decorate their walls inexpensively with screen prints or drawings; but whatever the medium or the cost, the impact on the ambience is unparalleled.

Artworks can do more than just decorate. The mobile hanging in the atrium, or the sculpture at its base also emphasize the quality of the space. A painting at the end of a corridor vista announces a change of direction. Stained glass running alongside a stair brings light where it is needed, and drama by day to those within the building, at night to those outside.

Psychosocial aspects

In ambience there is no clear boundary between the corporate and the personal. It is also hard to discriminate between elements which affect people's feelings and those which touch their senses.

Status

The cellular office and how it is furnished describes the status of the occupant. The large corner office, with wonderful views of the park, and antique furniture and paintings, sends messages of authority and hierarchy more clearly than any well-publicized pay settlement. The minimally furnished open workstation says the reverse. This kind of physical differentiation creates a climate that can undermine the liveliest of re-engineering strategies.

While each company has different aims and needs, workplaces can be designed to support organizational frameworks but discourage pointless status-seeking. Organizations are effective only where

---

HOW DO YOU PERSONALIZE A 'HOT DESK'?

You don't. Removable nameplates over the desk, screen-savers picturing your loved ones (and the dog), file trolleys covered in your favourite jokey stickers – all these miss the point. For hot desking means teamworking, and it is the team spaces – common rooms, corridors and kitchenettes – that can be used to show the personality of the team. The arrangement of furniture, the choice of pictures, the team bulletin board: these give the unique flavour. To take the home analogy: it is the living room showing the rich mix of family personalities, rather than the bedroom with its idiosyncratic individual display.

---

their technologies – including the physical workplace – are in tune with their culture.

Personalization

Status symbols may hinder, but other human desires need support. Personalization is the outward face of territoriality: the need to 'stake out one's patch'. While little is known of the value of defensible space in the workplace, it is clear that many people find the fluidity of today's work patterns unsettling. Their response is to withdraw into a cocoon of familiar objects.

Workplaces vary from the totally personalized private office, which looks just like home (or alternatively some fantastic dream), through the semipersonalized workstation with the pin-up, postcards and vase of flowers, to the totally impersonal – such as the shared workstation which belongs to nobody.

Most companies have clear guidelines on personalization, varying from no pinning up anywhere, through pin-ups inside screens, pinning up outside screens, to pinning up anywhere. To provide consistency, compliance and easy monitoring, it is best if management and user groups define the guidelines together.

The issues that need resolving are:

– Does personalization cut across company culture or image?
– Is personalization necessary to human well-being?
– Do bosses get personalization but not workers?
– Is personalization rather than 'team-ization' still relevant?
– How can personalization best be accommodated in today's workplace?

■ One British interior designer takes her clients round art galleries – usually the Tate Gallery – and then gets them to choose postcards of paintings that reflect most accurately how they want a specific area to feel.

■ Advertising agent Judie Lannon's office was furnished as a living room: soft furniture, colour and lighting; the desk set out of the way; and books and paintings. People came and relaxed. The room did not make a great design statement; rather, it said that its occupier was friendly and approachable.

Figure 7.7 Lynne Franks PR Ltd, West London: A garage has been converted to provide an open plan office for this public relations company. Offices, café and meeting rooms lie along the two sides, daylit through rooflights. The modest boardroom is made impressive with high-backed 'Oxford' chairs by Arne Jacobsen (with red, orange or fuchsia upholstery) around an asymmetrical glass table top on a miniature space frame base, designed by Tom Dixon.
Interior Designers: Ben Kelly Design

– Should people's mobile paraphernalia (like 'puppies') be personalized?
– Is personalization reasonable – or practicable – in an adaptable environment?

Privacy

Privacy relates closely to personalization, but is nevertheless an elusive concept.

Nobody really understands what anyone else feels about privacy; and rarely do people describing privacy analyse precisely what they mean.

The open door indicates availability; the closed one says 'please do not disturb'. Finding alternatives to the symbolism of the closed door is a conundrum of open planning. In some American companies staff don baseball caps to indicate times of high concentration. In other firms people simply go home to concentrate. But is that good enough; how satisfactory is a setting that denies privacy?

Careful analysis of privacy needs, their purpose, and how they may be met in design terms is central to the sensible workplace. The analysis starts from a consideration of the individual. Every person appears to have a personal bubble, an invisible aura, which is sacrosanct. Beyond the physical body is this sur-

THE MANY MEANINGS OF PRIVACY

Not to be seen, heard, overlooked, supervised
Not to hear, see, overlook or supervise
Not to smell or touch other people, nor taste alien flavours
To be able to work undisturbed, or without disturbing others
To have a chair of my own, a castle of my own
To have walls around me and a shut door
To have a low screen around me and no door
To have pictures of the wife and kids pinned up
To be able to leave a messy desk overnight
To keep my files by my desk
To have a window that opens
To have my own photocopier which nobody else touches
To have a smarter place than Jim, who is my subordinate
To have the best corner office in the building, with views over the river
To have the most expensive furniture in the office
To avoid anyone looking in from outside
Never to have the telephone ring when I am concentrating

rounding zone, which may be close to the skin or up to a metre further out; for it varies for different nations and cultures. The Japanese, for instance, work very close together, with no apparent privacy, but isolate themselves by avoiding eye contact.

Feng-shui

Feng-shui is now practised throughout the world. Cultures in the Far East have traditionally used this knowledge to create a psychic atmosphere that is believed to encourage well-being and prosperity – for the individual, the family and the business.

To some Westerners feng-shui may seem incomprehensible, but many of its recommendations make good conventional sense as well. These include clarity of circulation and sympathetic or effective positioning of furniture. Water, plants and mirrors, seen to enhance feng-shui, are normal elements of office design – though the inclusion of the frequently used chimes and crystal balls could be more difficult. Consideration of feng-shui is also an example of 'doing in Rome as the Romans do' – and understanding why – which is often so essential to business success in global markets.

Good manners

Open plans and intensively used spaces only work if people are considerate. Raised voices and prying eyes are upsetting; untidiness in shared space is unforgivable. At home there is generally a blend of consideration and tolerance. If the ambience of an office can provide the same feeling of shared ownership it gives a strong foundation for harmonious working.

Physical aspects

People using the workplace may be old, young, sprightly or have disabilities. How people get into a building and how they make themselves comfortable in it are the most fundamental physical aspects of workplace ambience. A building designed for the disabled will enable all those who use it.

Accessibility

Our eyes tell us where fire exits are, our ears hear the fire alarm, our noses smell smoke, and our legs carry us fast down the stairs – that is if we are not one of the millions of people worldwide who are disabled.

We forget that most people are disabled at some time in their lives: a leg broken skiing, a hand damaged gardening, workplace ailments, arthritis, old age. Valuable workers will be getting older, according to predictions, but we are being slow to respond to the needs of an ageing workforce.

In a perfect world, buildings would be completely accessible and usable. But that costs money, and there is a natural reluctance to do more than the minimum. So legislation is becoming increasingly prescriptive about designing for those with disabilities, with the deaf and blind joining those in wheel chairs.

Beyond necessity and legislation is ambience. In the humane workplace each person is respected, and her special needs and desires catered for. She is thus enabled to work at her best for the good of herself and the company.

The time to cater for disabilities is at the design stage. It can then be done for little or no extra cost. Imagining how the wheelchair user, or the person who is deaf, blind or partially sighted will move around and will know where they are, enables the designer to meet statutory requirements creatively and provide a safe and pleasant place for everyone.

The senses

How people feel about their environment stems initially from impulses from their senses. Senses transmit physical and psychological messages, but it is hard to differentiate between them. What is more, people react differently to the same stimulus. And stimuli may be interpreted differently and in particular ways. For instance, an aural message – the sound of a car – may be transposed by one brain into a silver VW Golf, smelling of dog and complete with wife in a foul temper; to another brain it is just a faulty gearbox.

Figure 7.8 Cable and Wireless, Mercury House, London: Typical office area with artworks illuminated by spotlights. *Architects: Austin-Smith Lord*

■ The experience which unites people with disabilities is not a shared physical experience, but a shared social experience of an environment which has been designed with barriers to prevent their full participation.

Women's Design Service: Accessible Offices

■ In one office people always sit down when they talk with each other, even if they are just passing by. Their voices are then contained by the sound-absorbent screens.

■ We always check the feng-shui of our Asian offices. If we didn't our Chinese staff would quit.

Executive vice-president, Citibank

■ A Chinese geo-mancer advised architects Sir Norman Foster and Partners on many aspects of the design of the Hongkong and Shanghai Bank headquarters, including the alignment of the entrance, internal layouts and furniture disposition – even on the day to move the bronze lions from the previous building. Its siting, with views out over water and its back to a mountain was considered most propitious.

ACCESSIBILITY CONSIDERATIONS

Planning

Approach to buildings – including car parking and changes of level
Internal spaces – widths of corridors, door openings and turning circles for wheel chairs
Doors – width, swing, weight, hanging, vision and kick panels
Stairs – width, treads, risers and handrails
Floors – non-slip materials, few changes in level
Toilets – number, size, heights, equipment
Grasp – door handles, window catches and taps (or levers)
Height – handles, switches, outlets, work surfaces, keyboards, reception desks and handrails
Hearing – visual alarms and indicators, and acoustic atmosphere
Vision – clear lighting, signage and visual indicators

(colour changes) for the partially sighted
Obstacles – projections which impede wheelchairs and the partially sighted

Materials

Materials – changes in flooring, colour, handrails, as signals
Reflectances – reduced for the partially sighted

Equipment

Keyboards – alternative to the QWERTY layout, and alternative input and hands-free devices
Monitors – contrast, adjustability, size
Filing – suspension filing systems (easier to use than drawers)
Meeting rooms – computer input devices for the deaf

It is therefore misleading to consider the sensory aspects of design – balance, smell, touch sound, taste and vision – as separate entities. Analysis can be useful, but not if overdone.

Another kind of overlap is the distances at which the senses are effective. Close to, they all overlap; but the further away the stimulus is, the fewer the senses that come into play. Thus distance affects how people sense each other: how well they smell, hear and see each other, and whether they are in touching range or not.

The distances shown in the figure opposite – and their implications – are fundamental to space planning. They show the spaces people need to operate in. For instance, the fact that a face-to-face distance of less than 2.5m is required in order to retain eye contact has a major impact on the design of any meeting space. The ordinary speaking voice carrying rather further than that affects the layout of workstations and acoustic screens.

Sometimes spaces are designed to keep people apart – to discourage interaction. In reception areas, seats may be well separated to achieve this. Conversely, in team spaces, close seating in a circular formation helps people to communicate.

Balance

Balance – or kinaesthetics – is how people's bodies respond to spaces as they move through them. Going from a carpet to a marble floor, up a few steps, or rising from a chair: all these activities demand

changes in the body's muscular responses. How steep a staircase is, how easy the handrail is to grasp: these convey important but often subconscious messages about the environment and can contribute to relaxation, or to stress. Even with all the other senses 'turned off' – by blindfold or whatever – the kinaesthetic sense remains. It is the most basic of them all. Perhaps that is why it often gets overlooked.

Smell

Smell goes straight into the bloodstream. Other sensory stimuli pass through the brain first. This explains

---

RULES OF THUMB: ACCESSIBILITY

Heights	*Centimetres*
Desk	70 (or adjustable)
Reception desk	80 (maximum, in part)
Steps	17 (maximum)
Handrails (on stairs)	84
(on level)	100 (maximum)
Door handles	104 (maximum)
Switches/alarms	120 (maximum)
Widths	
Wheelchair (with occupant)	75
Doors	76 (minimum)
	80 (desirable)
Corridors	120 (minimum)

why the smell of new-mown hay will conjure a total experience of a childhood summer in a way no sound or picture could achieve.

Smells can be unwelcome in the space immediately surrounding us – our personal bubble. Thus it may be that good ventilation can decrease the amount of physical space a person needs. It is certainly true that fusty air can affect performance. Conversely, some Japanese firms use the technique of aromatherapy to perfume the workplace through the air-conditioning system, and claim that productivity improves.

Touch

Shaking hands, opening a door, bumping into things, feeling a cold draught are all part of touch.

Culture affects touching, with the northern European touching much less than the Mediterranean or Arab. Some need and enjoy physical contact; others shrink from it. While touching in the workplace is a highly political subject, a touch on the arm can communicate complex emotions far more clearly than words alone. A relaxed and warm ambience can make touching seem much more natural and acceptable.

The touch of an object in the hand can send important messages. Choosing well-designed door furniture, with an interesting texture, a shape which fits the hand, and an easy movement, says that all those involved – manufacturer, designers, and sponsor – cared for the user.

Likewise with the chair in reception. The body is made welcome with a chair of just the right height and softness. The chair says 'although you will not sit here long, we still care enough about you to make this moment enjoyable.'

Bumping into things is another aspect of touching, and perhaps again relates to the personal bubble. Good design caters for free movement of and around furniture, and circulation routes that allow enough space to pass comfortably.

Cool air touching the cheek or a thin-stockinged leg can be welcome on a summer's afternoon – unlike an autumn draught which disturbs, or even causes a nasty cold.

Beyond physical touch there is a visual kind, where the brain combines sensation with memory: the pleasure of looking at a cool marble wall, or a supple leather armchair – and imagining.

Taste

Of all the senses, taste is the most personal. It happens privately, within the confines of the body. So what has it

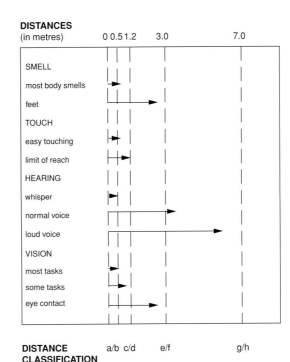

Figure 7.9 Distance and the senses. (after Edward Hall, 1966).
Key
a intimate distance - close
b intimate distance - not close
c personal distance - close
d personal distance - not close
e social consultative distance - close
f social consultative distance - not close
g public distance - close
h public distance - not close

possibly got to do with the design of the workplace?

The answer can be – really quite a lot. If there are places to prepare and serve good food and drink, then the atmosphere of the office is greatly enhanced. The ability to offer the visitor in reception a cup of freshly ground coffee, or to serve the staff a wholesome and elegant meal in attractive surroundings, brings taste into the whole sensory experience.

Hearing

Some people like loud pop music; others only listen to classical string quartets. Some hate noise; still others can work undisturbed through the loudest thunder. Piped music is sometimes found in the office, but people's tastes are so divergent that the personal 'walkman' works best.

Sound makes all the difference in the workplace, but the right balance is difficult to achieve. Much of the physical design – cellular offices, divisions, walls and screens – relates to controlling sound. Control, so that secrets are not heard next door; control, so that the noisy brainstormers will not disturb the creative writer.

A buzz in the staff restaurant persuades people they are in a lively place, and allows confidences to be

Figure 7.10 Ted Baker Ltd, Euston, London: The break-out area in the heart of the building, with its kitchenette alongside, has materials and lighting skilfully used to make up for the lack of daylight. Antique, art deco and specially commissioned furniture stands on the parquet floor (part of the old tannery office). Elsewhere natural polished screed sits alongside carpet, with pebble-dash and unplastered brick as wall finishes in reception. *Interior Designers: Ted Baker in-house team with Harper Mackay*

■ Standing with closed eyes in the entrance lobby of the Coopers & Lybrand headquarters in London, one could well be by the Victoria Falls – certainly not just above the underground railway, the sound of which is drowned by elegant waterfalls.

passed without being overheard. Noise in meeting or dealing rooms may help performance through increasing arousal, but usually noise in the workplace reduces effectiveness.

Calmness in the workplace mostly springs from low noise levels: carpets and other absorbent surfaces, quiet equipment, telephones that barely ring. Sound may be masked to an extent by the air-conditioning, or by artificially induced 'white noise', such as a fountain down the hall.

Sounds from outside can disrupt or improve the ambience. Loud aircraft or traffic noise can ruin the nicest office, whereas distant soft sounds wafting through the window can provide a valuable sense of context, time and place.

Vision

People can smell space, touch its walls, and react to sound within it; but the strongest signals come through their eyes (90% of the information a human receives). These messages travel faster than sound and are of a far superior quality. Seeing space tells its size, disposition and how to move around it. The impact of a space is largely what is seen: a small space may make a worker feel cramped, and in too large a space a team may rattle around and not become cohesive.

Sight keeps people in touch with the outside world. Through the windows they see the sky, and know the time of day and whether they are likely to get wet on the way home.

People react to bright lighting, strident colours and the play of water in a fountain. They notice comfortable furniture, the latest technology and the contentment on others' faces. The visual design of an office helps a worker decide – unconsciously – whether he likes it and the image it displays. His eyes tell him: 'Here is an organization where I am happy to work.'

The use of multimedia increases but also blunts visual awareness. With eyes taking over from hands

Figure 7.11 Designers Guild, London: This firm of fabric designers and wholesalers uses colour to greatly enhance its warehouse building. Trisha Guild's own office is also used for creative, brainstorming and 'works in progress' meetings. *Interior Designers: Spencer Fung Architects and Trisha Guild.*

RULES OF THUMB: COLOUR

Light colours. Reflect light, enlarge space, make it feel more impersonal and the walls further away. They may be considered feminine, but at the same time business-like.

Dark colours. Absorb light, and make spaces appear smaller and more intimate. They make walls feel closer, and are considered masculine and homely (in the way a pub is).

Warm colours. Reds and yellows, in all their shades, bring visual warmth to a space. However, while warmer hues can complement food and skin, and encourage sociability, too much red can overstimulate.

Cool colours. Blues and greens can make users believe a space is cold. However, pale unsaturated blues and greens are relaxing and refreshing, and look good with natural materials such as wood and leather.

Primary colours. Reds, blues and yellows are cheerful, unsophisticated, draw attention to themselves and can be effective where used with discretion.

Natural colours. The colour of natural materials, or the materials themselves, can be warm, friendly and lively without impinging too much. Naturally coloured materials tend to last well.

Neutral colours. Black, white and shades between can sometimes look rather sterile, but allied with other colours they become effective and timeless.

■ The information gathered by a blind man out of doors is limited to a radius of twenty to one hundred feet. With sight he could see the stars.

Edward T Hall

■ Henry Ford said:
'You can have your
Model-T any colour
you like – so long as
it's black.'
Why are all com-
puters grey?

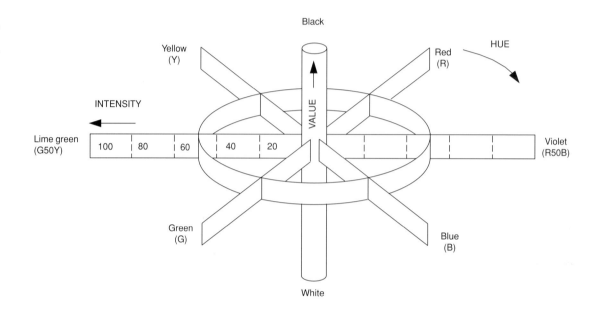

Figure 7.12 (Above and opposite) Colour specification.

Schematic model of the Munsell Colour System which forms the basis for many paint ranges.
Principal hues are red, blue, green and yellow, with intermediates of violet, turquoise, lime green and orange.
The model clearly shows colours that harmonise (adjacent) or contrast (diametrically opposite)

Figure 7.13 Cable and Wireless, Mercury House, London: Casual seating in the staff café.
Architects: Austin-Smith Lord

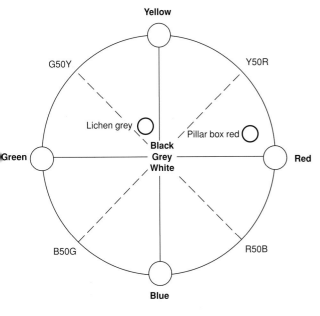

Diagram showing examples of colours:

Pillar box red: 1090 - Y90R
    Value (degree of blackness)   10%
    Intensity (strength of pigment)   90%
    Hue (mix of primary colours)   10% yellow + 90% red

Likewise, lichen grey: 2010 - G70Y

as the worker's chief tool, visual images are all important; but what do people actually see? Can people see without looking in the same way as they can hear without listening? Both involve conscious effort.

Colour

Colour is an important part of vision, but it is too often neglected in the workplace, despite the fact that it can influence motivation and performance. Unlike the home, the office tends to be sombre – with walls, floors and furniture in various shades of grey. Ceilings – though theoretically white – are made grey by shadows and perforations. Yet office workers are said to dislike white, grey and other neutral colours almost as much as they dislike strong ones.

Colour, used with style and knowledge, can turn a mundane space into a place of magic, and make an economical space feel luxurious. Colour is a powerful tool for the corporate statement, but more than this – colour can affect the way people perceive a space and react to it.

As with taste, colour is very personal, and may relate to childhood or cultural background. Green is considered unlucky by some cultures but the reverse by others. Yellow, black and white are each the colour of mourning in different countries.

The colour we see is light reflected off surfaces, so that two objects of identical colour but dissimilar textures appear quite different. Thus colours appear to change in different lights (warm tungsten or cool fluorescent; morning or afternoon sun) and in different situations (a grey chair will not look the same standing on a green carpet as on a red one).

Some of the best colour schemes use many different colours. However, when a variety of materials is used it is essential to check each against actual samples in good lighting conditions to ensure correct colour matching. Changes of carpet colour can be used to indicate fire routes, and hard natural materials – timber or slate – can be used where footfalls would not upset the acoustics. Timber work surfaces can be stained in a range of colours; and upholstery and screen coverings textured (so that stains show less).

Using colour creatively takes courage and discipline; but it is a cheap and effective way to enhance space, provide style, lift the spirits of the workers and demonstrate a company's image.

■ Gestalt psychologists claim that people become disoriented in surroundings where carpets, walls and furniture have the same colour – such as many offices.

Dilemmas

■ How compatible are individual needs for privacy and personalization with open and informal work patterns?

■ Do people need defensible space at work?

■ To what extent does the physical environment contribute to job satisfaction through processes beyond conscious awareness?

■ Do teams need pleasant surroundings and physical enclosure in order to cohere?

■ What should offices look and feel like when their focus is on group, congenial or social activities?

■ How much does colour really affect peformance and comfort?

■ Are organizations more effective when their structure is truthfully mirrored in the design of their workplace?

■ What effect do expected and unexpected noises have on workers' performance? How can they be controlled in open plan offices?

Chiat/Day Advertising Inc.
New York

workplace

DONATELLA BRUN

Figure 7.14 'The Store' counter for office supplies and equipment.

The New York offices of advertising agency Chiat/Day, are the epitome of today's location-free office: free-range working for all staff, in a space that looks like a fairground – or 'a street, with its complexity and dynamism'.

As its architect, Gaetano Pesce, says: 'I was convinced that one could make a working space more compatible with our time and with our communication tools, and that this would allow work to be simpler and more efficient. Creativity does need a special atmosphere, which may well be more like home.'

The single 2800m² floor of a Swanke Hayden Connell building in downtown Manhattan has not only mobile telephones, but mobile computer carrels that can be wheeled to the best place for any given activity. Their structure is a metal grid which is hung with a 2cm thick quilt to give sound and visual privacy when necessary.

There are no individual offices – only space which the 140 people use as their needs dictate. The 12 project rooms can be booked for an hour or for several days, and work with major clients is done in their own dedicated project rooms. A conference room is used for presentations or for just sitting around on the comfortable seating at one end, and a 'bunker' is used for strategic discussions.

Around the office there is a 'living room' with sofas and low chairs, a 'club house' café and an open 'piazza'. Photographic work may happen in the 'dog house' dark room, artwork in the 'print kitchen', audio-visual work in the 'broadcast suites' and research in the 'intelligence centre'. Equipment (mobile telephones and computers), materials and

■ At Chiat/Day we can work anywhere, anytime; but the downside of this is how do you switch off? With customers round the world one of them will always be wanting something.

Chiat/Day employee

Figure 7.15 Aimed at being 'more like home', the cafeteria has a fair-ground feel, and is used as an informal work area.

Figure 7.16 Location-free working is central to the operations of this advertising agency. Mobile computer carrels have quilts hung on metal grids to provide visual and acoustic privacy.

Figure 7.17 Sitting room work area.

Figure 7.18 'Dog house' dark room for photographic work.

post are dealt with at 'the store' – across a counter formed as the tongue in a bright red mouth.

Lockers become 'personal anchors' and contain not only property but photographs. Their doors are papier mâché moulded into faces. But elsewhere paperlessness is central to the culture, with most design work carried out electronically, a librarian adept at surfing the Net and telephone calls that follow wherever you go.

Colour and complex design are everywhere, including the floor. Staff (mostly in their twenties) react well to a workplace that has extraordinary views both within and without.

They react well too to a boss who sits among them, answering his own telephone. Jay Chiat says he is 'not in the business of telling elementary school kids what to do.' Rather, it is a self-directed university model. Hours are totally flexible, with people staying home if that is the right solution – the only measure being a job well done.

In moving to the new office, workers were brought onto a single floor from the previous four, and space was reduced by 50%. The difficulty which some experienced in adapting was helped by 'building a humane environment where people understand the need to participate emotionally and intellectually'.

As Chiat says: 'Change is good: it cleans out the cobwebs.'

Interior Architects: Pesce Ltd
Project completed: 1994

Figure 7.19 Layout.
Key
1 core
2 reception
3 audio-visual cluster
4 workspace
5 video-conferencing
6 client conference
   rooms
7 meeting rooms
8 piazza
9 bunker
10 library
11 art studio
12 lockers
13 computer room
14 store
15 clubhouse
16 dog house

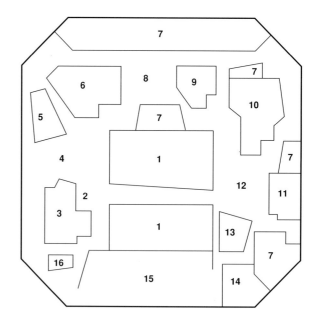

technics

The British Council, Madrid: This four-storey 'palacete', a listed building, has a light cone under a discreet rooflight that brings daylight into the centre of the building. An elliptical shutter automatically rotates to inhibit or encourage air flow, with hot air either being expelled or directed into the interior of the building according to need.
Architects: Jestico + Whiles

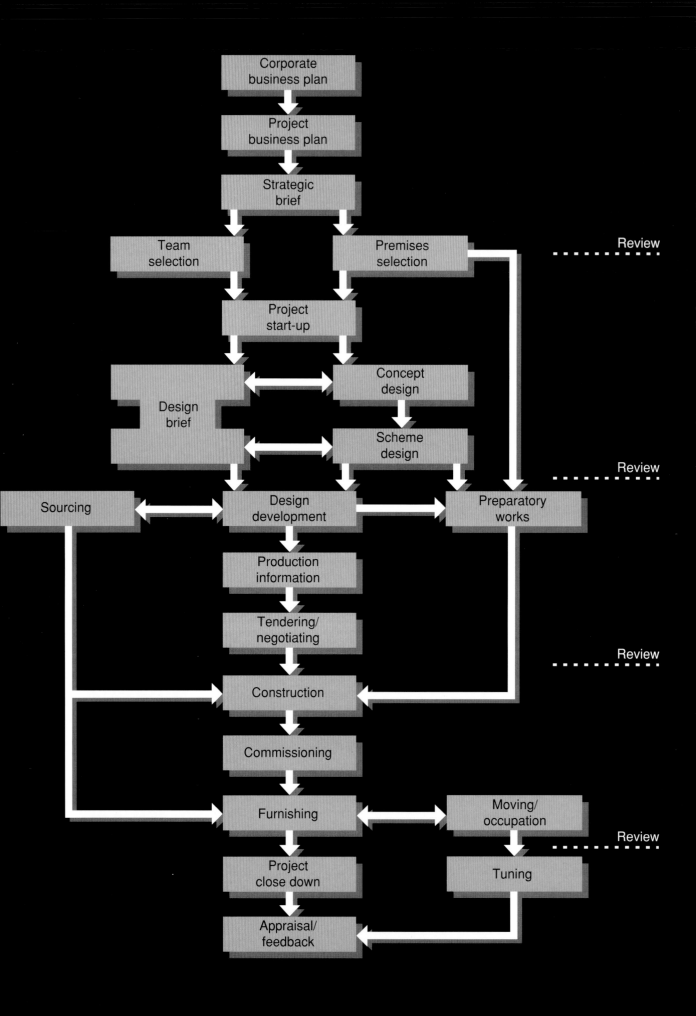

Chapter 8
Process

■ **The predesign stage**

The scope of the project

Project management

Choosing a building

The briefing process

■ **Design**

Design stages

Tendering and contracts

■ **Construction**

Preparatory work

Fitting out

Commissioning and furnishing

■ **Occupation**

■ **Dilemmas**

Can you tell me the way to Killarney?
If I were going there, sure and I wouldn't start from here.

Old Irish joke

Too many projects start from the wrong place – usually some way along the wrong road. The results: they do not fit their purpose well, quality suffers and time and money are wasted.

This chapter is about the logical process of design and construction, and its principal stages: predesign, design, construction and occupation. It describes how the needs of the office interior may be identified and quantified, and then met.

It also emphasizes the human dimension:

– the needs of the users and how to involve them throughout the process;
– building and leading a committed project team.

Maintaining vision, drive and control is critical to the process. Projects are inherently complex and multifaceted. They draw on the skills of many people and organizations, all with their legitimate – and often differing – interests. Keeping their insights and skills constantly focused on the same task allows the whole team to react well to opportunities, pressures and the unforeseen changes that always happen.

A building project interweaves many complex needs and aspirations: those of developer, sponsor, users and facilities manager; project manager and construction manager; building design team – architect, quantity surveyor, engineers, specialist designers; and contractors and suppliers.

Only when each part is balanced and moving in concert is a project truly successful. Success means partnership, with each of the three main players – sponsor, designers and contractors – achieving its own aims as well as the collective one. Problems and arguments may happen along the route: but as informed struggles, pressing for the right solutions, rather than as collisions.

Although this may seem foreign to a sponsor or user, it is really no different from events in their ordinary business. There are many parallels: the development of a new product, the establishment of a branch office, the restructuring of a department. All are deliberate changes, with clear goals. Likewise with a building project – only the 'language' is different.

■ A side-effect of companies deciding to operate 'new ways of working' is that they also change their ways of building. New thinking brings a refreshing new attitude, and that is good for the interior construction industry.

David King - Interior plc

Figure 8.1 Project process. Flow chart showing principal activities and review points.

Figure 8.2 The plait of partnership.

THE ORGANIZATION

SPONSOR
PROJECT MANAGER
FACILITIES MANAGER
USERS

BUILDING DESIGN TEAM

ARCHITECT
QUANTITY SURVEYOR
ENGINEERS
DESIGNERS
SPECIALISTS

CONSTRUCTION

CONSTRUCTION MANAGER
(MANAGEMENT) CONTRACTOR
(SUB)CONTRACTORS
SUPPLIERS

THE PRINCIPAL PLAYERS

Most of these roles need to be played on any project, but on small ones they may be combined.

Sponsor. The promoter of the project, usually the board of the organization. The ultimate source of decisions, responsibility and funding.

Champion. A senior representative of the sponsor, with personal responsibility for motivating the project and overcoming obstacles.

Facilities manager. The sponsor's representative for managing its premises. The source of much briefing data, and a link with the users. Responsible for the on-going operation and maintenance of the premises.

Users. All those who work in the office, from senior managers to cleaners. A primary source of briefing data. Where there are many visitors, their voice needs to be heard too.

Project manager. Appointed to plan, co-ordinate and energize the project. Either a member of the sponsor's staff with the right experience (sometimes the facilities manager), or an external appointment.

Designers. Usually outside consultants, although very large organizations may have their own in-house teams. Architects, interior designers, space planners; engineers (structural, mechani-

cal and electrical, information technology); and specialists such as lighting and catering consultants. We also include building and quantity surveyors.

Construction manager. A consultant appointed to manage parallel construction contracts, if that is the procurement route chosen.

(Management) contractor. A builder appointed to carry out the main body of the work, or to manage parallel construction subcontracts.

Specialist contractors. Specialist firms (especially HVAC and IT) appointed to carry out their specific part of the work. They may also be involved in its design.

Suppliers. Many items will be supplied for the main contract, and also specialist ones such as furniture. Again, the suppliers may be involved in special design work.

Statutory authorities. With office interiors the principal bodies are those concerned with construction standards, fire safety and general health and safety of the occupants.

Developer/landlord. If the sponsor does not own the building, it may be a new development or an existing leased one. In those cases the building owner may set particular obligations or constraints.

The predesign stage

Strategy starts with dreams: the driving visions and desires for a better workplace. These dreams must be defined, quantified and tested in order to give the project reality. Only when this has been done, and the dreams enshrined in a strategic brief, can the project process be mapped out with confidence. This predesign stage, so often treated cursorily, is critical for success.

The scope of the project

What is to be the main purpose of the project: is the new workspace primarily a business tool, a business asset or an enhancement of the corporate image? What are the opportunities, and the constraints? How much time is there? How much money? Who is going to do it all? Is it really needed?

This broad vision has to be established; and then within it the business aims of the project must be defined: strategic, operational, financial, human, physical and ethical. At the highest level these are a set of interrelated visions. If they are to be realized, they have to be enshrined in a project business plan: a range of objectives, with quantifiable targets, allocated resources and a management structure – a microcosm of the corporate business plan.

Causes

Reasons that make a project necessary may include the following.

– *Outside factors.* Proactive seizing of opportunities / reactive response to threats (including termination of leases).
– *Changes in size.* Growth / merger or acquisition / contraction.
– *Changes in organization.* New business activities / new methods of work.
– *Changes in image.* Raising the profile / economizing.

Responses

How an organization responds depends on the reasons for the project. Considerations are:

– *Location.* Single-site or multisite / existing building or different building / existing space or new space.
– *Scope.* New fit-out or refurbishment / total or partial / secondary services / simple redecoration.
– *Furnishings.* New / existing / a mixture.
– *Standards.* Minimal / normal / prestige.
– *Pace.* Single project or phased / normal or fast-track / incremental or cataclysmic.

Where a landlord or developer had no occupier in sight, the building may have been fitted out to 'developer standard'. This may well result in a considerable amount of stripping out and refitting – wasting time, materials and money (up to £12/m^2 at 1995 prices). Conversely, with an owner–occupier, or with pre-let space, resources and responsibilities can be allocated in a cost- and time-effective way.

LEVELS OF COMPLETION

Ask anyone connected with office development to give a definition of levels of completion, and it will be different from the last man's. The differences may be large, in terms of time, money and expectations – so it is essential to agree definitions at the outset. These guidelines may be helpful:

Shell and core. Building structure, cores and external envelope complete. All vertical services installed (water, drainage, gas, lifts, HVAC plant and risers, electrical risers). Perimeter heating (if any) installed. Toilets fully plumbed and finished.

Developer standard. As for shell and core. In addition, entrance hall, cores, staircases, toilets and other common parts fully finished. Office space left as shell and core, except that a part may be fitted out for display purposes.

Fully fitted. Appropriate when the space has been prelet before the shell and core have been completed. As for developer standard. In addition, partitions and doors, raised floors and suspended ceilings; horizontal services including HVAC ducting, sprinklers, electrical wiring (and possibly IT), luminaires and other service terminals; built-in furniture and equipment in special areas (e.g. reception, restaurant and kitchen); all finishes and decorations.

Fitting-out may encompass a wide mix of tasks, depending on the condition of the space and the ambitions (and budget) of the sponsor. Apart from interior rearrangements, it may on occasion include structural alterations.

Figure 8.3 Possibilities for office space.

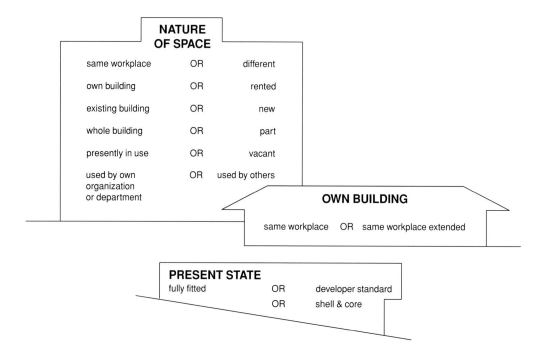

DEGREES OF FIT-OUT

Fitting-out may range from little more than redecoration to creating the complete interior of a new building. It may include:

All areas (i.e. including cafeteria, toilets, etc.)
Office areas only
Special areas only (e.g. reception, boardroom, cafeteria)
Mechanical services (e.g. HVAC, lifts)
Electrical services (e.g. light, power)
Electronics (e.g. telecoms, IT, BMS)
Partitions, ceilings, floors
Decorations
Furnishings (e.g. carpets, blinds, curtains)
Furniture and equipment
Accessories (e.g. signs, artworks, planting).

Project management

Project management is about:

- driving a project through to its successful conclusion;
- maintaining the proper balance between the four key project variables: scope, quality, cost and time;
- building, motivating and guiding the project team.

The last is the most important – and the most difficult.

Project leadership

Every project needs its champion. She may be the sponsoring organization's chief executive – who has the vision and the power; or a senior manager with an obsession (perhaps chair of a development committee). Her seniority gives her real influence, and her passion the will to use it – sometimes ruthlessly. Because of her the project gets the information, decisions and resources that it needs – and when it needs them. She promotes the virtues of the project to other decision makers. When the unforeseen occurs, she slays the dragons. Though not a full-time job, she must always be available.

In the early stages she is the one who communicates a vision and a purpose, encourages communication, creates an atmosphere of trust and mutual respect, and fosters strong bonds within the team. Good management is no longer enough; for supreme results a project must have heart as well as head.

Small projects may well be run by their champion; but ones of any size normally have a project manager.

Unlike the champion, the project manager must have constant involvement in the project, as well as complete commitment. His job is to define the tasks and set them in a programme; pick, build and manage the team; monitor and control progress; and deliver a well-designed and -built result on time and to budget.

For office interiors the project manager is likely to have either a management or a building background. Although some technical knowledge is important, the key attributes are clarity of thought and expression, determination and stamina, an empathy with people and shrewd judgement of risk. Representing the sponsor throughout the process, the project manager may either be an employee of the company or an outsider.

The facilities manager, who will ultimately be running the workspace, has a practical and long-term view of how the building should be designed. Her concerns are about durability, ease of maintenance and simplicity: a single workplace footprint, a limited number of different lamps (light bulbs), and access panels everywhere – even if they spoil the looks. She it is who understands – uniquely – how the parts come together, and what cause will have what effect – not just in tactical matters, but in strategic ones as well. She knows that skimping now will cost 10 times as much in the long run – let alone the disruption.

Sometimes a facilities manager runs the project; but though this has co-ordination advantages, the two jobs require rather different skills. Thus a separate project manager, working closely with the facilities manager, is usually the better option.

Project planning

One of the first jobs of the project manager is to identify and define the tasks that must be carried out. This analysis shows what skills are needed (whether in house, or from outside). It helps with the decision on how best to procure the project. It also allows the creation of a project plan and programme.

As the project planning moves ahead, so the tasks can be successively refined. At the start, however, they can conveniently be grouped under:

– Project management and control
– Project start-up (including project planning and team building)
– Briefing
– Design
– Contract administration
– Construction, furnishing and commissioning
– Moving in and settling in
– Appraisal and feedback
– Financial.

Careful task definition allows a task matrix to be developed. This device identifies the skills needed and helps to allocate the tasks appropriately.

Project procurement

Projects are carried out in one of four basic ways – two which separate design from delivery, and two which combine them. Appendix A describes the characteristics of each. The procurement route affects the selection of participants, their roles, and the timing of their efforts. Hence the choice of route – who is going to be contractually responsible for which activities – is a fundamental early decision.

Team selection

The task matrix, a project flow chart and a decision on the appropriate procurement route gives the project manager the basic data on which to base team appointments, whether internal or external. Terms of reference for each should clearly mesh with the others: no gaps, no overlaps. This ensures that all the tasks are covered, and later 'boundary' disputes are minimized.

Wherever possible consultancy contracts should be based on standard forms, with minimal variations. To prevent tussles over collateral warranties and other allocations of risk, the guiding principle should be to allocate risk where it can be best guarded against, and be cheapest to remedy. Risk management should be the aim, not punitive buck-passing.

The real safeguard, however, is proper selection of professional advisers (including the project manager). The principal subject areas to check are as follows.

'Economics'. Is the firm financially and managerially sound?
'Physics'. Is it technically sound, and experienced in this kind of work?
'Art'. Does it have the necessary flair?
'Chemistry'. Are they stimulating and rational people to work with?

Appendix B sets out the criteria in more detail.

A long list of consultants can be compiled from recommendations of friends, colleagues, and other advisers. The 'economics' and 'physics' are provided through references and company data. The 'art' element (of designers) may be ascertained through reviewing reports and pictures of previous projects, and then visiting them and talking to the occupiers.

Interviewing the ensuing shortlist allows candidates to present previous work and to discuss their approach to the project. It also lets the sponsor get a feel for the 'chemistry', and to double check the initial

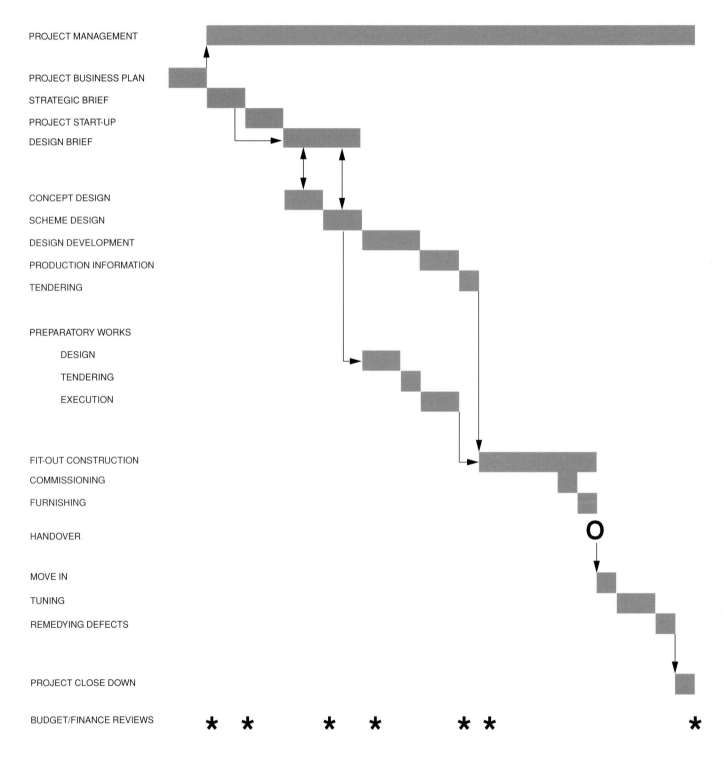

PROJECT MANAGEMENT

PROJECT BUSINESS PLAN

STRATEGIC BRIEF

PROJECT START-UP

DESIGN BRIEF

CONCEPT DESIGN

SCHEME DESIGN

DESIGN DEVELOPMENT

PRODUCTION INFORMATION

TENDERING

PREPARATORY WORKS

DESIGN

TENDERING

EXECUTION

FIT-OUT CONSTRUCTION

COMMISSIONING

FURNISHING

HANDOVER

MOVE IN

TUNING

REMEDYING DEFECTS

PROJECT CLOSE DOWN

BUDGET/FINANCE REVIEWS

Figure 8.4 project process : traditional (sequential) procurement.

appraisal. The sponsor is generally closely involved with choice of project manager and architect (or interior designer); but other appointments, including contractors, are normally screened by these two with a quantity surveyor, and recommendations then made to the sponsor.

The internal component of the team is an 'accommodation planning committee', consisting of internal facilities management and IT staff, and a small and carefully selected cross-section of office workers from middle management downwards. These people should be selected because functionally they represent large or complex departments, and because they have the right personal skills and experience to make an effective contribution. They need enough time off their normal work, not only for meetings, but also to act as focal points for comments from the workforce at large.

Starting up

The Danes talk about 'project start-up': a positive exercise in team building and induction, separate from carrying out the project tasks. The background to this is the strategic brief – required reading for all. The foreground is communications: how ideas, infor-

> ■ Plans are to give you something to deviate from.
>
> *Anon*

Legend:
- ● responsibility
- ◐ assistance
- ○ advice
- • no involvement
- ✔ approval

TASKS \ PARTICIPANT	SPONSOR	USER	FACILITIES MANAGER	PROJECT MANAGER	INTERIOR ARCHITECT	QUANTITY SURVEYOR	ENGINEER	SPECIALIST CONSULTANT	MAIN CONTRACTOR	SPECIALIST CONTRACTOR	SUPPLIER
PROJECT MANAGEMENT & CONTROL	✔	•	○	●		○	○	○	○	•	•
PROJECT START-UP	◐	◐	◐	●	◐	◐	○		•	•	•
BRIEFING - STRATEGIC	◐	◐	◐	●	○	○	•	•	•	•	•
- DESIGN	○	○	◐	◐	●	◐	◐	◐	•	•	•
DESIGN	✔	○	○	○	●	◐	◐	◐	•	•	◐
CONTRACT ADMINISTRATION	✔	•	•	●	◐	◐	◐		○	○	○
CONSTRUCTION, FURNISHING & COMMISSIONING	✔	•	○	○	○	○	○	○	●	●	●
MOVING IN SETTLING IN (TUNING)	○	◐	●	○	○	•	○	○	•	○	○
APPRAISAL & FEEDBACK	•	◐	●	○	○	○	○	○	•	•	•
FINANCIAL	●	•	○	◐	○	◐	○	○	•	•	•

Figure 8.5 Task matrix.

Figure 8.6 Basic data and their sources.

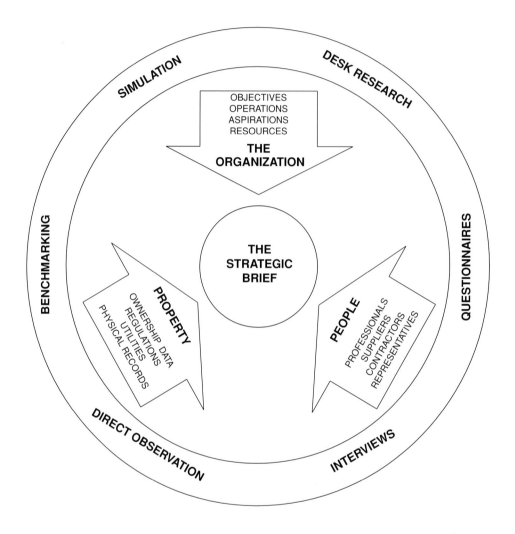

Monitoring and control

There are bound to be changes, but a well-designed process gives benchmarks against which to measure the deviations, and a route map that allows a sense of direction to be regained.

As the project proceeds, changes may occur due to external pressures, internal discoveries, creative new ideas, or the sponsor's new business intentions. The sponsor must be informed of how the proposed changes are going to affect scope, cost, quality and time so that it is properly equipped to make decisions (including how any savings may be spent).

However once on site, change almost always costs money, and may well disrupt the work flow and overall programme. This is particularly so with fitting-out, where the timetable is usually tight. Nevertheless, there is always the unexpected: delivery hold-ups, a damaged component, some defect in the building shell or services, a work dispute – these are common challenges.

The project manager can maintain control through close monitoring, with (simple) progress reports and regular meetings to discuss them (between client and consultants, and consultants and contractors). The need is to maintain an atmosphere of trust if hidden agendas with their accompanying surprises are to be minimized.

As the project proceeds, so the technical leadership shifts. At first it is likely to be operational and financial staff, then the designers, then the constructors – until, at moving in, it is the operational managers again. The project manager must orchestrate and control these transitions firmly but sensitively.

Promoting the project

Selling the project from the very beginning is essential. If everyone is committed, then the whole operation is easier. Therefore how, when and to whom the project is to be explained, and how confidential it needs to be (and for how long) all have an effect on engendering support.

The range of interested parties is broad: senior decision makers, managers and staff; customers and suppliers; neighbours and the general public. Each needs its own treatment, and the means of communication are wide: publications and press releases, formal and informal events, briefings and networking (social and electronic).

Keep everyone in the picture right the way through – explaining problems and difficulties, as well as successes. Use the move into the new place to celebrate, to thank everyone for their input, involvement and patience – and to raise the corporate image.

Choosing a building

There may be no choice: simply the task of refitting the existing space. Or it may mean moving to another part of the building, or to another building in the same complex. But when the choice is wider then location is the key: not just in terms of accessibility to customers and suppliers, and to transport, shops and cafés for the staff; but also the availability of easy routes out of town, parking, and supporting businesses. And does the locality convey the right image (more important in some industries and cultures than others)?

Whether a complex, a whole building or part of one, the cost, size, shape and condition must also be suitable. Aspects to consider are:

- circulation within the building, means of escape
- floor plans: critical dimensions, shapes, obstructions

- other dimensions (e.g. consistency of ceiling heights)
- natural and artificial lighting and ventilation
- the quality of existing mechanical and electrical systems
- the quality of existing IT, telephony and BMS systems
- advantages and drawbacks of the external surroundings
- how soon the space can be acquired
- whether there will be constraints on the fitting-out (e.g. deliveries, noise, security)
- whether existing items can be reused (e.g. partitions, ceilings, carpets).

The briefing process

The British call it briefing and the Americans, programming. But everywhere it is equally important. It starts at the very beginning of the project, and continues well into the design stage, producing a logical progression of documents as shown below.

- *Project business plan.* The sponsor's operational objectives, needs, method of work, budget and timetable, set out in business terms. It justifies the project and the use (and acquisition) of resources. Prepared by the sponsor.
- *Strategic brief (or predesign brief).* The project business plan, augmented by background data on the context of the project. It is written in a mixture of operational and design terms. It is the basis for selecting and subsequently informing the design team. It acts as a touchstone for all that comes after. Prepared by the sponsor, with help from advisers.
- *Design brief (or architectural brief).* Starting with simple information on the site and on accommodation needs, this brief is developed in dialogue between the sponsor and users, the design team and – probably – the statutory authorities. It will finish with detailed room requirements, and a detailed cost plan and critical path programme. It provides the design team with all the basic data for designing and executing the project; and it ensures that the sponsor has thought through the issues in enough detail to minimize afterthoughts.

The strategic brief

The strategic brief sets the scene for the creative solution of a problem. It sets out aims, facts and issues – not solutions. It contains sections on the following:

■ Unless an organization really understands what its purpose is and how it needs to go about achieving that, it cannot write a good brief.

Facilities manager, international organization

– *Objectives.* The prime (business) objective of the project / the principal supporting ones / associated business priorities outside the project.
– *Context.* Historical / regulatory / physical (including site and building data) / resources (data, skills, budget, timetable) / organizational attitudes and aspirations / other relevant activities and projects of the organization.
– *Issues.* Opportunities / uncertainties / constraints.
– Process. Approach / project management structure / principal tasks / skills needed (participants) / method of work / communications.
– *Initial action.* Sequence of events / priorities / project start-up.

Briefing data covers many aspects, and comes from a variety of sources. Appendix C sets these out in detail. Data can be gathered in many ways:

– *Desk research.* Archival material / public documents and directories / information from professional advisers, business colleagues, public bodies. Remote / can be time-consuming.
– *Questionnaires.* Sample surveys of management and staff. Easy initial involvement of all levels / good for quantitative information.
– *Interviews.* Individual, and focus groups. Good for understanding complex relationships / generate goodwill and involvement / time-consuming.
– *Direct observation.* Observations of actual as opposed to intended use patterns / checking of survey and interview data. Relatively inexpensive / hard to identify reasons for patterns (without further interviews).
– *Benchmarking.* Examining best practice elsewhere (visits, literature searches). Stimulates creative thought / establishes high standards / hard to get data.
– *Simulation.* Exploring options in models / computer simulations, full-size mock-ups. Generates strong commitment / avoids expensive mistakes / may give a glamorized impression.

With data collection for individual workers and workstations, the principal questions are:

– What activities are undertaken, and what space does each require?
– What other activities do they need to connect with, or be separated from?
– What furniture, equipment and storage do they need?

– What environmental conditions do they need?
– How does the pattern of activities change during the day, week and year?

Analysis of what people currently do, and use, is not only valuable for defining what they may need in the new workplace, but as a base line for later post-occupancy surveys. However, existing patterns should only be guides. Moving is a time for change, and old ideas, as well as rubbish, can be left behind. If similar analyses can be obtained from other organizations they can give new perspectives, and form useful benchmarks.

User involvement

Developing a brief makes people think, which is essential for a smooth project and a good result. The process should include the thoughts of all those involved, so that everyone understands and becomes committed to the brief. Top management must approve, so that they can champion the project. Users must be committed to the venture's success, and understand its ultimate benefits for them. Project management needs to know that it has the sponsor's support throughout the vacillations and vicissitudes of the project. Facilities management wants to be reassured that it will be given a workplace that is convenient to manage.

The design brief

The strategic brief defines the sponsor's needs – in strategic, operational, time and financial terms. At this stage it must be developed to reflect the needs of the users, and to put them into terms and criteria that all members of the building design team can use. The design brief should cover operational and activity needs, specification requirements and the constraints imposed by the building and by statutory regulations. Weaving through these are social issues such as provision for the disabled; a range of security matters from fire to terrorism; and the 'green agenda' – energy, conservation and sustainability. The conservation of historic buildings may also be a concern.

Developing the design brief is an iterative process; and it should be collaborative. A running dialogue between all the relevant parties ensures that each understands the other, and builds joint commitment. As the dialogue progresses, the information becomes progressively more detailed: moving from power loads per square metre to locations of socket outlets;

from numbers of desk workers to specifications for the desks themselves.

A good design brief is:

— comprehensive
— relevant and realistic
— clear in structure and description.

Briefing should overlap with concept design and outline specification, but it should never merge with them. The brief sets the questions: design and specification are a particular set of answers. If unsatisfactory, they do not prove the brief at fault; though if redesign cannot come up with an acceptable solution, then the brief may have to be reviewed. However at key stages the brief should be formally agreed – 'signed off'. This provides a firm basis for progress (and discourages backsliding).

NATURE OF THE DESIGN BRIEF

The design brief describes requirements and constraints in building terms. It enables the design team to develop detailed solutions to the users' needs. For an interiors project it is likely to contain:

User needs. Schedule of accommodation / zoning / circulation and linkages / statement on quality and aesthetics / 'green' policies.

Statutory requirements. Construction, fire, health and safety, fiscal and other regulations / particular restrictions in any town planning consent / listed building constraints.

Resources. Data / skills / budget / timetable.

Site. (As background information) Climate / surroundings / access / capacity of public utilities / physical characteristics.

Building shell. Structural, core and envelope constraints.

Building interior. Operational and technical requirements (down to room by room detail) / sponsor's preferences for materials, etc.

Building services. Operational requirements / energy conservation / existing constraints

Furniture and equipment. New items required / existing ones to be accommodated.

Project management. Project organization / responsibilities and authority / communications / method of procurement.

Design

Design stages

The main stages of design are concept, scheme design and design development. All are equally important.

The concept

Even in the replanning of a small department, the right design concept is a prerequisite for success. Enlightened companies see fitting-out as a catalyst: not so much an opportunity to carry out the same operations in a better environment, as the chance to look at how they might be done differently and better. Business process re-engineering and workplace redesign should egg each other on.

The concept design should be built around the four project variables, linked together by the project process:

— *Scope.* The relationship of the functional elements to each other, and to outside elements / how they are to be zoned and stacked / if they are to be phased / what need there is for adaptability or flexibility / expected useful life.
— *Quality.* The ambience of the workplace / its image to staff and outsiders / its degree of permanence / quality of finishes, fittings and furnishings.
— *Cost.* The outline budget / cash flow / external financing and its possible impact on the design / attitude to operating costs.
— *Time.* The overall programme / phasing / constraints (e.g. critical consents, holiday periods).
— *Process.* Tenure of the premises / procurement method / degree of in-house management.

Scheme design

'Balloons on a whiteboard' have to be converted to measurable designs; this is the scheme design stage. Scale drawings and specification notes can then be objectively tested and costed, and subjectively appraised by users. Perspective drawings, cardboard models, mock-ups and computer modelling can all help explain the project, especially to lay people who find plans and cross-sections difficult to understand.

Before the scheme design is formally signed off, it should be approved in principle by sponsor, users and facilities management, following a thorough testing to ensure that it is comprehensive, balanced and acceptable.

— Does it meet the operational needs of the users?
— Does it meet the requirements and constraints of both the strategic and design briefs?
— Is it within the budget?
— Does the work of the various consultants fit seamlessly together?
— Can it be built and furnished easily and to time?
— Does it fulfil the higher aspirations of the company?
— Are you sure?

REGULATIONS

As business becomes more international, the web of regulations becomes more complex. Not only is the range wide, but the force ranges from international law through industry codes of practice to company guidelines. Normally the higher levels take precedence over the lower (and what is developed as a national standard may become adopted as an international one); but in some cases (such as fire regulations) local interpretations may be powerful – and idiosyncratic.

International. Technical standards (e.g. ISO, CIE).
Regional. Laws (e.g. EU Directives).
National. Laws (e.g. UK Building Regulations), technical standards (e.g. BS, DIN).
Local. Laws (e.g. US earthquake codes), interpretations (e.g. UK fire regulations).
Industry. Codes of practice, standard specifications.
Company. Regulations, policies, guidelines.

Design development

During the development of the design, every small detail, dimension and description has to be worked out. The repercussions of choices and changes must be chased around the design, so that everything fits together. These decisions intimately affect every user: the height of a shelf, the cleanability of a skirting, the noise of a door shutting, the ease of replacing a lamp, the colours in a corridor. It is up to the designers and specialist contractors to say when decisions are needed; late changes can be very costly in time and wasted effort.

Fitting-out is usually rapid, and sourcing delays can have expensive commercial consequences. Quality and cost have to be balanced against time. Standard solutions using basic building materials can do much

to cut time and cost (dry-wall partitions are cheaper and often quicker than demountable ones). Specials can be cheaper than off the peg. Mechanical plant put together and commissioned off site, although more expensive, may save weeks on the overall schedule.

Production information

Working drawings, specifications, schedules and, usually, bills of quantities, provide the information needed to construct the project. Co-ordination between the various consultants and specialist contractors is arduous, but made easier with common standards (codes of practice) and common methods (systems of structuring information, CAD, standard specifications).

Signing off the production information is the final check: does it look right? Is the cost estimate right? Is all the information there?

Tendering and contracts

Tendering may be for the complete job, or for parcels of work that are fitted into an overall cost framework. Construction should not start without agreed prices.

The ingredients for satisfactory tendering are:

— a clear and complete description of the work to be done;
— a clear form of contract, which allocates risks fairly;
— carefully selected tenderers;
— enough time to tender properly;
— capable management of the tendering and negotiation process.

Where time is critical, and production information limited, conservative cover prices should be included for the missing items, so that a fair and balanced total picture can be seen.

Contracts

Contracts allocate responsibilities and risks, but their exact form depends on the procurement route chosen. In Britain the Joint Contracts Tribunal (which represents all sides of the construction industry) produces several suitable ones, relating to the scale and nature of the work.

Contractor selection

Selecting the right contractors (the main contractor and specialist subcontractors) takes much the same form as for consultants. Whether firms are recommended by other businesses in the area, by the consultants or are already on the sponsor's own register, they should provide prequalification information and be checked out.

The shortlisted firms should be given ample warning of the timetable for the whole process: tendering, negotiating (if required), contract award, mobilization and start on site. Both the size of the shortlist and the length of the tendering period should relate to the size of the job. Although there are no absolute rules, shortlists of between three and seven committed tenderers, and a period of three to four weeks are reasonable norms.

Tenders are evaluated by the professional team, which then normally recommends the acceptance of the lowest; although sometimes there may be valid reasons for accepting a higher one, or negotiating variations on particular items. Provided this is done openly and fairly, and within the terms of the tender invitation, there can be no real cause for complaint. The contract can then be drawn up and signed.

Negotiating and partnering

On occasion it is to the project's advantage to negotiate contracts rather than tender them − although even then the selection of the negotiating partner may involve some element of competition (such as tendering on a schedule of rates). It enables a sponsor to involve a contractor at an early stage, and incorporate its advice into the design and programming of the work.

Where the sponsor has a continuing programme of works then the relationship can be extended into a partnership arrangement, with each party guaranteeing the other continuity in return for economies of time and money.

Contract administration

The quicker the job, the more important contract administration is. Its principal aspects are:

- *Communications*. Methods of transmitting decisions and information to the right parties / recording decisions and progress / public relations.
- *Programme*. Mobilization / preconstruction activities such as accommodation works or stripping out / fitting-out contracts and their inter-relationships / commissioning and handover / moving in / principal milestones.
- *Monitoring*. Review procedures and meetings for progress, quality and expenditure / control of changes / monitoring of off-site works and of deliveries.

Construction

Preparatory work

Before construction proper can start, the space may need to be got ready, and a smooth flow of deliveries assured. Where the fit-out consists of improvements to an existing workplace, clear demarcation of responsibilities and territory between sponsor and contractors is fundamental. Particular aspects are security and insurance.

Accommodation works

With an existing building there are also likely to be preliminary works. It may be necessary to create temporary workspace, to devise alternative catering arrangements, to rearrange circulation routes, and to erect sound- and dust-proofing. Furniture and equipment may need to go into temporary storage; and it and other vulnerable areas may need additional security.

Sourcing

Construction activities on site are paralleled by off-site manufacturing and deliveries. In fitting-out, where so many components are delivered fully finished, sourcing may even be more critical than construction.

Prefabricated mechanical plant hoisted into place, sophisticated desking that can interlock in myriad ways, specially designed carpet with a range of unusual properties: the designer's palette expands daily. But once something complex and multifunctional is specified, the choice of sources diminishes rapidly. Genius in design may be followed by headaches in sourcing and maintenance. It is wise to have alternative sources, to use simple materials and components wherever possible. It is prudent to take only a small part of any one manufacturer's output, so as not to overstress it. It makes sense to let a main contractor choose its familiar subcontractors and suppliers, with whom it works smoothly and economically.

Fitting-out

Because of the high proportion of specialist work, fit-outs naturally break into a number of discrete work packages. These may be carried out by subcontractors under a main contractor, or by separate trades contractors co-ordinated by a construction manager. Sequence, physical and organizational interfaces, mutual support, communications: all these aspects need to be carefully considered from the outset.

■ A move is an opportunity to 'down-size' old files and equipment. When 200 people moved in Digital Equipment's office in Stockholm they got rid of 15 tonnes of paper and 457 obsolete PCs!

Who has to have finished before another starts? How does this component fit into that opening? Who needs an electrician in attendance?

The works may have constraints on space or access, and on dust, noise, vibration or working hours. The existing interior may have to be ripped out. Delicate equipment and expensive materials may well be installed.

Fit-outs are often carried out under tremendous pressure, so delays and changes can have serious effects. Fortunately interiors are sheltered from the weather, there is little 'wet' construction (e.g. concreting), and many of the elements are prefabricated off site. On the other hand, with an existing building there is the risk of surprises when it is 'opened up'. Changes may also come from problems of supply, or from the demands of the statutory authorities. What is important is that the cost and time implications of any change (even if apparently small) should be cleared with the sponsor before new instructions are given.

Commissioning and furnishing

Because the mechanical and electrical services are woven throughout the building, and are largely concealed behind access panels, false ceilings and raised floors, they must be tested, balanced and tuned before furnishing can begin. Just when the interior looked almost ready, walls. floors and ceilings are taken apart again.

Protecting completed work requires careful planning throughout the contract, but the nearer completion, the more critical this becomes. In technical areas such as dealing rooms and kitchens, the equipment needs to be commissioned as an integral part of the installations. Because some equipment (and its finishes) is delicate, it needs to be carefully protected from damage.

To further complicate matters, this is the point at which the users' equipment and furniture starts to arrive. Many of these items are valuable yet portable, so they need to flow smoothly from secure transit to secure zones. Completion may have to be phased through a series of the latter, so that once a zone is equipped the general workforce no longer has access.

Snagging – checking the completed work for any shortcomings – is done by the consultants and contractors, and a list agreed before the office is handed over to the sponsor. Some items on the list may need to be put right at once. If the works have been properly inspected throughout, these should be relatively minor. Other items will be held over until the end of the defects period, when everything can be dealt with at one time, with the least disruption to the users.

Occupation

Moving in

Moving in needs careful preparation: facilities staff taught how to run the systems and equipment; operational staff briefed on the new office's layout and general arrangements (using physical or computer models); and with supplies for both groups stocked and accessible. Information (paper or electronic) should be distributed in advance, so that uncertainty and apprehension are minimized.

The aim should be to make everyone comfortable and at ease from the very start. Smooth functioning of computer networks and telephone systems are central to this. They can also be the vehicle for further support: on-screen information, and the essential 'help line'.

The move itself is a major operation. It may be carried out by move contractors over a long weekend (even for a major company), or done in house over several months as IT is gradually recoupled. It takes time to plan, but the way it is handled makes all the difference, not only to how few man–hours are lost, but how people will feel about the building for years to come.

On moving day, thought should be given to the flow of belongings into the workspace: doors, corners and paintwork protected against knocks; set down areas allocated where boxes can be checked and distributed; temporary storage for empties; security, protection – and security again.

Once in the new workspace there can be 'hands-on' induction training, covering the use of the mechanical and electrical systems, the quirks of new furniture, and security and safety systems. Disabled staff can be shown the friendly features of the new workspace and given special assistance.

To help people find their way around, the normal means of orientation (such as views out of windows, and colour themes for different areas) may need augmenting with additional (temporary) signs.

Running in and tuning

A building is not a car: tens of prototypes tested to destruction and now 'one careful owner'. However routine, a fit-out is unique and untested – and serves many people. There are likely to be teething troubles, and sufficient money and manpower must be allocated to this period, so that it is properly resourced.

Closing down the project

While the staff are settling in, the project itself is closing down. Even in the best run project there may be outstanding items: late delivery of some piece of equipment, environmental systems needing adjustment, or damage caused in the move to be made good. Some of these properly lie within the scope of the project; others may be additions. It is necessary to decide which fall into the province of the project manager, and which into the on-going realm of the facilities manager (assuming them to be two different people).

Construction contracts have a defects period, at the end of which the contractors must put right all the items identified during the snagging inspection, and any other defects emerging subsequently. When this work is done and signed off, the final account can be drawn up by the quantity surveyor and contractors, with any claims (reasons why extra money is due) identified and settled.

Once the contractors have been signed off, it is the turn of the consultants. Provided that the work has gone well, and relationships are still good, it is a time for formal thanks to consultants and contractors, with the offer to act as a referee in future. It may also be an occasion for celebration: to thank all those who have contributed, from consultants and contractors to the statutory authorities; to show the results to customers, neighbours and the local community; and to get coverage in the media. Not least it is the moment to thank staff for tolerating inconvenience and accepting change.

As a part of the hand-over and closing down, the consultants and contractors should provide a set of records:

- operating and maintenance manuals
- as-built drawings and specifications
- a contact list of the consultants, contractors and key suppliers.

There may also be space-planning layouts, and an inventory of furniture and equipment. These records may be supplied on paper, or in electronic format – from as-built drawings on CAD disk to interactive maintenance manuals on CD-ROM. Some more detailed records may be kept by the consultants at their premises; and it is advisable to keep a back-up set of all records off site in case of catastrophe.

Reviews and feedback

The new workspace will have cost time, money and heartache. Was it worth it? Setting up a framework for feedback – a kind of 'briefing in retrospect' – allows the facilities management to:

- assess the success of the results;
- make modifications to overcome defects, or to improve performance;
- respond to the users' mood;
- prepare a better brief next time.

The framework should be in three parts:

- a sympathetic and responsive system for handling criticisms, complaints and suggestions;
- proactive and continuing arrangements for reviews and post-occupancy surveys;
- a system for implementing desirable changes.

Both the building's operational and physical performance should be reviewed. In operational terms, how well does each part function: prime workspace, ancillary and support areas and circulation? What is its ambience and image? How easy is it to run and maintain?

As for the physical construction: have the right materials been chosen, and designed well? Do the mechanical, electrical and IT systems work as they should, and are they user friendly? Are the furniture and furnishings wearing well – and are they liked?

This feedback should emanate largely from the users: through suggestions boxes, chats over coffee, focus groups and formal surveys. Within the project team itself, the project process should be assessed. Was the right team chosen? How good was the brief? Were contractual arrangements sound? Did people communicate with each other enough, and at the right times? What were the main successes, and how could they be replicated? What went wrong? Why? How could it be avoided in future?

Dilemmas

- If user input is critical for an effective brief, how will this be obtained where staff operate off site?
- What is the process for designing, monitoring and maintaining 'off-site' workplaces? Whose is the responsibility when they are 'third-party sites' (planes, hotels – or even ocean liners)?
- Can a partnership between clients, designers and contractors become the norm and, if so, will this speed up the rationalization of the fitting-out process?
- How can the increasing rate of change and obsolescence be set against the need to conserve physical resources?

Andersen Consulting
London

'Office for the nineties' (OFTN) is the name that Andersen Consulting gives to the 'just in time' working framework that it is developing. As a management consultancy operating worldwide, its own work methodology is central to the services it offers clients. Moving people around – 'constant churn' – can, it argues, encourage better and more creative working practices to emerge.

Its London office is in a seventies building situated halfway between the Law Courts and the Thames. This excellent location, with nearby rail, underground and parking (both dedicated and on the street) meant that rather than move to accommodate the firm's rapid growth, the partners decided to make the existing space work in new ways.

There are 1500 people based at the London office but, as consultants spend much of their time at clients' premises, 80% of these are usually out. Some form of desk sharing is a natural solution for this work pattern. In 1991 a working party (including user representatives and the appointed architects) spent nearly a year researching and designing the new concept. A pilot scheme for 166 people using half a floor (530m²) was implemented in 14 weeks, and opened in January 1992. Since then other areas have been refurbished in a rolling programme, with lessons learnt at each stage being passed on to the next.

OFTN is based on a high level of shared workstations. Only secretaries and administrators have totally dedicated workspaces. For the rest, there is a choice of short-term desking or larger 'corral' areas for longer work periods. These have continuous work surfaces so that spreading out is easy (if there is the need and few other people around). The partners have their own enclosed offices, but these are small

(originally designed as 9m², but subsequently increased to 13m² so that they can be used for meetings). They can be booked for general use when their owners are out. They are positioned towards the inside of the building, with a view through their glazed partitions looking over the secretaries to the windows beyond: a clear statement about where hierarchy is going.

General workstations are just over 3m² net a person (exclusive of storage), with an average of one desk provided for eight workers. There are four 'cells' – tiny two-person quiet rooms, and a secure project (or 'war') room. Telephone booths will soon be provided for confidential calls.

Clear desks are obligatory (for security as well as management) with storage against main walls to cellular spaces and in banks along either side of the central corridor. Each person has a full-height metre-wide cupboard with drawers and shelves, and there is coat hanging alongside the workstations. Paper processing areas with copiers, shredders, stationery and mail are located centrally, with venderettes alongside.

Figure 8.7 Part layout of typical floor.
Key
1 core
2 reception
3 quiet room
4 'corral'
5 short-term area
6 support workstations
7 cellular office
8 sculpture
9 copier

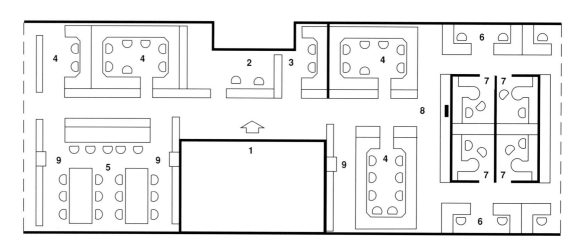

The concept includes relaxed seating areas, and also more formal ones around tables for spontaneous meetings. These areas may well become satellite cafés. There is one smoking room in the building, although clients are permitted to smoke in meetings if they wish. Restaurants and other facilities are shared with Arthur Andersen (the sister accountancy firm) next door.

OFTN is seen as the equivalent of a five-star hotel, providing a high-quality and highly serviced environment, and using a similar booking system. Excellent management is critical. Each floor has an administrator and a floor steward – facilities management immediately to hand. Property Director Tim Arnold describes it: 'Using OFTN is like leasing a car – you choose the model you want, when you want it,

and hand it back when you have finished with it. Cleaning out the ashtrays is someone else's problem.'

Workstations are networked, with docks for the consultants' lap-tops, and a telephone system that allows remote data access, voice- and E-mail, and DDI (direct dialling inwards). However, a concern about not losing the human touch discourages automatic answering: 'It could be a prospective new client who may well go elsewhere if all she gets is a machine.' Tim Arnold again: 'Technology removes the traditional attachment to the workplace, and enables productive work to be undertaken anywhere. People are empowered to choose the best place for the task in hand. OFTN is a reflection of this reality, not a cost-cutting exercise.'

The building is fully air-conditioned with solar

Figure 8.8 (Opposite) The cellular offices have glazed partitions in stainless steel frames. These, like the workstations and storage, were specially designed.

Figure 8.9 (Above) Sculptures act as focal points – outside the lifts against a curved sycamore wall, and at the far end of the central corridor.

■ One bank holiday weekend when the chippies were working frantically to a tight schedule, the construction manager went out and bought 'Big Macs' for everyone.

Figure 8.10 Low glass screens with decorative lines give a hint of privacy between different work areas.

blinds locally controlled. Lighting is by fluorescent downlighters in the ceiling and under high-level storage, augmented by task lighting at the workplace and spotlighting in circulation areas. Acoustic ceiling panels are neatly positioned, with jointless plasterboard margins around the tops of partitions. Acoustic privacy is provided in the cellular spaces by double glazing, seals round the doors and absorbent blanket in the ceiling void.

During the building works people were dispersed in pockets of free space all around the building – a kind of 'musical chairs'. This made moving back a relief, and perhaps mitigated any problems there might have been.

Using construction management allowed the client to stay in control of as many decisions as possible. A non-confrontational way of working with the contractors optimized the partnership approach in

which Andersen Consulting firmly believes.

This is a skilfully crafted environment, with the aesthetic being the epitome of elegance – low key but classy; beautifully designed to accommodate people and to make them feel valued, rather than just to impress.

The entrance lobby at street level is quite small, with comfortable seating, discreet displays and jolly girls behind the sycamore and red marble reception desk. The travertine walling, the marble flooring and the sycamore trim is carried into the lifts and then up to the refurbished floors above. The corridor runs straight through from end to end of the floor, but it is full of incident: space opened out, rooms closing in, different lighting and flooring changing subtly – from beige and green marble to gentle green in the work areas, and then to a bolder green pattern in the more public area.

TIMOTHY SOAR

■ The Japanese spend 75% of project time in preparation, and only 25% in implementation; Americans, it is said, do the reverse. With all building projects, time spent in proper brief development and preparation reduces time and costs on site, as well as providing a more effective result.

At one end of the corridor two ceramic works by Sutton Taylor excite increasingly as one approaches, and at the other the vast glass plate by Steven Newell forms a focal point. Both are precisely positioned and lit to emphasize the overall design. Artworks were chosen early in the design process, with the artists often involved in the design development. The firm's curator regularly brings works before a committee (which includes the architect): the collection has been built up over some 15 years.

Workstations and storage, designed by the architects, are fixed in position. Work surfaces in the enclosed offices are against the far wall, surrounded by storage (while practical and space efficient, this demands that people sit with their back to the door). Sycamore with maple lipping is beautifully used for work surfaces, shelving and storage. Glazed partitions (with minimal incised lines) are framed generously in

stainless steel. Colour, apart from the green carpet, comes from burgundy drawer fronts and multi-coloured (though predominantly red) chairs. Planting sprouts from the top of storage units on either side of the passageway (the units have curved tops to discourage dumping – a detail that occurs throughout).

Legibility was a key design factor, with materials used to orientate the visitor (panelling opposite the main lift – a painting opposite the staff one); but underlying this is solidity – rather like the image of an old-fashioned bank. But this place is not old-fashioned at all – just providing a feeling of continuity and reliability in the ever-changing world of modern consultancy.

Architects: The Chadwick Group
Art Consultants: Art Guidelines
Construction Manager: Mace Ltd
Programme started: 1991

Figure 8.11 A 'corral', with low storage along the central corridor. The curved top and planting discourages 'dumping'.

Chapter 9
Space planning

Aims in space planning

Measurement

■ **The building shell**

Nature of the building

Building form

■ **The organization's needs**

■ **Putting it together**

Zoning and stacking

Circulation

Grids

Design

■ **Dilemmas**

Space planning is changing: not just to underwrite new management practices, but to provide a different quality of service. It is no longer just about squeezing in regiments of 'bums on seats', but about creating a workplace where people can interact productively.

The 'bums' must still be fitted in as neatly as possible, but the division between cellular and open plan working is softening, with team space beginning to supersede the individual workstation as the unit of design. Space planners are contending with new issues: when is the individual office really necessary; how cordless can the workplace be; should people move, or the furniture; should the workstation footprint become more standardized, or less?

Any planning of space is hypothetical: the space may be used as intended, but equally it may end up being used in quite another way. It will surely alter as the tide of commerce ebbs and swirls into unforeseen opportunities. Space planning is important, but only as a tool to a workable set-up; not as a straightjacket inhibiting growth and change.

So organizations ask for flexibility; but this need not mean moving furniture and partitions. Instead, people can move around – to whatever space fits what they are doing, and which is free at the time. Power and data connections become the main restrictions. Flexibility of body encourages flexibility of mindset, so that the restaurant becomes seen as a place where staff can meet to work at any time, whether they eat or not.

In this climate space planning is becoming increasingly creative, with workstations clustered and grouped, with tight spaces and open spaces, spaces for concentration and spaces for discussion; simple regimentation being replaced with layouts that reflect clearly the different activities for which they are being used. At the same time it is increasingly pragmatic and cost-conscious. Lavish provision against every eventuality has given way to shrewd assessment of what is likely: '95% of the performance for 75% of the cost'.

Skilful and imaginative use of space can only be achieved by good design. This chapter sets out to encourage informed discussion between users and designers, by providing pointers on the critical aspects of the process.

Aims in space planning

The essence of space planning is fitting an organizational structure into a building structure. Very occasionally it is a new organization; but usually it is an

■ In 1994 the British Council for Offices produced its 'Specification for Urban Offices'. This set out realistic performance norms, to counteract the excessively high standards of the 1980s, when developers aimed at providing maximum flexibility for all the possible needs of occupiers. We refer to these norms here and elsewhere in the book.

Figure 9.1 Automobile Association, Basingstoke: Full height banks of paper storage are still needed despite an increasing use of electronic systems. *Architects: Watkins Gray International*

existing body that needs to relocate, or to replan its present space.

The reasons for this may include:

— accommodating growth or contraction;
— accommodating restructuring of the organization;
— encouraging interaction and team working through space layout;
— encouraging interaction through circulation routes;
— providing spaces that enhance the lives of those who use them;
— increasing the ratio between net usable and gross internal areas;
— reducing overall space per person;
— rationalizing and reducing the number of work-station footprints;
— increasing (or decreasing) the number of open plan workstations;
— providing for shared workstations;
— providing maximum occupancy of all areas including support spaces;
— rationalizing furniture and equipment;
— reducing reconfiguration costs;
— reducing operating costs (for example by using natural light and ventilation).

In parallel with considering the organization's requirements, however, it is necessary to look at the existing building, if there is one: what its characteristics, opportunities and restrictions are. It is only by relating the two that the feasibility of the project can be assured.

Figure 9.2 Area measurements (After Alexi Marmot Associates).

Measurement

Space measurement has a language of its own – or two. In Britain the construction industry has been fully metricated for a quarter of a century; but letting agents persist in talking of space in square feet – perhaps because the numbers sound bigger! So thinking about space often means thinking in both languages, and converting effortlessly between them.

RULES OF THUMB: MEASUREMENT CONVERSIONS	
Rough conversions are:	
Metric	*Imperial (feet)*
Length	
1 metre (m)	3 feet + 3 inches + $^{3}/_{8}$ of an inch, 3.3 feet
30 centimetres (cm)	1 foot
3m	10 feet
Area	
1 square metre (m^2)	11 square feet
0.09m^2	1 square foot
9m^2	100 square feet
Floor loadings	
1 kiloNewton per square metre (kN/m^2)	20 pounds per square foot

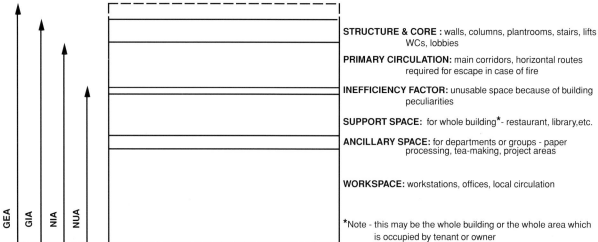

STRUCTURE & CORE : walls, columns, plantrooms, stairs, lifts WCs, lobbies

PRIMARY CIRCULATION: main corridors, horizontal routes required for escape in case of fire

INEFFICIENCY FACTOR: unusable space because of building peculiarities

SUPPORT SPACE: for whole building*- restaurant, library,etc.

ANCILLARY SPACE: for departments or groups - paper processing, tea-making, project areas

WORKSPACE: workstations, offices, local circulation

*Note - this may be the whole building or the whole area which is occupied by tenant or owner

GEA - Gross External Area: whole building around outside of outer walls
GIA - Gross Internal Area: whole building to inside of outer walls
NIA - Net Internal Area: gross internal area less all structure and cores
NUA - Net Usable Area: net internal area less primary circulation

Ways of measuring space in a building vary considerably, and these too have their own terminology. The principal measures are as follows.

- *Gross internal area (GIA)*. Area within internal faces of external and atrium walls, including core area, but excluding roof plant and totally unlit spaces. The same as gross floor area (GFA).
- *Net internal area (NIA)*. GIA but excluding core area. The same as net floor area (NFA) and net lettable area (NLA).
- *Net usable area (NUA)*. NIA but excluding primary circulation.
- *Core area*. Lifts, stairs, common lobbies, plant and service areas, ducts, toilets and the area of internal structure.
- *Primary circulation*. Major routes within the NIA linking fire escapes.
- *Secondary circulation*. The routes connecting workspaces and cellular offices to the primary circulation.

The building shell

Whether searching for new premises, refurbishing existing ones or developing a new building from scratch, understanding the building envelope is a prerequisite for creating an effective interior.

Nature of the building

Types of building

The large company probably wants to occupy a modern building, whether existing or purpose built. Even for such a company, however, and certainly for smaller firms, older buildings – possibly over a century old – may prove a good option. Looking at this range, office buildings fall into the following categories.

- *New build:* owner–user. Flexibility for change should still be built in. Another firm's tailor-made building can misfit badly. The newest may be naturally ventilated, with good daylighting.
- *New build:* speculative. Often built to the lowest common denominator, with money spent where it shows (even those to 'developer standard'). Usually air-conditioned.
- *Refurbished:* post-war. May be of utilitarian construction with poor insulation standards. Naturally ventilated, often with good daylight. With advancing technology, limited storey heights can be sufficient. Cheap.

- *Refurbished:* prewar. Well built, with good storey heights. Naturally ventilated and daylit (but often inadequately). Floor plans may be inflexible.
- *Refurbished:* nineteenth century – office. Well built, with good storey heights, and frequently considerable character.
- *Refurbished:* nineteenth century – domestic. Often well built, with character, but generally small spaces constrained by load-bearing walls.
- *Refurbished:* nineteenth century – industrial, civic. Factories, warehouses, churches, hospitals. Generally solidly built, with considerable character and a range of space sizes and types. Industrial buildings likely to have simpler and more flexible floor plans than civic ones.

These types are common in Britain, but are mirrored in other countries.

General considerations

Where an existing building is being considered for complete or partial occupation, the sponsor needs to review the factors that can have an impact on its use, whether directly or indirectly. External considerations – such as a noisy neighbour – may well affect the way the interior can be used.

┌───┐

CHECKLIST: BUILDING SELECTION

Surroundings. Amenities / noise / pollution / overlooking.
Orientation. Sun / wind / view.
Adjacencies. Neighbours / co-tenants.
Size. Floorplate shape and size / number of floors / clear floor height (to underside of beams).
Usefulness. Amount of net space available for workspace / column grid and obstructions.
Flexibility. Modular planning / future needs / technical changes.
Access. Entrance / circulation / lifts / staircases.
Shell. Condition / maintenance / aesthetic and image.
Settings. Condition / suitability / aesthetic and image.
Security. Perimeter / entrances / fire escape / security systems.
Services. HVAC / power distribution / sanitary provision / energy efficiency.
Electronics. IT / telecommunications / building management systems.

└───┘

■ When Leo Burnett, an advertising agency, was looking for new offices, architects Fletcher Priest provided 'virtual walk-throughs' of several unbuilt projects. As a result, the right building was picked at an early stage, both satisfying its developer and allowing Leo Burnett to influence the design – including major changes, such as escalators from street level.

Figure 9.3 External constraints that may affect suitability of a building.

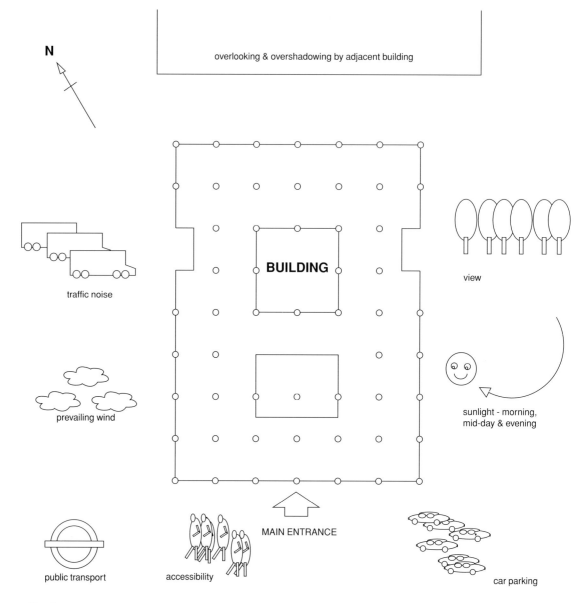

Plan form

The depth of the building, window to window, the core position and the general shape and size of the floorplate are central to the way the layout can be planned.

Deep floorplates (over 20m between windows) are flexible, have short communications and encourage maximum interaction. Shallow ones (less than 15m) can provide natural light, ventilation and views out, and can easily accommodate cellular offices. Offices in between these limits can combine the advantages of both, and thus be excellent options.

Suitable dimensions are:

Window to window   15–18m
Window to core   6–12m (9m preferred)

An atrium turns a deep plan into a series of shallower ones, bringing natural light and views, if not natural ventilation, into the centre of the building. The bottom of an atrium may also form part of a single large floor. Some building frames are designed to allow the atrium to be in-filled at the lower levels to provide deep floor space should this be needed. However, atria can restrict the way floors are planned, in the same way that cores do.

Building form

The shell, services, settings (partitions, ceilings and floors), furniture and furnishings of a building have different lifespans and amortization rates (though the two may not match). Thus to reconfigure the divisions within a space may well make financial sense after six years, but major alterations to the air-conditioning may need to wait longer.

Structure

The form of a building is influenced by the site and local planning regulations, by its original users' needs, by its structure and by the propensities of its designers. Small old buildings may have bearing walls, with relatively short floor spans and spaces constrained by the walls. But most offices will be of frame construction – either reinforced concrete or fireproofed steel. The principal structural constraints are then the floor to floor height, the spacing and location of the columns, and the location and bulk of the cores.

Too great a floor-to-floor height increases the bulk (and cost) of the building; too little prevents the use of suspended ceilings and raised floors to carry essential service runs. Conventionally, ceiling voids

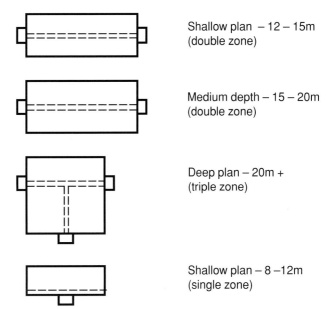

Shallow plan – 12 – 15m (double zone)

Medium depth – 15 – 20m (double zone)

Deep plan – 20m + (triple zone)

Shallow plan – 8 –12m (single zone)

contain HVAC and lighting, and floors power and IT. In both the space required is tending to reduce: ceilings because of a return to natural ventilation; and floors because of the advent of structured cabling (and cordless communications). This makes some of the low-ceilinged buildings of the 1960s appear viable again – but natural ventilation may not be enough for the increasing density of computer use.

In some naturally ventilated buildings, the prudent

Figure 9.4 Building depths.

Life spans of different elements of a building

	Years
Shell	40–75 (or more)
Services	15–25
Settings	5–7
Furniture	5–15
Equipment	2–5

	FLOORPLATES: COMPARATIVE CHARACTERISTICS		
Characteristics	*Depth of floorplate*		
	Narrow (12–15m)	Medium (15–20m)	Deep (20m+)
Ease of subdivision	Excellent/allows for 100% cellular offices with a view	Good/allows for 60% cellular offices with a view	Poor/allows only 20% cellular offices with a view
Range of layout options	Poor/cellular layout	Good/allows for variety of sized groups and open plan or cellular layout	Poor/open plan layout
Individual control of the environment	Good/opening windows/ natural ventilation	Fair/opening windows at perimeter/central air handling	Poor/total air-conditioning/ central control
Natural light and view	Good	Fair	Poor
Cost of occupancy	Fair	Good	Poor

From Worthington and Konya

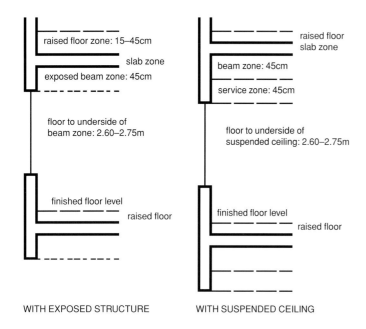

WITH EXPOSED STRUCTURE

raised floor zone: 15–45cm
slab zone
exposed beam zone: 45cm
floor to underside of beam zone: 2.60–2.75m
finished floor level
raised floor

WITH SUSPENDED CEILING

raised floor slab zone
beam zone: 45cm
service zone: 45cm
floor to underside of suspended ceiling: 2.60–2.75m
finished floor level
raised floor

Figure 9.5 Vertical dimensions (after British Council for Offices, 1994).

are making provision for the installation of HVAC, should this later prove necessary. Where HVAC is run in the floor void, the structural ceiling can be exposed. This increases room height without increasing storey height, aids daylight distribution, allows cooling through using the slab as a reservoir, and – depending on the ceiling's form and height – may improve acoustic conditions. It also strongly affects the feel of the space. A low ceiling in a small office can be fine, whereas it is claustrophobic in a large space.

Buildings have often been designed to take high floor loadings ($5kN/m^2$) everywhere. But this is costly, and loadings can be reduced to about half that, with limited areas (say 5% of the whole) boosted to $7.5kN/m^2$. This effectively means that many buildings can then only take exceptionally heavy floor loads – such as filing centres or equipment rooms – in specially designated areas.

Columns normally form part of the structural grid (sometimes measured to their face rather than their centres). Columns set back from the external walls, with cantilevered floors, can create spaces that are difficult to use (the 'building inefficiency factor'). Wherever possible walls should coincide with columns. Column spacings of 6.0m, 7.5m and 9.0m give a reasonable compromise between flexible column-free space and structural cost.

Cores

The position of the core in a building is a major influence on how the floorplate may be used. The stairs,

lifts, ducts, plant rooms and toilets may form a homogeneous centre – a true 'core', or they may be spread around in a manner which proves more or less efficient for the projected use of the space.

Escape stairs are rigidly controlled by fire regulations, but the positions of lifts and other staircases generally relate to easy access to all floors, and to keeping primary circulation routes to a minimum. Lifts in the centre of a deep plan building reduce the space taken up by primary circulation; whereas lifts at the edge of the floorplate allow greater flexibility in how the space is used, but increase the amount of circulation.

Ducts seem to take up an unreasonable amount of space (except to engineers), but well-placed ducts of adequate capacity can ensure that all parts of the floorplate are properly serviced. Air distribution and exhaust require the largest ducts. 'Wet' ducts serve toilets, cleaners' cupboards, catering facilities and fire points, with main power, telecoms and data risers running to switch- and patch-panels in separate 'dry' ducts.

Toilets usually occur at every level, on primary circulation routes and frequently near stairs. Others are often found near the main entrance and alongside the restaurant. They are normally part of the basic building, and have been designed to comply with standard regulations based on the estimated building population. Only if the fit-out is going to significantly increase this number, or special additional facilities are needed – a crèche or an executive flat – is there a need for radical change.

Building fabric and services

The external skin of a building affects the interior design through the size and placing of the windows. Continuous windows influence the planning grid through their mullion spacing; infrequent window apertures may prevent cellular subdivision around the perimeter. If the window heads are high then it may be difficult to insert deep suspended ceilings; low sills discourage placing furniture close to the external wall, and the lowest prevent the insertion of raised floors. High sills, which might otherwise be oppressive, can become acceptable when raised floors are installed.

The service most likely to affect the interior design is HVAC, as it may not be possible to alter main horizontal trunking or, when they exist, perimeter terminals (whether they be fan coil units or strip radiators). Both HVAC and natural ventilation may affect how easily cellular offices can be created.

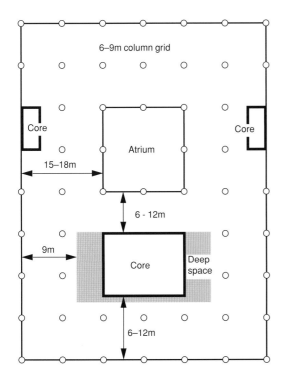

The organization's needs

The brief is not a rigid set of instructions, but rather a statement of intent which develops during the design process. At its simplest it forms the basis for the initial space planning. Much can be shown in schedules and diagrams:

- schedule of accommodation
- adjacency matrix
- proportional bubble diagrams
- flow diagrams.

Total space

At feasibility stage, the amount of space required needs to be roughly estimated, but with enough precision for informed decision-making. With companies having very different requirements, and buildings varying in usability, there is no absolute standard. However, if the net internal area (NIA) is divided by a suitable gross area per person (say 15–20m²), this provides an indication of the number of people that a particular building – or floor space – might accommodate.

Work and other spaces

Having established a broad estimate of total space, the particular needs of every activity can be considered in general terms. The main element of the workplace has been the individual workstation, whether open plan or in a cellular office, with meeting areas separated out. Multiples of this small module have been the traditional way in which space is initially parcelled out. However, using team or group areas containing spaces for the various activities can provide a more useful planning module. Even though larger – and thus a coarser module – it reflects more realistically the way office space is now being used.

With deep buildings it is common to allocate a proportion of the NIA furthest from the windows for ancillary spaces used for filing, paper processing and tea-making – places where people are not permanently working.

Relationships

Between departments and functions, and within the bigger departments, relationships and linkages are essential components of organizational and space planning. For each linkage the following questions need to be asked.

- Does it involve the physical movement of people or objects?
- How important is it?
- How frequently is it activated?
- How many such linkages does the function have?

Where IT has eliminated the need for physical linkage it no longer has a bearing on space planning.

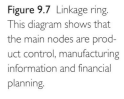

Figure 9.6 Plan form and dimensions (after British Council for Offices, 1994).

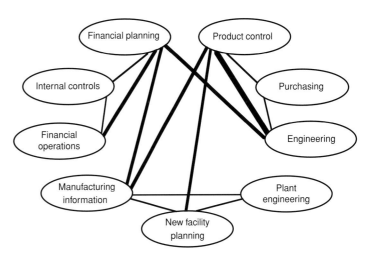

Figure 9.7 Linkage ring. This diagram shows that the main nodes are product control, manufacturing information and financial planning.

Figure 9.8 Adjacency matrix.

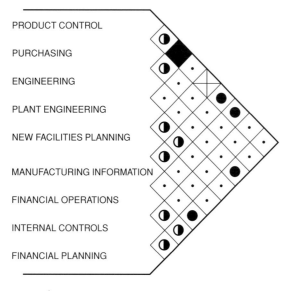

PRODUCT CONTROL

PURCHASING

ENGINEERING

PLANT ENGINEERING

NEW FACILITIES PLANNING

MANUFACTURING INFORMATION

FINANCIAL OPERATIONS

INTERNAL CONTROLS

FINANCIAL PLANNING

Key to linkages:

◆	◈	◖◗	⋄	⊕
Essential	Important	Desirable	Unimportant	Prohibited

An adjacency matrix can establish the relative importance of physical linkages. It shows the relationships between pairs of functions, and highlights which functions have many important relationships. It can also show which functions need to be kept apart. A similar matrix can plot frequency of contact. A linkage ring quickly shows the number of linkages each function has.

With this information a bubble diagram can be developed showing graphically how the various functions of the organization are linked. This can be combined with the initial space analysis to show the relative sizes of the functions as well. Topologically, this diagram is the space plan.

Putting it together

Fitting an organization into a building means approaching the problem from two directions simultaneously: how much space do a certain number of people need (additive approach), and how many people can the building hold (subtractive).

These crude approaches need to be reconciled before more detailed study can begin.

Zoning and stacking

Zoning and stacking are the initial broad brush approach of fitting the proportional bubble diagram of the organization into the available space: zoning on the horizontal plane and stacking, floor by floor. Perhaps the customer relations department needs to be near the main entrance, the boardroom away from the noisy main road, the design studio facing north. When all that is achieved individual floors may be too empty (or too full) – the 'planning factor'. Such space wastage forces compromises. Linkages and departmental area estimates have to be reviewed, and maybe even ways of working reconsidered. Does Accounts really have to be that close to Sales? What would happen if the hot-desking ratio were raised to 6:1? Even so, after several attempts a small planning factor is likely to remain.

The specification and design of a building can also affect arrangements: floor loading has already been mentioned. Cafeterias needing additional ventilation and access to wet ducts should be in well-serviced areas or, failing that, in places where additional services can be introduced economically.

Figure 9.9 Proportional bubble diagram showing relationship between workgroups, and their relative sizes (redrawn from the *New Metric Handbook*).

Key		
1 Product control		7 Financial operations
2 Purchasing		8 Internal controls
3 Engineering		9 Financial planning
4 Plant engineering		10 Procurement
5 New facility planning		11 Plant
6 Manufacturing informa-tion		12 Electrical & mechanical
		13 Invoice control
		14 Staff
		15 Order schedules

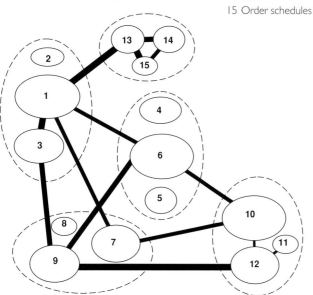

Stacking relates to the position of lifts and stairs, and to the ease of physical communication between floors. Ease is as much a matter of perception as of reality. An atrium with staircases in it, or clearly visible glazed lifts, reduce the psychological barriers between floors. Views across atria make other floors seem less distant. Cheerfully lit stairs that are conveniently located and not too steep make waiting for a lift seem unnecessary.

While zoning and stacking are largely about making it easy to move between functions or departments, there is a more subtle opinion that promotes a degree of separation. People on planned journeys do then have a chance of random encounters. Where fostering these is part of a company's culture, or even of its method of work, then the shortest distance between two points may not be the best.

Circulation

Circulation forms the arteries of a building. Routes should be wide enough for people, wheelchairs and trolleys to pass easily, but they may also have lay-bys. These allow bulky loads to pass, and people to stop and chat.

The design of circulation routes is central to the feel of an office. A star arrangement is inherently more hierarchical than a grid. A narrow corridor, well lit and with a high ceiling, may appear more inviting than a wide one with bland lighting and an oppressively low ceiling. Lay-bys, broad intersections and curved walls are other ways in which circulation routes can be enlivened.

Grids

Office buildings are likely to contain several kinds of grid as shown later.

— *Structure*. Beams and columns.
— *Shell*. Window spacings/window mullions.
— *Services*. Floor electrical outlets/HVAC diffusers/lighting luminaires.
— *Settings*. Systems for raised floors/partitioning/suspended ceilings.
— *Planning*. Workstations/room layouts.

Planning is likely to be simpler and more economic where grids are multiples of each other and relate to the dimensions of building components. For space planning common modules are 90cm, 120cm and 150cm, but there are many variations. Ninety centimetres is based on the width of a door frame, and gives a high degree of flexibility, but has many joints

---

SPACE PLANNING: ADDITIVE AND SUBTRACTIVE APPROACHES

Additive

At its simplest this takes a gross figure of 15–20m^2/person and multiplies it by the projected working population[1] to arrive at a required NIA (net internal area).
A slightly more accurate approach is:

12–14m^2/person × working population[1]
   = NUA (net usable area)
Add: 20–25% primary circulation[2]
      10% partition allowance[3]
      10% 'building inefficiency factor'[4]
Total[5] = NIA

Notes
1 Working population is adjusted to take account of desk- and job-sharing, to arrive at 'full-time equivalent' members of staff (FTE).
2 Circulation is influenced by the shape of the floorplate and the position of the stairs.
3 This allowance depends on the degree of open planning.
4 This is caused by awkward plan shapes or positions of columns and ducts making efficient use of space difficult.
5 Two further allowances may need to be added:
   (a) 'Planning factor' – difficulty in fitting work groups exactly on floors without slack or overspill.
   (b) Allowance for expansion.

Subtractive

	per cent
Gross internal area (GIA)	100
Less: core area	(20)
Net internal area (NIA)	80
Less: primary circulation	(15)
Net usable area (NUA)	65

Divide by 12–14m^2 to arrive at the FTE working population that can be accommodated.

Although difficult at the fitting-out stage, reducing circulation areas (or even cores) produces a welcome improvement to the NUA.

RULES OF THUMB: CIRCULATION

Widths for horizontal circulation in metres

Primary circulation	1.5–2.0+
Secondary circulation	0.9–1.5+
Tertiary circulation	0.55–0.75+
Lift lobbies	3.0+

Fire escape: maximum distance in metres

Direct distance to single escape	18
Travel distance to alternative escapes	45

Distances on ground floor may be increased
Distances may have to be reduced for large
open spaces

Design density	1 person/7m² of NIA

Figure 9.10 Fire escape routes. Maximum travel distances from the furthest point (alternative exits or only one).

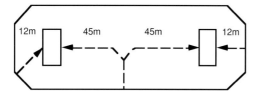

and elongated panel proportions. Most sheet materials come in 120cm widths, which makes this module economical to build. It may well suit small installations, or those which are purpose made. But the 150cm grid is the most common, and leads to economical planning of space. Partitioning and furniture systems are generally designed to work with one of the common grid sizes.

In highly compartmented offices partition positions are almost inevitably governed by the window mullion and column grids. This may result in inefficient space planning if these grids lead to a coarse module. In offices that are largely open plan, however, space planning can escape this domination.

Partition and ceiling grids should relate to each other, for aesthetic and practical reasons. Offset joints or framing members are unsightly; and offset framing makes it difficult to fit sound and fire barriers above suspended ceilings. Where there is no suspended ceiling and the structural slab is coffered the same problems arise if the coffer and partitioning grids are offset.

Design

True quality in design comes from a balance between the practical, the aesthetic and the intangible. During the design process these three aspects need to be kept circulating, each being considered for itself and in relation to the others. The final solution is then a balance: an interior that works well and looks beautiful, costs the right amount and is completed on time – and which also has a really good feeling.

ASPECTS AFFECTING THE DESIGN

Practicalities. The building: opportunities and constraints.
Space: size, accommodation needs / adjacencies / circulation.
Environment: light / air / noise.
Resources: cost and timetable.
Aesthetics. Image / style / materials / details.
Intangibles. Ambience / comfort / security / joy.

Armed with the strategic brief (and in particular with data on the building that is to house the new workspace), the schedule of accommodation, adjacency matrix and proportional bubble diagram, the designers can begin to develop a design concept. In parallel they should draw out more information from the users on the way their departments function, and the fine details of the space, furnishings and services that they require. It is out of this dialogue that the architectural brief develops and the designers get a real feel for the organization and its people.

Although the design must focus on the particular organization's needs, these can be 'benchmarked' by considering what others are doing. Appendix D shows space-planning criteria for some recent projects.

As with scientific discovery, so with design: the four stages in the process are research, assimilation, the creative leap and development. For the building interior, the design concept is that creative leap. The concept responds to practicalities, aesthetics and feelings with sketches, descriptions, models or computer projections which show how the pieces fit together, and how the place should look and feel.

This tangible concept stimulates all those involved to remember what they have forgotten to feed in, before the project has gone too far. Small inputs of this kind are part of the design process, and can be constructively assimilated. It is when massive afterthoughts are hurled at a still fragile concept that damage can be done.

By the time the space layouts have been agreed, the design information will be augmented by a

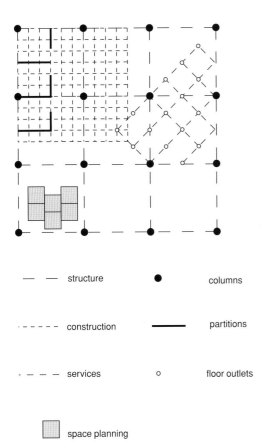

— — structure   ●   columns

· - · - · construction   ▬   partitions

· — · — services   ○   floor outlets

▨ space planning

dossier of detailed user requirements, technical sketches and specification notes. These form the basis for the full construction information.

Although this next stage is often seen as the province of the designers, continuing user involvement is essential. Technical drawings and specifications are often difficult to understand, but if the sponsor does not properly monitor the detailed development of the scheme, then it can lose control of the project and of the result. As architect Mies van der Rohe said: 'God is in the details.' But so may be the Devil; it is up to the users to keep watch.

Figure 9.11 Grids in offices (redrawn from the *New Metric Handbook*).

Dilemmas

■ What kind of organization needs deep plan, flexible and highly serviced space; and what kind would benefit from a shallower building with natural light and ventilation?
■ Should space planning be based on the individual or the team?
■ What are the space-planning implications of different patterns of working: mobile, static or peripatetic?
■ When people cost so much more than space, is space reduction worthwhile at the expense of worker comfort?
■ In the open office, how can people escape from an unwelcome visitor?

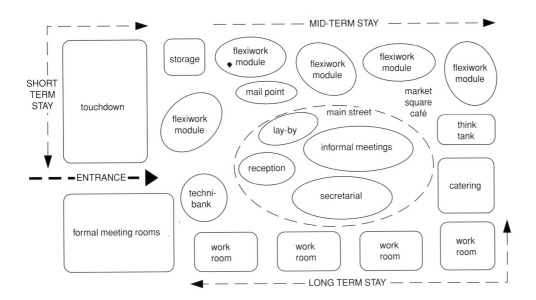

Figure 9.12 Concept diagram. 'Unitel' mobile work centre designed by Morgan Lovell.

The Automobile Association
Basingstoke

workplace

GRAHAM CHALLIFOUR

The Automobile Association is not only responsible for the world's largest patrol and breakdown service, but for insurance, broadcasting throughout Europe and publishing. It has been in the business of helping motorists since 1906 when 'scouts' patrolled on bicycles. Founded as a self-help organization, service to members and a thrifty philosophy are central to its ethos.

Of the 12 000 people which the AA employs to serve its 8 million members, 2200 are based in Basingstoke. The move to the new national headquarters building in 1994 will eventually allow the seven buildings currently in use to be reduced to four.

Norfolk House is an 89 000m² building housing about 700 people on three floors. These include personnel, finance and public relations sections, and the secretariat. Part of the top floor is the Committee (board) area with high-quality meetings rooms, boardroom, offices, support staff workstations and an open seating area (where four Charles Eames club chairs provide a touch of elegance).

Moving from predominantly cellular accommodation, only directors and some senior managers now have private offices (130m²). Most managers are out on the floor, their 10.5m² workstations having only fairly minimal meeting space. Staff workstations are 5.5m². Shared desking is being piloted; but a layout that encourages people to move rather than the furniture has reduced churn costs from over £1m a year to a few pence.

Structured cabling and a patching system allows easy movement to a new position.

Described by one director as 'the best air-conditioning I have ever come across' the VAV system includes a 'thermal wheel' that collects heat and humidity from the exhaust air and passes it to the 90% fresh air being drawn into the building. BMS points every 3.5m allow a fine degree of control, so that local tweaking for individual needs is possible.

Lighting (by fluorescents, with virtually no task lighting) is centrally controlled to go off at the end of the normal working day. However, a bleep warning allows people enough time to override this with a nearby switch. At night there is only emergency lighting, but lights on circulation routes are switched on from central control when security staff do their rounds.

The building – which was commissioned by the AA – cost £24m including furnishing and IT. The main contract took 18 months and the fit-out a further six. Moving in was carried out over six consecutive weekends. Staff stopped work at lunchtime on Fridays and were fully operational again by 8am on Monday morning.

The architects, the AA design staff and the furniture suppliers worked together to develop the interior layouts. Components were kept to the minimum – only the cellular offices, meeting rooms and committee areas have different furnishings. The process for furniture choice was precise. After the

■ Younger people adapt more easily to open plan working than those who are older – even where they are of equal seniority. It seems that the young accept the principle that space does not need to go with hierarchy.

AA Manager

criteria had been agreed a 'trawl' was made of the furniture market, while a layout and basic workstation module was produced in house.

Figure 9.13 (Opposite) Managers responsible for millions of pounds worth of business have open plan workstations. These are extended to include additional storage, a meeting area and rather higher partitions than elsewhere.

CRITERIA FOR FURNITURE SELECTION

Create a good working environment
Have 15–20 year life expectancy
Provide adequate cable management
Be simple to reconfigure
Guarantee of lifetime manufacturer support
Screens to be easily recoverable

A simple questionnaire culled a long list of potential manufacturers into those firms believed capable of fulfilling the brief. A comprehensive 'invitation to tender' included a standard form for pricing; this simplified evaluation. The invitation included contractual terms and conditions, workmanship standards, design criteria, the specification and a bona fide declaration.

Three companies were then asked to set up a typical workstation and office/meeting room in an area where the ceiling, lighting and carpet were those intended for the new building. Each supplier made a presentation outlining the advantages of its products and confirming that they conformed to all requirements. As details of the contract had been negotiated in parallel, there was no delay once the supplier had been selected.

The mock-ups were used to obtain user feedback, which included a preference for rosewood finish rather than oak. The quality of the rosewood

veneer, used in open plan areas as well as cellular offices, is one of the 'pay-back' elements that has made the move to open plan more palatable. Workstations are specifically designed so that whether people are left or right handed they have sufficient spreading space where they need it. A single task chair is used throughout, except for back pain sufferers who may choose an alternative.

Carpets were chosen with the same care as the furniture. Here criteria included rub, wear, impact resistance and stain removal. The supplier, appointed early on, recommended absorbent matting around venderettes and entrances, and in the lifts. Dirt sinks to the base of these mats, which are then washed monthly – two mats for each position make this simple.

Architects: Watkins Gray International
Contractors: Higgs and Hill / Lovell Construction

Figure 9.14 (Above, left) Mail handling is a major operation in an organization with eight million members.

Figure 9.15 This national headquarters houses 700 people on three floors. Only directors and some senior managers have private offices. These have glazed fronts to allow light penetration into the building. Furniture has the rosewood finish chosen by the staff.

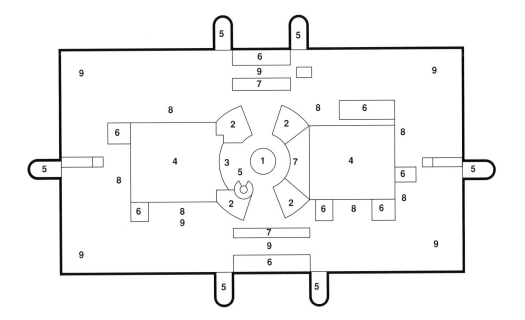

Figure 9.16 Layout.
Key
1   void to reception
2   core
3   waiting
4   void
5   staircase
6   cellular office/s
7   meeting room/s
8   executive workstations
9   workstations

Chapter 10
Settings

- **The set**
  Floors
  Walls
  Doors
  Storage
  Ceilings
  Finishes
  Ironmongery and service terminals
- **Set dressing**
  Windows
  Accessories
  Landscaping
  Art works
  Signage
- **Light fittings**
  Ceiling fittings
  Architectural lighting
  Wall fittings
  Free-standing lights
  Task lights
- **Dilemmas**

An office interior is a series of settings, like sets for a film, designed to accommodate specific action, and to tell a particular tale. With new work practices, this description is all the more apt. Like a film or stage set, an office has three visible elements:

- *The set.* The floors, walls and ceilings that shape the space.
- *Set dressing.* The furniture, furnishings and accessories that make it usable.
- *Lighting.* The light and light fittings that make the space functional, and contribute to its ambience.

Hidden away – usually – is a fourth element, which makes it all work: the services.

Interiors need to change as much as stage sets. Users ask for flexibility, to move walls and alter installations; but a high level of flexibility is expensive and can be disruptive. What is more realistic is adaptability: the ability to rearrange furniture and equipment within reasonably sized and shaped spaces and, when absolutely necessary, to move walls and services without affecting the structure or primary installations.

This chapter considers the function and construction of floors, walls and ceilings, and the impact of furnishings and lighting on the set. Services and furniture have separate chapters of their own.

The set

Walls divide: floors and ceilings hide – this is the chant for most office spaces. In the typical office fixed or movable walls define cellular spaces, and the main pipes, wires and ducts run above or below the structural slab, concealed by raised floors or suspended ceilings.

Careful thought needs to be given to the detailed design of where the hidden services emerge. Outlets, switches, controls, sensors, grilles, heating or cooling elements and light fittings – the 'service terminals' – are the visible ends of the concealed pipes and wires. This interface between the invisible and visible is critical for a successful office interior, not only in terms of aesthetics, but also of function.

Floors, walls and ceilings often need to conform to a planning grid, which is determined by:

- the efficient planning module for workstations and rooms;
- the column and window spacing of the building shell;
- the component sizes of floor, wall and ceiling systems.

Figure 10.1 BHP Petroleum Ltd, Piccadilly, London: Finishes vary from the black marble with white insets of the floor in reception to metal panels behind the desk (screening coat storage). PVC-faced steel partitioning provides large colourful surfaces which allow magnetic map-hanging by the many geologists who work here.
Design Consultants: Murray Symonds Associates

Figure 10.2 Telekurs, Broadgate, London: The 900m² offices of this Swiss communications company are made to feel generous by the flowing ceiling and floor planes, and transparent partitions. *Architects: ORMS*

In a new building these can be balanced to arrive at a rational result; in an existing shell, or where a tight budget or timetable demands the use of off-the-peg components, painful compromise may be necessary.

Floors

The floor deck of a modern office building usually has space for pipes and wires below it, or above it under a raised access floor system. Raised floors are common in Britain; in many other countries there is only a grid of wiring ducts built into the floor slab, providing more limited flexibility.

When raised floors were first introduced, underfloor cabling networks were purpose made and frequently changed, with the new cabling often just laid on top of the obsolete. The normal raised floor system 15cm high was soon unable to cope, so heights were increased to 20cm. Permanent structured cabling has allowed floor systems to reduce to a reasonable height again, except where dealer floor cabling or air supply has to be accommodated.

Floor systems are normally classed as 'shallow' if their cavity is less than 15cm overall, and 'deep' if it is greater. Shallow floors can be made of timber panels on timber or metal battens. Deep ones usually have a metal frame – with timber or metal infill panels – on adjustable metal legs.

The main selection criteria are:

– *Loading.* The system must be strong enough to take the required distributed and point loads without deflection or damage; and where it stands on legs these must be able to transfer point loads to the structural deck without buckling or penetration.
– *Access.* Access to the void is necessary for voice, data and power leads, and for maintenance and recabling. Leads may run through grommets in the floor, or be plugged into flush or tower socket outlets. Access to the cabling may be by flush access plates, or by removal of whole floor panels.
– *Permeability.* The system should provide vertical underfloor barriers to prevent the spread of sound or fire. However, if the void is to be used as an air plenum, the floor panels need to have openings to allow the necessary air flow.
– *Finish.* Finishes normally need to be modular, to allow easy access. Other factors are ease of maintenance and, in computer areas, freedom from the build up of static electricity.

Until recently the difficulty of installing underfloor wiring in older buildings has been a drawback. The handsome boarded floors of nineteenth century

MARCUS HILTON

Figure 10.3 de Beers Industrial Diamond Division, Ascot, Berkshire: In this research laboratory and offices a special dust extraction system allows close working between scientists and technicians. The glazed wall acts as a unifying feature in encouraging teamwork, and lets customers see what is going on.
Architects: ORMS

buildings wear well and look good, but need severe surgery to install cabling. The advent of cordless equipment is reducing the need for this, and giving such buildings a new lease of life.

Walls

As well as dividing spaces, internal walls may need to block vision, sound or fire. Visually they are one of the most important elements of an interior, so appearance is also a major factor in their design. Internal partitions can be fixed or demountable, but the difference is becoming increasingly blurred. It may well be quicker and cheaper to move a 'dry-wall' partition than to dismantle and re-erect a sophisticated panel system.

Fixed partitions

Heavy fixed partitions like brick- or block-work bear on the structural slab or another wall, whereas light ones of stud and plasterboard may stand on a raised floor. Heavy walls are normally plastered, and stud partitions may be plastered too. Alternatively, the latter may simply have filled joints. This is quicker and cheaper, and can be demolished and rebuilt with reasonable ease.

All these walls have an unbroken continuity of surface which looks good, can allow for curves and fancy profiles, and helps sound insulation. But wet plasterwork is messy and slow, both to build and to change. The dry-wall option is therefore being increasingly used.

Figure 10.4 Prudential Assurance, Holborn Bars, London: The refurbishment of 13 000m² of office space in this listed building also involved new construction. On the fifth floor five executive dining/meeting rooms and the corridor in the middle can become a single space, with the acoustic partitions stored in special recesses.
Architects: DEGW

For good sound insulation partitions should continue – in some form – to the structure both above and below. For some activities sound insulation is critical, with lawyers demanding complete privacy in all client areas, and music publishers perhaps needing acoustic isolation. Otherwise high-performance sound insulation may be required for a few meeting rooms only.

Demountable partition systems

Factory-made partitions can be quick to install, are relocatable and can provide adequate sound reduction levels. They may be glazed or solid, and incorporate sophistications such as acoustic double glazing with blinds in the cavity. However, they can be expensive and have a life of not much more than five years (depending on construction and wear). Their standard sizes may not be compatible with the planning grid of the office. Sound and fire insulation, demountability and floor, ceiling and module-to-module fixing generally vary with materials, detailing and unit price. With both sound and fire insulation it is essential to differentiate between the performance of a single panel (which can be high), and the wall as a whole – which may have significant leaks above, below and between panels.

Slow delivery can be a problem with off-the-peg partition systems, as can the possibility of the range being discontinued. These and other aspects can be checked using an appraisal and selection system similar to that described for furniture (Appendix E).

Mobile partitions

Boardrooms, conference rooms and auditoria may be divisible by partitions that take only moments to open or close; but if good they are expensive. They normally run between floor and ceiling tracks. It is relatively easy to bear the weight of a heavy system on the floor track, though it may need a removable capping for when the partition is open. Conversely, while a hung system allows the floor finish to run through unimpeded, the top track has to be robustly mounted. If the panels are constructed of acoustically effective material and there is some mechanism for sealing the joints once the partition is in place (pneumatic seals are sometimes used) then a reasonable acoustic performance can be achieved.

CHARACTERISTICS OF PARTITION SYSTEMS						
				Construction		Ease
Description	Construction	Sound insulation	Wear	Speed	Cost	of moving
Fixed						
Block or brick	Plastered/fair faced	Good	Good	Slow	Low	Bad
Stud and plaster	Plasterboard on timber or metal studs	Moderate	Good	Slowish	Low	Bad
Stud and sheet	Studs with timber or metal sheets	Adequate	Good	Moderate	Low	Moderate
Demountable						
Frame and panel	Timber, aluminium or steel, with solid or glazed infills	Very variable	Adequate	Fast	Medium	Fast
Panel and panel	As above	As above	As above	As above	As above	As above
Mobile						
Track and panel	Metal frame, timber panels	Adequate	Adequate	Fast	High	Fast

Doors

Some of the best looking doors are full height, which avoids the problem of what happens between the top of a 2m door and the ceiling. The tall door (even for a WC cubicle) is a cheap way of getting a sense of grandeur. Curiously, the oversized door can make a small room seem larger; this applies to width as well as height. Where wide doorways are needed for moving furniture, a normal door with a hinged vision strip alongside is an effective solution.

A door may be solid or framed, of timber, glass or metal. It may be a standard or a special, or come as part of a system. Viewing panels are obligatory on escape routes; it may also be company policy to allow a limited peep into every room. Toughened or laminated glass should be used to resist impact, with wired or other heat-resistant glass providing a fire rating where that is necessary.

Storage

Storage for working files and personal effects generally has a marked impact on the layout and appearance of the workspace. However, the effect of clean desk policies and shared workstations has led to grouped storage for teams and less fixed storage at the workstation itself.

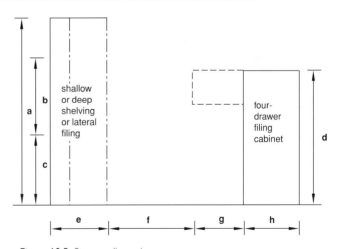

Figure 10.5 Storage dimensions.

Key		centimetres
a	maximum reach (for the average woman)	195
b	optimum shelving zone (for storage of heavy items)	75–80
c	low zone, easy reach	70–75
d	maximum height for seeing into a drawer	140
e	depth of shelving	30–60
f	aisle width (allowing for door opening)	90–120
g	clearance for filing drawer to open	45–75
h	filing cabinet	50–80

Note: lateral storage has twice the capacity of filing cabinets, so floor loadings need consideration.

CONSIDERATIONS
FOR STORAGE

What type of article?
How much?
How heavy?
How voluminous?
How specialized
(e.g. artwork)?
Where?
How accessible?
How often?
How safe?
How robust?
How mobile?

Beyond individual storage there is a need for local storage: office supplies and equipment, slide projectors and screens, outdoor clothing and even extra chairs (excess furniture can be stored further away, or even off site – some manufacturers provide a 'banking' service). Storage for cleaning and maintaining the building is also necessary, in convenient but unobtrusive positions.

Whether cupboards, cabinets or shelves, storage may be built into fixed walls, be part of a prefabricated partitioning system or be freestanding. Whichever it is, it is likely to form a visual 'wall'(indeed, integrated storage systems are often called 'fat walls').

Built-in storage is usually cheaper than freestanding, and can be made more robust and secure; but it is less flexible. It is normally part of the fit-out contract, whereas freestanding storage is chosen along with the furniture.

Design considerations include the loads that storage elements put on the floor (which may be a raised system), working space in front of them for opening doors and drawers, and – with freestanding units – stability against toppling.

Ceilings

Suspended ceilings are the conventional way of tidying up the underside of ugly structure and services, and of providing an acoustic absorber and a plane of artificial light. But if the underside of the floor deck can be designed in an orderly way and left exposed, floor to ceiling height can be increased (with the possibility of effective uplighting), and both capital and maintenance costs should be reduced.

While there are signs of this trend in new naturally ventilated buildings, in the majority of offices the suspended ceiling is still the norm. It may be constructed of timber joists and skimmed or taped plasterboard, but usually it is made up of a lightweight metal grid, hung from the structure, supporting ceiling panels and the service outlets (such as luminaires, air diffusers and sprinkler heads).

Grids are usually of aluminium or steel, with infill panels of any number of finishes and characteristics. Rectilinear panel systems are the most common, although in special areas linear strip or 'egg-crate' systems are sometimes used.

Figure 10.6 CDP, Soho, London: Curved walls, 'storewalls', and 'smart' columns containing services are used to sculpt the office landscape. *Architects: Harper Mackay*

NICHOLAS KANE

Flat panels may be square or rectangular, with the suspension grid either part of the design, or concealed. Service outlets are usually integrated in the ceiling plane. Unless luminaires have low brightness louvres the 'checkerboard' appearance can be unattractive. Acoustic absorption ranges from excellent to reasonable. Fire and moisture resistance, and robustness in handling are necessary; thermal performance may also be important.

Linear strips are usually metal, with the strips clipped to a system of counter-battens. They can give a directional elegance to a space, but it can be hard to integrate service outlets, and their acoustic performance may be less good than flat panels. Egg-crate systems, on the other hand, allow free movement of air into the ceiling void, with acoustic (and ventilation) benefits.

Plastered ceilings can take on more interesting shapes than modular ones, so are often used in important areas. They are good for sound and fire insulation, but acoustic absorption is low, and access to the ceiling void for service maintenance can be difficult. However, they are usually low in cost and need

little maintenance. Because they are reminiscent of home, they also soften an office environment.

Finishes

The finishes are what people see of the 'set', and they are also the bits that get dirty and worn. Function and appearance go hand in hand.

Floors

Floors must wear well, be safe and communicate the desired image. Materials include timber, marble, vinyl sheet – and even perforated steel – but in British offices by far the most common floor finish is carpet. In Europe, however, hard finishes are becoming more common, on the grounds that they are less likely than carpets to harbour pollutants.

Choice of flooring depends on performance, appearance and cost.

Performance
– *Safety.* Non-slip surface / evenness / freedom

DENNIS GILBERT

Figure 10.7 Sony Music Entertainment, Soho, London: Each floor of this office is dedicated to one of the group's record companies. Its logo on the wall, display areas, undulating ceiling and wood block floor changing to carpet, all emphasize the individual identity of the particular record label, while retaining a sense of corporate image.
Architects: Harper Mackay

Figure 10.8 Chemical Bank, City of London: Stainless steel, polished ceramic floor and walls faced with metallic laminate make a durable but dramatic servery for the staff restaurant.
Architects: Pringle Brandon

Figure 10.9 Prudential Assurance, Holborn Bars, London: With uplighters designed by the architects in association with the manufacturer, satisfactory lighting conditions were obtained despite relatively low ceilings. Much of this open plan office space uses furniture brought from elsewhere, which is moved around the space as needs dictate.
Architects: DEGW

from uneven wear / non-inflammable / non-toxic materials (including fixing adhesives).
 — *Resistance.* Abrasion / point loads / impact / wheeled traffic / chemicals and fats / sunlight / vermin.
 — *Convenience.* Resilience / comfort / traction.
 — Environmental. Sound absorbent / impact absorbent / heat resistant / non-static / hygienic / non-dusting.
 — *Installation.* Compatibility with subfloor / speed of installation.
 — *Maintenance.* Ease of cleaning / ease of repair/replacement / continuity of supply.
Appearance
 — *Colour.* Colour range / consistency of colour.
 — *Pattern.* Non-directional/directional/gridded / pattern range / man-made or natural.
 — *Surface.* Textured/smooth / matte/reflective.
Cost
 — Material cost / installation cost / maintenance cost (regular/periodic) / ease of partial repair/replacement (e.g. carpet tiles versus broadloom).

Finishes range from soft carpets to exceptionally hard ceramics. They come in tiles, strips (e.g. boards) or sheets; or can be jointless. Tiles are easy to replace or to make access through; wood strip floors denote quality; broadloom carpet (or sheet finishes) has a generous and relaxed scale; and monolithic finishes can be extremely hard wearing. When tiles are used in rigorous situations such as lavatories, kitchens or laboratories, the jointing needs to be as durable as the tiles.

Jointless finishes range from heavy-duty epoxy screed to seam-welded plastic sheeting. Both may be

taken up the wall to form an integral skirting. Monolithic terrazzo flooring is one of the most durable finishes (though using terrazzo tiles eliminates the long drying-out time).

Wood can make an attractive finish, whether parquet or strip. With proper maintenance it wears well, though it can suffer from indentation. Access through wooden flooring depends on its format and how it has been laid.

Natural stones, including marble, slate and granite, all look good and are hard wearing, but may need special treatment to protect against staining. They can also be noisy, and tiring on the feet.

Resilient floorings – whether in sheet or tile form – are normally PVC, rubber, linoleum or cork. They are all medium-hard materials which vary in durability and other characteristics. PVC is now the principal plastic used in flooring; but the thinness of the sheet requires a smooth subfloor. Linoleum, as a natural material, is increasingly popular.

Carpet (tiles or broadloom) comes in various grades, only the heavier duty ones being suitable for offices. Circulation areas should have the top grade. Costs relate as much to look as wear; a very hard-wearing carpet may be cheap but, being totally synthetic, look unattractive. Offices often use resin-bonded felt tiles, but tufted carpet looks better,

and woven carpet (such as Axminster) better still. A wool–synthetic mix (80% wool) is desirable, but expensive. For any carpet a good underlay (synthetic or natural) greatly improves performance and sound reduction.

People do not stop to wipe their feet when they come into an office building, so door matting should do this for them. Ideally there should be a primary barrier to take heavy dirt off shoes, in the form of gridded, brushing or scraping matting; and then a secondary barrier to absorb moisture. In choosing entrance matting, maintenance and cleaning is of special importance. Mats should be sunk flush with the surrounding floor finish.

Walls

Plastered walls are cheap to finish and maintain. A coat of paint every couple of years can keep even places of toughest wear looking fresh. Special paint finishes and fine wallpaper add quality, but they cost more and generally wear less well. Plastic-coated wall coverings are practical, but are often of limited appeal. Special plaster finishes add interest and are hard wearing but costly.

Walls may be faced with marble, stone, tiles or mosaic. All provide hard-wearing and effective finishes, at a cost. It is prudent to overorder so as to have a supply of matching replacement material for repairs.

Solid or veneered wood panelling can be fixed to masonry or stud walls, or may be integral in demountable systems. It can be treated with stains, sealer, oil or wax and, if well maintained, can improve with age. Laminated panels offer enormous choice in material, colour, texture and design, but need well-designed edge detailing for looks and durability.

In special areas unusual materials can be used to effect: stainless or stove-enamelled steel, powder-coated aluminium, glass in its many varieties, mirrors and glassfibre. Many of the most striking interiors have used glass structurally or decoratively in various ways. However, being fragile and potentially dangerous, it may need framing, toughening or laminating to be safe.

Ceilings

Beyond painted plaster, there is a wide choice of ceiling panels with different characteristics and cost. Few people like an obtrusive grid overhead, so choose panels with butt joints and a textured rather than strongly directional design. Ceiling panels often come self-finished, but may later be redecorated in place. If they are acoustically absorbent, their performance will diminish with each repainting.

Special finishes used on walls can be carried onto the ceiling if there is a suitable base, but may contrast strangely with grilles and sprinklers.

Ironmongery and service terminals

Ironmongery ranges from door handles to curtain tracks. 'Service terminals' we use to describe all the points where concealed pipes, ducts and wires meet the office interior. Because they are specified by different specialist consultants and suppliers it is hard to co-ordinate their appearance – and this shows. For example, there are several variants of 'polished chrome'. Different tradesmen can create inadvertent juxtapositions on what had been a carefully designed wall. Users can add overlooked items after the contract is finished.

To achieve a satisfactory result the essentials are to:

– ensure all items have been listed and considered;
– define co-ordinating dimensions and 'location zones';

IRONMONGERY AND SERVICE TERMINALS

door ironmongery
cupboard ironmongery
cloakroom fittings
curtain tracks, blind fittings
signage: warning signs, locational and directional
  signs, nameplates

luminaires
light switches and sensors
emergency lighting, exit signs

ventilation grilles, air diffusers
thermostats

power socket outlets, floorplates
IT socket outlets
information 'touch terminals'

lift indicators, call buttons

fire and smoke sensors
fire alarms, fire bells
fire hosereels, extinguishers

internal and external security systems: sensors,
  alarms, CCTV cameras

■ Acid etching or sandblasting glass panels are decorative ways of providing a feeling of privacy and enclosure. Obscured areas can occur on the line of sight (both seated and standing), with clear glass above and below.

Figure 10.10 Talk Radio, Soho, London: Main circulation route delineated by a splayed wall in polished plaster. The wood block floor is used throughout. Low-voltage spotlights accentuate the deep blue of the wall, with compact fluorescent downlighters used elsewhere.
Architects: Harper Mackay

– select a limited range of finishes, and check samples for consistency with each other.

In many instances certain items may already be in place, such as window and door ironmongery, air diffusers, luminaires, lift indicators and fire protection systems. These have – somehow – to be integrated into the overall design. The list below covers the groups of ironmongery and allied items which may need to be considered. It excludes the most basic items, like hinges and latches.

Set dressing

Windows

Windows are the nostrils and eyes of a building, bringing in fresh air, sunshine and views of the world outside. However they can also cause draughts, glare and lack of privacy, and become dark reflective pools at night. Their function and attractiveness can be changed quite radically through careful treatment –

TIMOTHY SOAR

Figure 10.11 Wickens Tutt Southgate, Bayswater, London: The curve of the reception desk pulls the visitor into the building and towards the blue glass borrowed lights, which look through to the accounts office behind. Opposite is an angled wall with back-lit apertures neatly displaying the wares of this design and corporate identity consultancy.
Architects: Apicella Associates

daylight can be controlled and their appearance softened with blinds, sheers or curtains.

If the architect has not designed solar control into the skin of the building, it is up to the interior designer to do what he can on the inside. Blinds are the most common internal means of solar and privacy control in an office, though curtains and sheers – lightweight translucent curtains – can play their part.

Curtains (or drapes) are normally only found in top-executive offices and boardrooms, if at all, as they are expensive and to many seem too domestic

for the workplace. Sheers on the other hand are cheaper and look good by day as well as at night.

Fabrics for blinds, sheers and curtains (and their backings) must comply with fire regulations, principally in retarding the spread of flame. Regulations vary not just between countries, but even between adjacent fire authorities. Although most contract fabrics are pretreated to comply with the regulations, fabrics from other ranges can be treated to meet the criteria. However, many treated fabrics can then only be dry cleaned (and even this can affect the treatment).

Figure 10.12 Ernst & Young, Rolls House, City of London: Described as 'a symphony of white', this reception area clearly displays in its details a caring ethos. PCs are concealed behind the curved stainless steel panels of the reception desk, spotlights are precisely positioned, and flowers are elegantly arranged.
Architects: Austin-Smith Lord

■ Scottish Nuclear at Livingston in Scotland has special plant pots that are claimed to clean the air as a fan pulls it through the plant roots.

■ In the headquarters of an international bank, every meeting room has an elegant reproduction sideboard. Precisely centred under each one is a grey enamelled waste bin, with a white plastic bin liner draped in it.

Many blinds, sheers and curtains are opened and closed manually; but motorized controls are used for large installations, or where solar control is under the building management system.

Existing windows may be protected against the effects of bomb blast by covering the glass with a transparent adhesive film, which holds the broken glass together; or by using voluminous, weighted sheers, which catch the glass shards before they can do damage.

Accessories

Waste-paper baskets, desk tidies and filing trays are the loose items that can mar an otherwise elegant setting. They may be useful or decorative, and often vary with organizational culture. Each activity needs them, from the flower vase in reception to the coffee-maker in the meeting room. Catering accessories in particular play a significant part in conveying the right message to staff and visitors. Co-ordinated restaurant and servery equipment and tableware – including china, glass, cutlery and linen – reinforce the overall design concept. When choosing accessories key considerations are function, aesthetics, quality, durability, ease of storage and standardization.

Landscaping

Landscaping around a building, and within it, is the icing without which no respectable cake exists. But not just icing: landscaping adds living things to inert steel and glass. As one sociologist put it: 'Outside is best, so if we can't be there we must look out at trees and plants, and bring as much of it as we can into the building.'

Plants

Plants can decorate, humanize and soften a space, and divide one area from another. They can also act as humidifiers; but their acoustic effect is debatable. An atrium can easily become a 'business winter garden', with interesting and even rare plants flourishing there, and providing visual refreshment for those looking in, those working there and those just passing by.

Planting is best set up and maintained by specialists. Good natural light is needed – or special lighting to a level of between 600 and 700 lux, with temperature at 21°C and humidity at 45–50% RH. Plants dislike draughts, radiant heat or hot ducted air. An automatic system ensures that watering is done regularly, and in the right amount. Carefully chosen containers, like other accessories, can enhance the effect.

Flowers

A single daffodil in a vase on the desk, a fine azalea or a superb arrangement of flowers from a manager's garden, clearly send messages of good will, personal attention and style. Flowers bring colour to the office, and while the life of cut flowers is short, the pot plant, well maintained, can last for months. Properly lit and ventilated locations for plants and flowers should be designed into the scheme to avoid the gauche effect of vases and plants positioned as obvious afterthoughts.

Artworks

Few living rooms have bare walls: likewise – increasingly – the workplace. The executive in her private office has long chosen pictures for the wall, but now artworks for the whole office are part of any refurbishment budget. Some organizations have a positive buying policy, and have established fine collections.

'Per cent for Art' – the policy of devoting one per cent of the project budget to artworks – is not a bad yardstick. Art of course includes sculptures in the courtyard outside, fountains and rugs in reception, and stained glass panels looking onto the street; as well as paintings, drawings and prints hung on walls throughout the building.

Artworks mean thinking ahead, so that they are an integral part of the design. The interior designer needs to choose positions for sculpture, ceramics or paintings, and to indicate their size and importance – ideally in liaison with the artists. The locations need proper lighting to enhance the object without dazzling the viewer and, if the work is valuable or fragile, appropriate security measures.

Often a committee is formed to choose artworks. Sometimes its members find the works themselves, but more often a specialist is employed. The committee agrees the type and style of works with the consultant, with an overall number and cost. The consultant then presents her proposals by colour slides, or with the works themselves, to simplify the committee's choice.

Artworks can be hired or even borrowed. Areas like reception and the restaurant can provide temporary exhibition space; but here again lighting and security need to be considered from the start. Although this takes continuing organization, it is a low-cost way of having art around, and of building links with the community.

Signage

Signs save lives when fires break out, and make a strange building legible to the first time visitor. A sign may be obligatory and written in letters 15cm high; or it may be wordless, like the comfortable chair in reception which says 'welcome'. Signboards placed carefully can make it easier to get around. In a small organization, or one with little mobile working this may be unimportant; but in a large building, with transient staff, clarity is essential (though signs need not be institutional).

Signage for the handicapped is improving all the time: changes in flooring, for instance, can indicate the positions of lavatories, and signs can be incised for finger reading. In tomorrow's office it will go further: touch screens will talk to those with sight and hearing limitations; the exit sign will bleep when the fire alarm goes off and, for the deaf, lights will flash.

Signage includes:

- *General.* Exit, fire escapes, toilets.
- *Reception.* Company logo, staff information, visitor information.
- *Circulation.* Maps, directions, arrows, lift displays.
- *Offices.* Names, numbers, groups, departments.
- *Notice boards.* Events, management notices.
- *Restaurant.* Menus, events.

Signage should be part of the main contract and not an afterthought. Properly considered it provides valuable clarity and unity to the interior. Aspects to consider include positions (and sight lines), sizes, typefaces, legibility, materials and durability.

Light fittings

The principles of office lighting are covered in the next chapter, but light fittings (or luminaires) – a very particular kind of service terminal – are a major element of any work setting, and need considering with it. Luminaires include:

- ceiling fittings
- architectural light fittings
- wall fittings
- freestanding lights
- task lighting.

Ceiling fittings

Fluorescent downlighters have been the normal way of lighting commercial spaces for decades. Initially hanging from the underside of the structural slab, they are now an integral part of most suspended ceilings. Improvements in lamp and luminaire design make them economic to install and energy efficient – and unobtrusive. But their light remains uniform, bland and can cause glare on VDTs.

With higher ceilings, fluorescent or metal halide uplighters may be installed (though an even, matte and reflective ceiling is needed). This indirect light can be more sympathetic than downlighting, and the colour of the ceiling can be used to modify the colour appearance of the light. Its evenness and slightly lower intensity make it good for use with VDTs, though the bright ceiling can distract the eye, and the

Figure 10.13 Cable and Wireless, Mercury House, London: A large 'G' carved into the travertine walling indicates the floor level.
Architects: Austin-Smith Lord

Figure 10.14 Lloyds Bank, Canons Marsh, Bristol: At the headquarters for Lloyds Bank Retail Banking, exposed concrete ceilings act as reflectors for uplighting, as well as maximizing the thermal capacity of the structure. Energy is further conserved by good daylighting and natural ventilation, and by using dock water for cooling.
Architects: Arup Associates

PETER COOK

Figure 10.15 Mercury Communications, Red Lion Square, London: Sofas, flowers, rugs, and artworks on the wall and hung from above all decorate this reception area. *Architects: Austin-Smith Lord*

light on the work surface can be bland. For both these reasons, and where high working light levels are needed, it may have to be augmented by task lighting.

Ceiling spotlights add sparkle and accent. However, not only do they add heat, and glare if wrongly positioned, but they are energy inefficient. Recessed luminaires with compact fluorescent or metal halide lamps can provide interest more economically. Fibre-optic lighting of pictures can be effective, although its energy efficiency is extremely low.

Recessed wall washers can emphasize the form of a space, and turn the wall into a source of reflected light. Except in areas such as reception or the restaurant where drama may be desirable, walls need to be light in tone and probably neutral in colour. Curiously, wall washed dark wood panelling can appear gloomier than under ordinary lighting.

Architectural lighting

'Architectural lighting' describes light sources that are built into the fabric or fittings of the interior. It is

inherently inflexible, but can be used to create particular moods or special effects. It is found, for instance, as concealed cornice lighting in high-ceilinged spaces or uplighting on top of storage walls. Architectural lighting can achieve an atmosphere while using simple fluorescent lighting (with its low running costs). Fluorescent lighting is especially useful in places where heat would be hazardous, such as near curtains.

Wall fittings

Wall-mounted luminaires are also inflexible, so can only sensibly be used where the wall is permanent, like cores. Uplighters can provide interesting illumination, and may be combined fittings with an element of down light. Uplighters can also be mounted on the columns in the general workspace to bring a bit of variety to large areas.

Fittings range from extremely utilitarian bulkhead fittings on escape stairs to highly decorative gilded sconces in the chairman's office. Wall fittings are sometimes used to illuminate artworks, but do not add a great deal to either the picture or the space as a whole.

Freestanding lights

Standard lights add interest, sparkle and extra light in specific areas such as executive offices, meeting rooms, restaurants or coffee bars. They are fairly rare in general office spaces (especially as their wires need managing). They are often used decoratively – both as objects in a space, and as light sources. In offices they are mostly uplighters, unlike standard lights in a home.

Task lights

Task lights provide light where it is needed, and the user has total control. However they may take up valuable desk-top space, unless they are fixed above – either as an adjustable fitting, or beneath high-level storage.

They enhance lighting in a number of ways: the colour appearance of the light may be slightly warmer than the ambient (fluorescent) light; the light comes

from a lower, and point, source, so can create modulating highlights and shadows; and the light may be turned on and off more frequently, thus giving change in the course of the day.

Dilemmas

■ How much flexibility is really needed; and can this best be achieved with demountable settings, with cheap rebuildable ones, or simply by moving people around?
■ How can modular ceilings be designed to minimize their gridded appearance without losing accessibility?
■ What is the right choice between the durability and hygiene of hard flooring and the comfort and acoustic qualities of carpeting?
■ Should the 'dark pool' of nighttime windows be counteracted by blinds and curtains?
■ How can signage be clear without being too institutional?

Figure 10.16 Talk Radio, Soho, London: The reception area, with its rug by Helen Yardley, can be opened up into the managing director's office and boardroom by means of folding doors, providing a big space for parties or presentations. The mixture of architectural cornice lighting and recessed spotlights creates a welcoming atmosphere. The red curved wall on the right screens and marks the entrance, while the blue wall which continues down the corridor separates off the studio space.
Architects: Harper Mackay

Ernst & Young
Chicago

Management's goal was to consolidate three offices without increasing space costs, as well as to present a unified and positive image of the firm to our clients and to the business community.

Mike Thompson – Ernst & Young, Chicago

Ernst & Whinney's merger with Arthur Young in 1989 created one of the most powerful firms of accountants in the world. In 1992, 1350 of its employees moved from three buildings in Chicago to the Sears Tower. Seven floors, each of 4600m², now provide accommodation for 2000 employees, a quarter of whom are 'hotelers' (with a desk ratio of 5:1).

The hoteling concept was developed with psychosocial consultant Michael Brill of BOSTI. In carrying out 'bed checks' he found that 40% of the employees were spending 60% of their time out of the office, and were thus candidates for shared workspace of some sort. Focus groups then developed goals for the hoteling concept.

All seven floors have identical floor plans. Cellular offices run all around the perimeter at a ratio of 2:1 to open workstations.

Conference rooms are in the corners (occupation of prime corner offices being a contentious issue) and there is a service cluster on the south side, a large conference room on the north side and a mixture of offices and cubicles in the middle. Offices are 18m², 9m² and 6m² for partners, managers and staff respectively, with extensive storage in the corridors. The service cluster contains paper processing equipment, mailing facilities and office supplies, and 'concierges', who are responsible for bookings and other administrative support services.

Technology includes a computer-aided facilities management (CAFM) system to deal with bookings. Employee profiles are built into its database, so an employee giving his name ensures that not only is a name plate and personal telephone number assigned to his space, but that files are moved from his personal locker to the desk. To find out who is where, an electronic locator system is accessible from the lobby and from each workstation.

All workstations are networked for both Macintosh and MS-DOS, and jacks are provided for the hotelers' notebook computers. Wiring is designed to support all protocols for a long time ahead, and includes a fibre-optic backbone and unshielded twisted-pair copper wiring (delivering 100 megabits per second to every terminal).

The move to the new premises was carried out during the season of slow business. The equipment was installed by 50 auditors themselves – who had a great time, coming to work in jeans and gaining a sense of ownership.

Interior Designers: Sverdrup Interiors
Contractor: La Salle Construction Inc.
Project completed: 1992

SUCCESS FACTORS FOR HOTELING

The focus groups identified these factors:

Identical looking hoteling and non-hoteling space
High-quality administrative support services;
Convenient locator system
Reservation system requiring as few details as possible
Connectivity to the computer network regardless of space assignment or computer type
Remote access to the computer network
Personal storage space
Easy movement of belongings to assigned space
Accommodation for 'after hours' and 'quick drop-in' visits

Figure 10.17 Name plaques are colour coded to show the 'mega-module' location on each floor and the lift corridor (in red). The location is also given in braille.

Figure 10.18 Each 'hoteler' has a locker for files, documents and personal belongings. These have a pull-out desk surface so that they can function as temporary workstations.

Figure 10.19 These accountants occupy seven floors of the tower, and operate a 'hoteling' system. To assist this, lift lobbies have directory monitors providing employee locations, and a map showing the position of offices, conference rooms and other facilities.

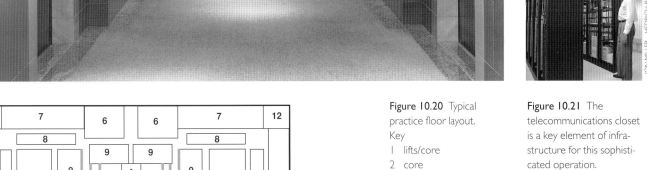

Figure 10.21 The telecommunications closet is a key element of infrastructure for this sophisticated operation.

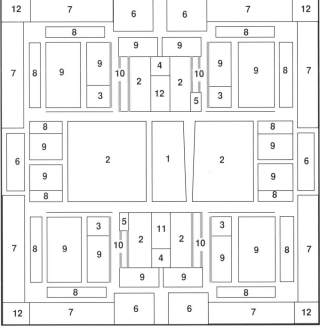

Figure 10.20 Typical practice floor layout.

Key
1 lifts/core
2 core
3 copy/print
4 telecommunications
5 coffee
6 staff workstations
7 partners' offices
8 admin. support clusters
9 managers' offices
10 hoteling lockers
11 service centre
12 meeting room

Chapter 11
Building services

- **Lighting**
  Aspects of light
  Daylight
  Artificial light
- **Heating, ventilating and air-conditioning**
  Ventilation
  Heating and cooling
- **Acoustics**
  The nature of sound
  Acoustic control
- **Power distribution**
- **Plumbing**
- **Lifts and escalators**
- **Fire and security**
  Fire
  Security
- **Information technology**
  Cabling
  Business systems
  Building management systems
  Facilities management systems
- **Dilemmas**

Today's educated and articulate worker demands an effective and comfortable workplace. Earlier we dealt with the ergonomics of the work setting: this chapter addresses the mechanical and electrical systems which service that setting, and the information technology that enables businesses to operate.

The engineering services in a building consume some 40% of its construction budget. Telecommunications and information technology (computer networks and building management systems) can cost the same again or more, depending on demands.

The principal elements of the serviced environment are:

- lighting (natural and artificial)
- heating and cooling, ventilating, air-conditioning (HVAC)
- acoustics
- power distribution
- plumbing and sanitary services
- lifts and escalators
- fire and security systems
- telecommunications (data, images and voice)
- information technology (systems for business operations, building management and facilities management).

Often these are integrated, interactive and conflicting: windows producing draughts and glare as well as light and ventilation; artificial lighting giving off heat as well as illumination.

Engineering services not only interact with each other, but also with the fabric of the building, the people and equipment inside it, and what is going on outside. Much of their purpose is to produce stability out of this complexity – reliably and humanely. To do this they need to create conditions that:

- protect people from harmful effects
- enable them to operate well
- make them feel physically and psychologically comfortable.

Workers like control of their own destiny: whether it be to turn on the light, turn down the heat, open a window or telephone an efficient and obliging facilities department. Light switches and heating controls help, but what does control mean where one person's fresh air is another person's draught, or where those near the window want it closed and those away from it are much too hot?

Figure 11.1 Western Morning News, Plymouth: This 'galleon' is the flagship of the largest newspaper publisher in southwest England, and contains administrative, editorial and production functions. The main entrance is a bridge or 'gangplank', with views into the building as the visitor crosses. *Architects: Nicholas Grimshaw and Partners*

In most fit-outs the basic environmental and service elements are already fixed. The building's carcase incorporates windows, lifts and toilets; at least the main framework of heating, air-conditioning and power distribution is established; and the building's structure itself defines how easily new elements or changes can be accommodated. The principles of these environmental systems should be respected and supported (unless they are being replaced). For instance, where natural ventilation is fundamental to the building's concept, the position of partitions must relate to the planned air flows. Likewise, where daylight is a primary light source, surface finishes of the right reflectance are needed.

The same issues affect the serviced environment as the rest of office design. The principal ones are management's drive for efficiency, the worker's desire for autonomy, and socio-economic pressures towards a 'greener' workplace. Building services have to be cost-effective, under personal control and ecologically acceptable.

Lighting

Light influences perception, mood and behaviour; so lighting, whether natural or artificial, is a crucial element in the design of the workplace.

People like natural light, and the nineteenth century artist's studio with its northlight window provides an excellent model of what good daylighting can achieve. However, all around the world offices are built with deep plans, and often little variation between facades of different orientations. Since daylight is fickle and not always there, it is given secondary status. Artificial lighting is on all day, mainly from ceiling-mounted fluorescents – cheap to install and to maintain, and energy efficient – but often unflattering to both the interior and the occupants.

Now much is changing. European Union regulations include stringent measures on VDT screens and glare. Energy efficiency means making good use of daylight. Ways of controlling daylight entering the building are improving all the time. People too are changing, demanding daylight, sunlight and views out through windows not far distant from their desks.

Aspects of light

In the workplace there are two lighting tasks: the general lighting of the space (ambient light); and any additional lighting that may be needed at the point of work in order to do it properly (task light).

Apart from these functional tasks, there has to be the right light to meet basic human needs:

– contact with the world outside (is it raining or shining, noon or dusk?)
– orientation to the space inside
– ability to see hazards
– enjoyment of attractive surroundings
– awareness of the companionship of colleagues
– feeling stimulated.

All this means enough light, and of the right quality. It needs to be suitable for the task, reliable and controllable. At the same time it should offer some variety, and be 'easy on the eye'. And this at a modest cost in both money and energy consumption.

Characteristics of light

The properties of direct light include:

– *Illuminance*. How much is coming from the source.
– *Direction*. Whether it is diffuse, or gives shape and shadow to objects.
– *Colour appearance*. Whether it appears 'warm' (like direct sunlight) or 'cool' (as under a deep blue sky).
– *Colour rendition*. Whether it makes colours appear the same as in daylight.

As it reflects back to the viewer further characteristics emerge:

– *Brightness (luminance)*. The amount of reflected light reaching the eye.
– *Contrast*. The difference in brightness between adjacent objects. If there is too much it creates glare, making the work difficult to see (a brightly lit polished mahogany boardroom table will make white paperwork on it dazzling).
– *Veiling reflections*. Such as bright windows reflected in a VDT, making the screen hard to read.

Illuminance

The amount of light needed depends on the activity: seeing well enough to move around a building needs much less light than reading or doing intricate tasks. The eyesight of the viewer is another factor: older people need more light than the young.

Regulations lay down the amount of illumination that must be provided, but they do not say that lights must be switched on. The result may be overprovision yet a substandard reality, with neighbours arguing as to the merits of having the light on or off. To overcome this waste there is a trend towards lower ambient lighting levels, with locally switched task lighting.

Definition
Unilateral light, such as direct sunlight or a sharp spotlight gives clarity and life to what it illuminates, but can throw harsh and obscuring shadows unless moderated by a gentler light from another direction. Generally, for office work, diffused light is preferable.

Colour appearance
This affects what things look like. A woman's face changes dramatically between being viewed in warm candlelight or the cool midday sun. Light's spectral composition depends on the 'colour temperature' of its source. The skilled manipulation of this, through the use of different light sources, can make a space appear friendly or formal, exciting or intimidating.

Colour rendition
Seeing colours precisely as they are is usually not critical in an office, except where colour processes are involved. Natural light provides the most balanced spectrum, and thus where good colour rendering is needed artificial light tends to ape natural light, or be combined with it. In areas such as restaurants special

COLOUR TEMPERATURE	
The lower the temperature, the warmer the light appears.	
	Kelvin (K)
Candle	2000
General light source (GLS) incandescent lamp (150W)	2700
Tungsten halogen incandescent lamp	3000
'Warm' fluorescent lamp	2500–3000
Metal halide lamp	3000–5000
'Cool' fluorescent lamp	4000–5000
Late afternoon sunshine	4000
Summer midday sunlight	5500
Overcast sky	6500–7500
North light/blue sky	8000–8500

lighting may be used to enhance the colours of food and make it look appetizing.

Where artificial light is being used with natural, it generally looks best when the colour temperatures of both are about the same. However, in the evening, when artificial light comes on as daylight fades, a warmer light may be desirable.

Daylight

Because windows are an integral part of the building shell, the amount, quality and nature of a building's daylighting is largely fixed before fitting-out begins. However, with daylight having a major impact on the building interior, its seasonal penetration into an office needs appraisal: positively – which areas have reasonable natural light; and negatively – where glare is likely.

Daylight penetration is affected not just by the amount of glazing, but by the head height of the window (and to an extent by the profile of the window surround, and the reflectivity of adjacent surfaces). Daylight is generally considered to penetrate 5m into a building, but taking a 45° angle from the window head to the working plane provides a more useful measure.

The positioning of partitions and furniture is critical to the way in which daylight is drawn into an interior. Keeping partitions, screens and tall furniture perpendicular to the window wall and using pale reflective colours on the floor, walls and ceiling (in that order of importance) all help.

A well-designed building will have integral sun control measures where the orientation demands

■ Glare from low sun, as in winter or at sunset, may be more difficult to cope with than full summer sunlight high up in the sky. Low latitudes, like Northern Europe or New Zealand, have more problems with this than the tropics.

Amount of light for a detailed task, related to age	
Age	*Quantity of light*
20	L
40	2 × L
60	4 × L

RULES OF THUMB: LIGHTING LEVELS	
	Lux
Bright sunshine	100 000
Bright cloudy sky	20 000
Dull overcast sky	5 000
(2% daylight factor of above	100)
Studios and drawing offices	Up to 750
General office space	400–500
Reception area, kitchenettes, etc.	300
Corridors, toilets, changing rooms	100–200
Store rooms	100–150

Figure 11.2 Sunlight, day-light and air in the natural-ly ventilated building.

Key

A sunlight deflected by louvres, or

B alternatively sunlight is deflected by 'light shelves' as part of the window

C and bounces up onto the ceiling and into the room

D sunlight may also be reduced by 'light shelves'

E and by special glazing

F the window head limits how far light pene-trates into the room

G fresh air comes in at low level

H hot air goes out at high level

J the structure will cool the air

K the floor void may have room for auxillary ventilation

L blinds reduce light and glare (and may provide privacy)

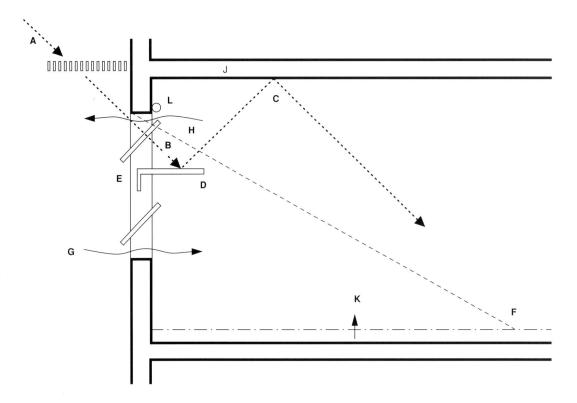

them. These may be part of the building fabric – lou-vres, grilles and overhangs, or part of the building skin – shutters or special glass. If such screening devices do not exist, it may be possible to install internal blinds as a part of the fit-out. Automatically con-trolled systems, while being more precise, have more parts to go wrong. Local (manual) adjustability is user friendly, but may cause neighbours to fall out, and looks messy. Shutters and blinds may restrict air flow within naturally ventilated buildings.

Artificial light

The quality and economy of artificial light sources is improving all the time – with lamps (bulbs) and lumi-naires (light fittings and fixtures) having a wide variety of characteristics.

Lamps

Lamps commonly used in offices include the following.

– *Fluorescent.* Linear/circular/compact; with or with-out integral starters and control gear. With high-frequency ballast units they can be dimmed and are without visible flicker. Effect tends to be bland, but concealed with light bouncing off wall or ceil-ing, they can form a most effective light source.

METHODS FOR CONTROLLING DAYLIGHT		
Many of these are incorporated in the building shell.		
Building fabric:	Overhangs/fins	
	Louvres	Fixed/movable
Building skin:	Shutters	Roller/casement
	Glass	Solar/prismatic/smart*
	Plants	Vines/trees
Internal:	Blinds	Venetian (horizontal or vertical)/roller/sunscreen
*Changes in response to an electric charge, or automatically to light.		

– *High-intensity discharge (HID)*. Metal halide HID gives very good colour rendering, and some variants of high-pressure sodium lamps (SON) give reasonable rendering; others are unsatisfactory for office use. Lamps tend to be slow to strike and warm up, and are therefore often coupled with other lamp types in one luminaire.

– *Incandescent*. Ordinary tungsten GLS bulbs/PAR (parabolic aluminized reflector)/tungsten halogen/low-voltage lighting (tungsten and tungsten halogen). Because of their high-energy consumption and low lamp life these now tend to be used only in special situations.

Fibre-optic cable, cold cathode ('neon') and other low or high-pressure lamps are likewise only used rarely in offices.

Luminaires

Luminaires (light fittings) may be built in, surface mounted, hung from the ceiling or freestanding, and illuminate downwards, upwards or specific tasks. They may spotlight objects, and be used together in many ways to create decoration, magic or a precise mood.

– *Downlighters*. The simplest, most efficient method of lighting a space, downlighters fit easily into a ceiling grid. There is an infinite range, varying from flush louvred fixtures to neat recessed lamp holders.

– *Uplighters*. The ceiling lit by reflected light is the nearest thing to a natural overcast sky – but similarly unstimulating. As a result, luminaires are sometimes hybrids, with an element of direct downlight as well. Uplighting is often integrated in the building fabric, with fittings positioned above cornices and on top of high-level cupboards. Freestanding uplighters are useful for boosting local lighting levels, and for providing accent light. In all cases the fittings have to be far enough below the ceiling to achieve a broad and even spread of light: hence uplighting needs relatively high ceilings.

– *Task lights*. Task lighting may consist of downlighters fixed to the underside of high-level cupboards, or adjustable fittings either fixed to the workstation or freestanding – space hungrily – on the desk top. They may be directional or provide all round lighting.

– *Spotlights*. Spotlights may be recessed, surface mounted or hung from ceiling or track. They can be used to provide general sparkle or focused illumination.

CHARACTERISTIC — LAMP

CHARACTERISTIC	tungsten	halogen	low-voltage	fluorescent	H.I.D.
colour rendering	good	good	good	poor	good
versatility	good	good	good	moderate	moderate
directional control	good	good	good	poor	poor
dimming/switching	good	good	poor	moderate	poor
efficiency	poor	moderate	poor	good	moderate
cool running	poor	poor	poor	good	moderate
lamp life	poor	moderate	poor	good	good
compact	moderate	moderate	good	moderate	good
no control gear	good	good	—	—	—
ease of relamping	good	moderate	moderate	good	good
capital cost	good	moderate	poor	good	moderate
running cost	poor	poor	moderate	good	moderate

KEY: ■ good   ◪ moderate   ☐ poor

Figure 11.3 Characteristics of different lamp types.

CHARACTERISTIC — LUMINAIRE

CHARACTERISTIC	downlighter	uplighter	task light	spot light
simple	good	good	poor	moderate
energy efficiency	good	good	poor	poor
built in	good	good	moderate	moderate
range	good	good	good	good
adaptable	good	good	moderate	moderate
fits ceiling grid	good	—	—	moderate
directional control	poor	moderate	good	good
supplementary source	poor	poor	good	good
range of effects	poor	moderate	moderate	good
dramatic	poor	moderate	good	good
glare free	poor	moderate	moderate	poor
no 'hot spots'	good	poor	moderate	poor
soft light	poor	good	moderate	poor
cost	good	good	poor	poor
ease of relamping	moderate	moderate	good	moderate

KEY: ■ good   ◪ moderate   ☐ poor

Figure 11.4 Characteristics of light sources.

Other systems

Track systems are used to support spotlights and accent lights, and may be decorative in themselves. Where there are only limited fixings, linear systems can be hung from the structure. These tubular systems have built-in fluorescent luminaires, and can support additional spot lights and compact fluorescents. Fibre-optic lighting is rarely used in offices as its specific characteristics can usually be provided more cheaply by other means.

Figure 11.5 Combination of lamps and luminaires.

LUMINAIRE / LAMP

LUMINAIRE	tungsten	halogen	low-voltage	fluorescent	H.I.D.
downlighter	good	good	good	good	poor
uplighter	good	good	poor	good	good
task light	good	good	moderate	good	
spotlight	good	moderate	good		poor

SUITABILITY

good — moderate — poor

Decorative lighting

Decorative lighting may be provided by a combination of sources to add impact, glamour or dramatic effect to an interior. This can be achieved by using fixtures which themselves have a strong design element, or by arranging standard fixtures in a decorative manner.

Special lighting

Particular locations call for special lighting: audio-visual suites, serveries, art displays. In such installations technical criteria dominate.

Emergency lighting

Emergency lighting illuminates escape routes and signs; standby lighting provides light for critical business activities in the event of power failure. Emergency lighting incorporated within the normal luminaires is visually preferable to two sets of fittings. It needs its own separate source of power, but if this is provided by integral batteries the cost of supplementary wiring is eliminated. Statutory regulations not only control the amount and location of emergency lighting, but also its maintenance.

Lighting controls

Task lights are controlled by the user; but ambient lighting is generally controlled centrally, with local switching – either manual or by movement sensors. Central control normally relates to the time of day and possibly external lighting conditions (with sensors on the roof), and varies with company needs. A normal pattern might be:

06.00–09.00h	50% lighting in circulation and open plan areas
09.00–19.00h	full lighting in circulation and open plan areas/cellular spaces locally switched
19.00–20.00h	50% lighting in circulation and open areas/default off in cellular offices without movement
20.00–06.00h	50% main circulation lighting only

When daylight reaches a certain level, central controls may switch off banks of lights near windows and half the lighting in adjacent areas.

Maintenance

Lighting regulations now cover maintenance as well as design and installation. Lighting systems should therefore be designed to make maintenance easy. Lamps should be replaced at regular intervals, as efficiency and colour appearance deteriorate. A limited variety of lamps simplifies relamping and storage. It should be easy to clean luminaires without disrupting the workers below. Maintaining the designer's lamping schedule ensures that the lighting concept is adhered to; this prevents the look of the place from being totally altered – for example, by substituting cool fluorescents for warm ones.

Heating, ventilating and air-conditioning

Air enables us to breathe; but it is also helps keep our bodies at the right temperature. Heating, cooling, ventilating and air-conditioning (HVAC) systems are responsible for satisfying these demands. Successful HVAC systems provide comfort, control and economy.

Comfort

There must be enough air, and it needs to be fresh and clean. There should be no draughts. The blend of

■ Working intensely, he is thinking hard and moving not at all. Suddenly the lights in the office go out. That infrared-eyed devil sensor is at work – and has turned the lights off as there is no movement.

temperature and humidity should create the right conditions for the skin. People should be able to dress comfortably and conventionally: neither the greatcoat nor the bikini is a realistic solution.

Freshness may require blocking or removing pollutants from the air. These pollutants include solids (dust, micro-organisms, pollens), vapours (gases, fumes – which may also contain solids) and fluxes (microwaves, ionization, ultraviolet/infrared rays).

Control

Workers need to be physically comfortable in order to perform effectively; they also need to be psychologically at ease – to feel in personal control of their environment.

HVAC is largely controlled centrally; but increasing sophistication can allow a degree of personal control locally (in the office or at the workstation) and can cater for variation (such as opening a window). But it is unwise to expect the ordinary worker to understand the overall HVAC concept in detail and react accordingly. At best his intuition will tell him what to do in his own part of the building.

Economy

HVAC is intimately bound up with energy conservation, both in terms of operating costs, and the social issue. Its design also has a major impact on the capital cost of buildings.

The economic considerations mean that the major HVAC decisions are taken when a new building is first conceived – possibly long before its fitting-out is contemplated. Only in a major refurbishment is it likely that HVAC strategy will form part of the design. For most fit-outs it is a case of 'going with the flow' – the air flow.

In HVAC terms, a fit-out is limited realistically to these aims:

- to integrate successfully with the HVAC strategy for the building;
- to help achieve the goals of that strategy;
- to produce visually and acoustically unobtrusive results.

Ventilation

People like to open windows. Fresh air is nicer, and it's cheap. But satisfying this desire is not always possible. The sealed building may already be there – and for good reasons: dust, traffic fumes and noise, or wind

MODES OF VENTILATION	
Natural	External wall openings (conventional windows)
	External wall openings (ventilation flaps or grilles)
	High-level venting ('stack effect')
Mechanical	Extract fans (special areas only)
	Total extract system
	Plenum ventilation system (air input)
	Displacement
Air-conditioning	Low velocity
	Low velocity (with terminal reheat)
	High velocity (with terminal reheat)
	High velocity (dual duct)
	High velocity (variable air volume – VAV)
	Fan coil units
	Induction units
	Window-mounted package units

(natural ventilation is usually impractical above the fourth floor).

Narrow buildings in countries with temperate climates and cool air, such as Britain, may well be able to operate without air-conditioning; but in places like Chicago (where temperatures range from –30°C in winter to +40°C in summer) air-condtioning is essential. With deep buildings, atria not only bring light into the centre, but can usefully act as air stacks with warm air rising naturally out into the sky (or return air being pulled upward into air handling plant at roof level).

With close examination of the building's characteristics and the office's needs, department by department, it is possible to devise an economical 'mixed mode' system, using full air-conditioning only where and when it is absolutely necessary.

When fitting out the interior the design issues are: not impeding air flows, minimizing air noise, providing reasonable maintenance access and catering for special areas.

Air flows

Air flows are a fundamental part of any natural ventilation strategy. It is not just a question of cooling and freshening the air around people; the air currents may also be purging the heat from the building fabric,

■ If it gets hot on the top floor, the design may assume that those on the north side of the ground floor will open their windows to admit cool air. But why should they if they are not yet hot?

William Bordass – environmental engineer

■ In many places around the world air-conditioning is still a sign of privilege; and as most people want to be privileged, they want air-conditioning even when it is unnecessary.

or gaining coolth from it at other times of the day. Curtains and blinds may prevent air entry; partitions may obstruct its path; wrong doors or windows left open may negate the stack effect. Air circulation is equally important with artificial ventilation, but here at least it may be possible to rebalance the system to mitigate mistakes made in designing the fit-out.

Noise

Apart from blinds that rattle or flail about in high winds, papers that cascade to the floor and doors that slam, natural ventilation makes little noise inside the office. High-velocity air-conditioning, on the other hand, can be a noisy companion. Any new ducting needs careful acoustic design, as do outlet grilles. And anything with a fan, such as an extractor, a fan coil unit or a package air-conditioner, is a potential source of noise.

Not that all noise need be eliminated. A certain level of plant noise provides an undistracting background hum that masks more irritating noises. In fact, one of the side-effects of natural ventilation (and also of chilled ceiling systems) is the significant reduction in background noise, which can result in the need for additional acoustic treatment.

Access

Where possible ceiling ducting needs to be routed above primary circulation routes, particularly where there are elements such as dampers needing adjustment and maintenance. Fan coil (and induction) units around the external walls, need access for the same reason, and can thus inhibit placing desks hard against the walls.

Special needs

Spaces in an office that need extra fresh air, more powerful extract, or both, include machine rooms (photocopying and printing), meeting rooms, smoking areas, restaurants and kitchens, kitchenettes and toilets. These are likely to have mechanical ventilation at the very least. Many will be newly located in the fit-out plan, so the ability to run ducts to them becomes an important space-planning consideration.

Heating and cooling

To function effectively, the body needs to keep within a very narrow temperature band. It is amazingly clever at maintaining this stable temperature. It can

---

HEATING AND COOLING MODES

Some modes depend on incidental heat (or cooling)

Natural	Solar gain	Heating*
	Occupants	Heating*
	Air (summer)	Heating*
	Air (winter)	Cooling*
	Radiation to night sky	Cooling*
	Below ground mass	Cooling*
	'Wind chill'	Cooling*
	Lakes and wells	Cooling*
Structural/mechanical	Machines	Heating*
	Lighting	Heating*
	Hot water – at varying pressures (radiators/heat exchangers)	Heating
	Steam (heat exchangers)	Heating
	Electric heaters	Heating
	Cold water (chilled panels and beams)	Cooling
	Building mass	Heating and cooling*
	Thermal wheels/heat exchangers	Heating and cooling
	Treated air	Heating and cooling
Air-conditioning	All methods described earlier	Heating and cooling

*Incidental source.

be helped by the addition or removal of clothes, or by an environment which provides reasonable air and radiant temperatures, relative humidity and air movement: the 'comfort zone'.

The heat comes from the sun and the air; people, lights and machines; and the heating system. Cooling (the withdrawal of heat) can be done by the air and the night sky; the mass of the building, the ground, or water; and the cooling system.

As with ventilation, heating and cooling can be helped by nature and by the sophisticated use of the building fabric, but again the integrity of the environmental design concept must be maintained.

Heating, cooling and ventilation are interlinked. For instance, the thermal inertia of the massive parts of the building – floor slabs and core walls – can be used to dampen down diurnal temperature variations – provided that they are not screened off from air currents by suspended ceilings or panelling. The interior design can also have an impact through the fineness of its zoning. This can range from simple perimeter zones related to orientation and a single zone for deep internal space, to special rooms (e.g. boardrooms) or workspaces with their own controls.

Acoustics

Here we define sounds as what people want to hear, and noises what they do not. The aim with office acoustics is to make the former audible and intelligible, and to block or mask the latter.

The acoustic environment of sounds and noises forms three concentric zones: immediately around the worker, the whole workplace, and the outside. In these zones are both sounds and noises, thus creating six kinds of sources (though what seem to be desirable sounds may – in other contexts – be unwelcome noises).

The nature of sound

Sound is a form of energy transmitted by vibration. This is transferred from one medium to another; so that sound waves (air vibrations) passing through the air in one room can cause a partition to vibrate, and set up new air waves in the next room. In general, structure-borne sound is more potent than airborne.

Sound energy is diminished by mass (insulation), by dissipation (absorption) and by distance (which allows general dissipation). Just as certain frequencies are more obtrusive to the human ear, so different frequencies can best be diminished in different ways.

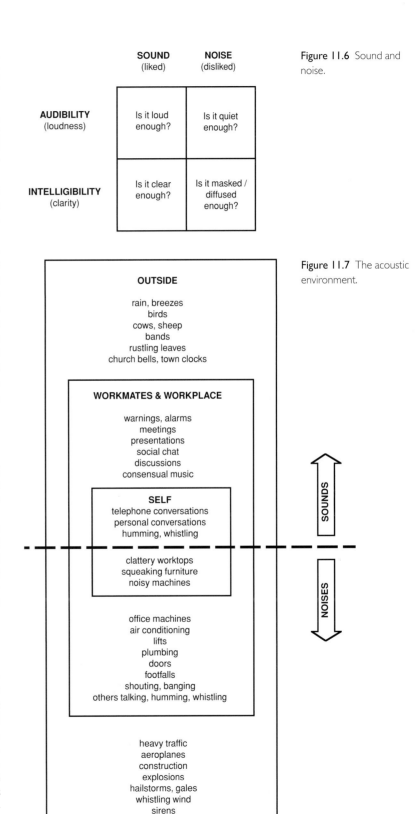

Figure 11.6 Sound and noise.

Figure 11.7 The acoustic environment.

Sound is measured in decibels (dB – or dBA), on a scale in which each increase of 10dB represents a doubling in loudness.

In large rooms like conference rooms and restaurants sound may reverberate, so that sound reflections off hard surfaces some distance from the listener take time to die away. Whereas early reflections (such as those off a hard ceiling above the listener) reinforce sound, late reflections merely confuse it and reduce intelligibility.

Acoustic control

Enhancement

Good sound transmission needs a direct and unobstructed path, with the transmitter (live or electronic) aimed at the listener. This direct path can be reinforced by hard surfaces providing early reflections, such as the uncluttered top of a boardroom table. With audio systems, the quality of the loudspeaker (and the input microphone) is important.

In particular places, where either audibility or intelligibility are at risk, electronic reinforcement may be needed: warning systems in machine rooms, or loudspeaker systems in conference and presentation rooms.

Reduction

Noise control is best done at its source; then along its transmission path; and only as a last resort at the receiving end.

Noise can be absorbed by porous or limp materials, and diffused by multifaceted surfaces. In the typical office the ceiling is the principal absorbent area, with soft-finished screens an important adjunct. If people face them rather than the general space, then telephone conversations are rapidly absorbed before they can affect others. The effectiveness of carpets depends on how densely furnished the office is; nevertheless carpets are important in eliminating the noise of footfalls at source. Soft furnishings and curtains provide modest additional absorption.

A busy office is by its nature multifaceted, with desks and chairs at a variety of angles; books and files on shelves and worktops; and soft people in soft clothes everywhere. All break up the noise and dissipate its energy.

Where complete sound attenuation is needed – to keep unwanted noise out, and private conversations in – not only must the wall or partition be well designed, but also well made. Flanking transmissions must be countered (unlike water, sound flows upwards as well as sideways and downwards), with acoustic barriers running to the structure rather than just between floor and ceiling. Acoustic performance is measured by the total construction, rather than by the theoretical noise reduction through a typical cross-section, so that though there is nothing like mass to reduce sound, the joints must perform equally well.

'White noise' can mask unwanted distractions such as chatting neighbours. The hum of air-conditioning (operating at a preset noise level), the murmur of distant conversations, and machine and street noise can all act as white noise, as can fountains: muzak is not the only answer.

Figure 11.8 Noise paths around partitions. Acoustic path through

A ceiling void

B ducts

C gap at the top of partition

D through partition construction

E gaps / joints at ends / between panels

F floor void (not usually a problem unless used as air plenum)

G gaps under partitions (only with demountable systems)

H structure-borne sound only likely for direct machine vibrations

X for effective sound insulation, floor and ceiling voids must be sealed along the partition line

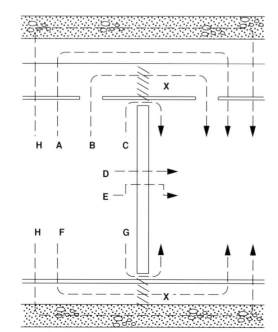

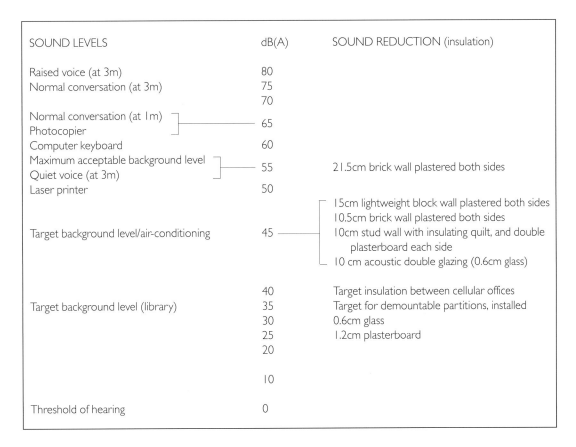

Figure 11.9 Office sound levels and reductions.

SOUND LEVELS	dB(A)	SOUND REDUCTION (insulation)
Raised voice (at 3m)	80	
Normal conversation (at 3m)	75	
	70	
Normal conversation (at 1m) ⌐	65	
Photocopier ⌐		
Computer keyboard	60	
Maximum acceptable background level ⌐	55	21.5cm brick wall plastered both sides
Quiet voice (at 3m) ⌐		
Laser printer	50	
		15cm lightweight block wall plastered both sides
		10.5cm brick wall plastered both sides
Target background level/air-conditioning	45	10cm stud wall with insulating quilt, and double plasterboard each side
		10 cm acoustic double glazing (0.6cm glass)
	40	Target insulation between cellular offices
Target background level (library)	35	Target for demountable partitions, installed
	30	0.6cm glass
	25	1.2cm plasterboard
	20	
	10	
Threshold of hearing	0	

Power distribution

Office machines are getting smaller in size but greater in number. So it is the distribution of power that is changing, more than the amount required. Generally it is just 'small power': 240V single phase, feeding normal socket outlets. Only in special locations such as kitchens and workshops may 415V three-phase supply be needed.

Any overcapacity in the system should be in the intake, the main risers, and their distribution boards

on each floor. These elements are the most costly and disruptive to change later. To speed the installation of horizontal cabling, prefabricated wiring harnesses (a technique borrowed from the motor industry) can be prepared off site and then laid in cable trays, either above the ceiling or, more commonly, beneath a raised floor.

Plumbing

Toilets and kitchens are normally built well before the fitting-out stage. Their specific service and waste requirements, such as main waste stacks, hot-water supply (including high-temperature water for kitchens, grease interceptors, etc.) limit where they may be located. They only need altering if they are outmoded or the building occupancy has increased.

Other 'wet' facilities – kitchenettes, serveries, vending areas, special process areas such as darkrooms, executive toilets and showers – can be added during the fitting-out, though the choice of location may be restricted.

RULES OF THUMB: POWER DISTRIBUTION

Occupancy	1 person/14m^2 of NIA
Small power load	25W/m^2
Floor outlets	1 per 5–10m^2

If underfloor, keep main horizontal runs under primary circulation routes, for ease of access.

■ Surveys show that in the overspecified offices of the 1980s, peak power loads rarely reach 15W/m^2 – about half the design load. Average loads are around 7.5W/m^2.

■ 'I can see you haven't used one of our washrooms yet, Sergeant Curtis,' chuckled Dukes. 'He's right,' said Helen. 'Everything is automatic. And I mean everything. Let's just say that this is a paperless office environment.'

Philip Kerr: Gridiron

■ At advertising agency Leo Burnett in London, the escalators between street level and the first floor reception area were introduced to increase speed of access and make the office feel more welcoming.

TOILET PROVISION	
British Council for Offices: best practice	
Single-sex toilets	1 person/14m² NIA
	60% men
	60% women
Unisex toilets	1 person/14m² NIA

In refurbishing older buildings it may be necessary to renew the hot-water supply system, as old and poorly insulated systems encourage Legionnaire's disease. To prevent it, hot water should be distributed at temperatures above 60°C, and stored in insulated cylinders near draw-off points.

Lifts and escalators

Lifts and escalators usually form part of the shell and core contract, though they may be replaced in a major refurbishment. Escalators are expensive in both money and space.

People need to move vertically: staff, visitors and, in an emergency, firefighters. Goods movement includes office, catering and maintenance supplies, furniture and waste. Lifts of both sorts should provide adequate capacity, acceptable frequency and swift loading and unloading. The design of the loading area, and the provision of clear and timely information can speed up loading.

Because facilities like conference halls and reception suites can generate heavy peak loads – often of important people – they should be located at or near ground level, to minimize dependence on lifts. Like-wise, careful stacking of departments encourages staff to use stairs for short journeys.

In offices of over 10 000m² a separate goods lift is essential; and if there is much movement of furniture and equipment one is desirable in smaller buildings. Because goods lifts can generate dirt and noise they should have working lobbies separating them from the main office areas, and a separate loading bay at ground floor level. Lobbies opening into broad primary circulation routes make trolleying easy and minimize damage to walls and corners.

Fire and security

Despite the efforts of building technologists, offices are still subject to a variety of hazards, from bombs to mice. Many of these can be countered by the right management policies, but the fabric and systems of the building have a part to play.

Fire

Death, destruction and disruption are the harsh penalties of a major office fire. People must be saved, the building and its contents protected, and the operations (and thus profitability) of the business hampered as little as possible.

Dealing with fire involves:

Avoidance
Statutory regulations control the use of inflammable materials in construction and furnishing; and well-installed and -maintained office machines rarely burst into flames.

Warning
Smoke and toxic gases are the killers. Smoke detectors, with heat detectors in high-risk areas, give early warning. In addition, manual 'break-glass' alarms are required in offices. Building management systems can

RULES OF THUMB: LIFTS	
Office lift systems should accommodate the morning peak, with the aim of moving at least:	
1/6 of the building's population in 5 minutes	Owner occupied
1/8 of the building's population in 5 minutes	Multitenanted
Desirable maximum waiting time	30 seconds
Actual car capacity (as % of rated capacity)	80% (standard lifts)
	70% (scenic lifts)

trigger the alarm, precisely locate the fire (helping both evacuation and the subsequent firefighting) and alert occupants, facilities management and the fire brigade.

Bells are the normal warning signal but, for the deaf, should be augmented by flashing lights.

Escape
Escape routes are governed by statutory regulations, which now include the concept of 'refuges'. Fire is particularly frightening and disorienting, and smoke may rapidly reduce visibility, so exit routes must be well signed and show clearly the direction of safety.

Control
Smoke is as big a hazard as flame. Fire-break partitions running from structural floor to structural ceiling prevent the spread of smoke through floor and ceiling voids. Direct venting — especially at high level where hot smoke will go first — stops it building up.

Fire-retardant materials (especially surface finishes) slow the spread of flame; and dividing the building into fire-resisting compartments contains the fire and limits the dangerous 'flash-over' caused by intense radiant heat.

Firefighting
Manual extinguishing is only effective if carried out by properly trained staff; initial firefighting is best left to automatic systems (e.g. sprinklers, gas dousing). Civic firefighters need safe routes into and through the building, with a firefighters' staircase (and lift in tall buildings) with protected double lobbies.

Recovery
Most organizations now have disaster recovery plans. Refurbishing the workplace is one element, and involves:

- making the premises secure and safe
- appraising the damage
- salvaging key equipment and documents
- removing debris
- fitting temporary weather protection
- deciding whether to replicate the old or not
- phasing the work and reoccupation.

Security

Security risks can be divided into theft from the premises, and attack at them — either by people outside the organization, or within it. Informal surveillance plays a major part in security, and can be helped by eliminating unnecessary visual barriers (using low screens or glazed partitions, and carefully placing tall storage units), and by creating circulation routes that provide a natural overview.

Theft

So many different things can be stolen:

- business equipment (computer theft 'to order')
- office supplies
- personal effects (the handbag-snatching 'stair-dancer' in multitenanted buildings)
- documents and information (industrial espionage and hacking)
- people (kidnap).

In all cases proper control of the office perimeter, easy informal surveillance and secure localized storage makes management's task easier.

Attack

It may be arson, bombing or vandalism, or smaller enemies — rodents and insects. Perimeter security and good storage again form a large part of the answer.

Perimeter security

A limited number of entrances, with no bypasses and a stringent monitoring system keeps the office perimeter secure; sensitive inner zones may also need restricted access.

'Smart' ID cards may be swiped to allow people through doors, turnstiles or designated routes. Where they are necessary bag checks take up space — both for the checking table (or machine), and also for people waiting.

Storage

Secure storage ranges from lockable drawers for personal effects to strong rooms for archives. The principal issues are location, construction, locks and surveillance. The following points are to be considered.

- Are these four security factors in balance (no weak link)?
- Have all risks been taken account of (fire, explosion, damp, theft, vermin)?
- Is a second line of defence needed (to prevent ingress, or escape)?
- Is the storage convenient to use, or will its complexity deter people?

■ After a major fire in one of their offices the computer company Digital decided to switch to locationless working, with a consequent saving in premises costs of £2m a year.

■ Each of the open plan floors in the Standard Life Tanfield building in Edinburgh is the size of the Murrayfield rugby football ground. For this to be allowed, fire escapes are at closer than normal centres, and the domes overhead have automatic smoke vents.

■ A public office building, designed with terrorist threats in mind, was instead subjected to ram-raids through its curtain walling to steal valuable DTP equipment.

Information technology

The 'intelligent building' is a somewhat loosely used term. Here we take it to mean a building with electronic systems in it for running:

— the business
— building management
— facilities management.

These different systems may be present — and integrated — to varying degrees; but they share the objectives of operational efficiency, energy efficiency and ease of making changes. They share one further matter: cabling.

Cabling

While the technologies of telephones and computers continue to leap forward, that of their linkages struggles to keep up. Once there were a few wires in walls and ceilings; now floors and furniture are stuffed with them. Their power supply has remained simple and relatively unchanged, but the lines carrying voice, data and images have ramified.

The main types of carrier are: copper cable, fibre-optic cable and 'cordless'. Each has its uses and its limitations. Fibre-optic's high carrying capacity may be used for the fixed vertical risers, and twisted-pair copper wiring for the flexible horizontal runs. Because copper cable suffers from electromagnetic interference, IT wiring should be kept well separated (at least 0.5m) from power cabling. It may also need shielding to prevent 'electronic eavesdropping' by competitor businesses.

In Britain IT cabling is normally run within floor voids and in furniture systems; but in densely fur-

nished offices, or buildings without voids or ducts, ceiling runs may be more practical, with drops to the workstations through 'power poles'. In shallow and lightly serviced offices wall raceways at dado or skirting level may be enough.

With cordless technology there is the possibility of eliminating some horizontal wiring, and improving the freedom both of the designer and of the worker.

Even with cordless installations there are main junction points. Although the PBX is now a desk-top unit, there still has to be an intake panel (or room) for the external telecommunications, cable TV and satellite links. On each floor there should be at least one patch room or panel — where the IT network can be reconfigured — easily accessible but properly secure and shielded from electrical interference.

However, power remains hard wired and needs to provide a smooth and uninterrupted supply to the electronic equipment (and alarm systems), or to batteries being recharged. Business and BMS systems may require standby batteries or generators.

Business systems

Business systems cover a spectrum of purposes:

— *Voice*. Telephone / public address / voice mail.
— *Text*. Electronic mail (E-mail) / fax / telex / simple desk-top publishing (DTP).
— *Image*. Complex DTP / computer aided design / closed circuit television / audio-visual presentation / video-conferencing.
— *Data*. Data transfer / databases.

In any but the smallest office personal computers will be networked together, which means a large amount of wiring. Because of this, when a move is needed, the tendency is to leave wired up furniture in place, and to shift staff around (made simple through electronic patching). Where 'hot desking' and 'hoteling' occur — without cordless equipment — patching is the only practical solution, with staff logging on at whatever workstation they have been allocated.

Building management systems

The simplest kind of intelligent building merely looks after itself. The basic elements are lighting and HVAC; to these may be added fire and security. A more complex building management system embraces the following.

— *Energy*. HVAC / artificial lighting (normal and emergency) / solar control (external and internal)

RULES OF THUMB: IT AND TELEPHONE CABLING NETWORKS

— Work to same occupancy and outlet guidelines as for power distribution (say one outlet/8m2).
— Risers to be within 80m cabling distance of any part of serviced floorplate.
— IT riser cables to be designed for saturation loads.
— Telephone riser cables to have 30% spare capacity, with space left in riser tray for doubling the capacity.

CORDLESS SYSTEMS: ADVANTAGES AND
DRAWBACKS

For:

Allows the use of old buildings that are difficult to
rewire.

Reduces churn: workers move rather than partitions.

Tenants on short leases do not have to invest in
cabling systems.

Installation costs are 10–15% lower.

Staff are no longer tied to their desks, which
allows free movement and a variety of work
postures.

Personal communications services (PCS) telephones give the number to the person, not
the place – so they can be contacted anywhere (office, home, on the move).

Result is far fewer unanswered calls.

Which means reduced return calls (savings on
telephone bills of up to 30%).

Combining PCS with notebook computers means
mobile data transfer is possible.

Against:

Slower speeds than wired systems make image
transfer impractical (e.g. CAD, DTP, video).

Lack of common standards yet – but Digital European Cordless Telecommunications (DECT) is
gaining ground.

System depends on (short-lived) batteries in
handsets.

Battery recharging.

Questions over safety of radio microwaves.

/ demand prediction.

– *Security.* Fire detection / fire alarms / fire-fighting
(sprinklers, dousing systems) / access control
(staff and visitors, deliveries, special secure areas)
/ intruder detection (perimeter and entrances,
circulation and general areas, special secure
areas).

– *Circulation.* Lift monitoring and control (including
emergency control).

Systems have sensors or monitors at the points
where variations may occur (e.g. changes in daylight,
intruders), linked to control points where suitable
responses may be made – manually, automatically, or
a combination of both.

Building management systems should be robust,
simple and understandable, and provide clear feed-

back. Too many fail through being oversophisticated
and unintelligible, or because they do not satisfy the
users. The truly intelligent system is clever enough to
allow humans to think they are in control of their
individual environments. However, for energy efficiency it then surreptitiously draws the building back
to the ideal state.

Facilities management systems

With so much of building design and operation being
computerized there are potential benefits for facilities
management. CAD floor layouts can quickly generate
furniture inventories and schedules of light fittings.
Schedules in turn can form the basis of purchase
orders. Power and fuel consumption records can
support better briefing when the next fit-out comes
around. What is important is that this potential
should be anticipated: that during the design and fitting-out data should be assembled and recorded in a
way which is useful to the future operation, maintenance – and adaptation – of the space.

However, with computer-based data being fed in
from so many sources, there are legal issues: copy-
right, responsibility for changes (to drawings, specifications), lack of confidentiality, illicit access to (and
possible tampering with) records. A secure, logical
and just system is needed before data integration is
put into practice.

Dilemmas

■ Do users – management and staff – want closely
controlled, bland working conditions; or do they
want more natural variety – with the penalty of
occasional discomfort? To what extent will 'green'
policies affect this choice?

■ How can lighting best enhance the interior while
still providing sufficient illumination wherever it is
needed?

■ What effect do expected and unexpected noises
have on workers' performance? How can they be
controlled in open plan offices?

■ How will the voice-activated computer affect the
acoustic environment?

■ What are the implications of cordless IT for the
other building services?

■ Which environmental element is the most critical? In what circumstances?

■ What are the environmental requirements of
home working? What regulation is there likely
to be?

■ In our cordless
office, the average
telephone call is
60m long.

*Digital Equipment
Company, Stockholm*

■ Benefits of BMS.
Energy saving –
happy staff – ease of
reconfiguration –
information about
performance – high-
er quality of opera-
tions and service.

■ Drawbacks of
BMS. Higher capital
cost – more to go
wrong.

Western Morning News
Plymouth

workplace

The Western Morning News Company, part of the Northcliffe Newspaper Group, is the largest news publisher in southwest England. However, its site in the centre of Plymouth had become increasingly impractical, so it decided to relocate to a business park and build its own production and printing facilities and headquarters offices.

The new building is a 'galleon', with a curved plan, supportive masts and convex glazing. There is also a tower rising 22m above the ground, housing a conference room with an unparalleled view over sea and rolling hills.

Of the 15 000m², a third is office space, situated in the 'prow' of the building on three floors, with cellular spaces on the inside looking into the atrium, and open plan advertising, editorial and accounts areas curled around the outside. The 400-strong workforce includes management, editorial, advertising and

Figure 11.10 (Left) The ground floor restaurant is alongside the reel room – the bottom part of the three-storey printing process. The high ceiling uses ductwork decoratively.

Figure 11.11 (Opposite) One-third of the building is office space. The atrium has cellular offices all round, and at the bridge level reception townspeople can be found sitting down to place their advertisements and notices.

■ The region has a strong sense of identity; it dislikes London. We need to stand up for the interests of the region. It's west versus the rest.

Colin Davidson – editor, Western Morning News

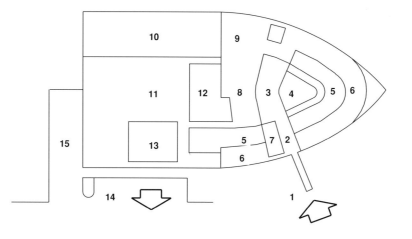

Figure 11.12 Layout of entrance floor.
Key
1 entrance bridge
2 entrance
3 reception
4 atrium
5 offices
6 advertising area
7 core
8 interim composing room
9 plate making
10 press hall
11 mechanized publishing
12 core, stores and offices
13 packing and collection
14 van loading
15 articulated lorry loading

production staff, operating round the clock.

The single pedestrian entrance is across a bridge that straddles a moat around the building and leads directly into the atrium. A highly dramatic space becomes homely with timber desks and shelving. Little old ladies in faded summer dresses placing their advertisements look perfectly at ease alongside the high technology. The restaurant – again with a fine view – is on the lowest floor, and the gym is cleverly placed so that visitors can admire the antics of the users while crossing the bridge.

For this is a very transparent building: even the printing machinery is visible for the enjoyment of the world outside. Many of the internal walls are glazed too. The curved glazing reduces reflections, and overhangs, louvres and planting all control heat gain and glare – to an extent. Sail-like blinds are manually wound across the windows as they are needed, with two nautical handles: one to close the blinds, the other to open them.

The workstations were specially designed by the architects. All cabling is within the floor void and comes up through 'standards' which support worktops – set at keyboard and desk heights. Workstation positions relate to the curve of the building. Enclosed offices have suspended ceilings, but elsewhere ventilation ducts are generally exposed and hang from the ceiling.

The company chose its architect with care, considering the work of several firms before appointing Nicholas Grimshaw and Partners. Close collaboration with the sponsor and thorough discussions with all levels of staff helped the architect produce a comprehensive brief.

The management contractor was chosen with the same thoroughness, as were the specialist contractors. Though local companies were favoured, they had to show that they could operate under 'fast-build' disciplines to produce a high-quality result, that they had experience of the complex work involved and that they were competitive. A fully integrated computer system used on site was an essential ingredient of the process.

Managing Director Jerry Ramsden championed the project all through: 'We were keen to try for a building that would give the company a high profile, strong identity and a good public image within the West Country.' This he has achieved – handsomely.

Architects: Nicholas Grimshaw and Partners
Management Contractor: Bovis Construction Ltd
Project completed: 1993

■ On a fast-build and technically difficult project such as this, an in depth 'hands-on' approach, dealing with queries instantly, is the key to success.

Clive Wood –
Bovis Construction

Figure 11.13 The top floor advertising area is in the 'prow' of the building, with fixed desks following its curve. Windows are cleaned by an abseiler, and on the south side blinds are wound across as needed.

Chapter 12
Furniture

Types of furniture
■ **General office furniture**
Chairs
Personal workstations
Free-standing furniture
System furniture
Cable management
■ **Special furniture and equipment**
Reception areas
Executive offices
Meeting areas
Eating areas
Serveries
Kitchens
Refreshment points
Toilets
Support spaces
■ **Home office furniture**
■ **Procuring furniture**
User inputs
Choosing suppliers
Supplier services
Design
Regulations
Budget
Trials and mock-ups
Tendering
Installation
■ **Dilemmas**

Choosing furniture is a real can of worms.

A facilities manager

With several hundred furniture products on the market, selecting furniture is much like choosing a car – deciding on your needs and budget, asking around, looking at brochures, admiring the shape and checking performance. You then aim to find dealers who are reasonably local and who not only offer a competitive price, but prompt delivery and good after sales service.

At least you know what you want the car for. With office furniture, however, there are now such different approaches: the free-address workstation that fits anyone, or the personalized one designed to fit someone particular; a focus on the individual workstation, or on the team and its meeting space; allowing teams to furnish their areas with what works best for them, or restricting choice to what the facilities department can bulk purchase.

And the chief executive, does she still display her stripes with quite different furniture from everyone else? Is boardroom furniture chosen for function and style, or just to look more expensive than that elsewhere? Is office furniture necessary at all? Robustness and wire management apart, why not use domestic furniture, or at least furniture that is human and colourful and not just different shades of grey?

Workplace disorders, VDT use and pressure of work are other factors that have focused attention on the workstation – rightly so. Yet free-range working and technological advance are changing the physical parameters of getting the task done. As one well-known furniture designer says: 'Once we are walking around talking to our computers, we may as well go back to the hard-backed kitchen chair.'

Advances in IT have made it even easier to move people than furniture; so some organizations are now building fixed workstations. The advantages are that they can be purpose made to fit specific activities, can be more lightly engineered than movable furniture systems, and the wiring can be permanent. As a result they can also cost less than loose furniture.

So while there is pressure – correctly so – to ensure that all office staff have good working conditions, these conditions need not necessarily be just for the conventional workstation. Nevertheless, most organizations – and their employees – are still in the main-stream; and this chapter looks chiefly at the kind

Figure 12.1 PowerGen, Coventry: On the ground floor, work areas flow into the atrium. Glazed balustrades above allow a clear view all round. The scale of the uplighting is in keeping with the space and, unusually for an office, the ceiling is one of the most elegant features. *Architects: Bennetts Associates/Fletcher Priest*

Figure 12.2 Designed by Bill Stumpf and Don Chadwick to fit both the worker's body and their desk, the Aeron chair combines revolutionary functionality and use of materials. 'A chair to kill for.' – Joshua Burrill, computer consultant. *Reproduced with the permission of Herman Miller Ltd*

■ Once you have sorted out all the nitty-gritty criteria of practicality and cost, pick three or four chairs and let four or five people use them for a week at a time.

Margaret Hayes: OFAS (Office Furniture Advisory Service)

■ Herman Miller's approach to the project was most refreshing. They really tried to meet our requirements, and were as concerned as we were about quality and image. If they felt something was not right they would say so, and they encouraged the setting up of pilot areas.

David Hinton – The Automobile Association

of furniture which is needed in those workplaces, and how to go about getting it.

Types of furniture

Furniture in the workplace is used for core activities – by the individual or by the team – and for ancillary or support functions. Increasingly, some of these activities may also take place at home.

Workplace furniture is normally categorized as:

- seating
- freestanding individual products
- freestanding modular systems
- screen or panel hung systems
- storage systems
- ancillary area furniture
- support area furniture
- built-in (workstations or special pieces).

Furniture for the individual covers all aspects of the workstation; for the team it includes break-out, meeting and conference room items; and for ancillary activities it is likely to be specialized, and often built in. That for support activities covers the widest spread of all, from auditorium seating to mail room sorting tables.

General office furniture

Chairs

Some companies use a dozen different chairs to fulfil different functions, and others just two: a task chair on casters at workstations and the same body on a sled base used everywhere else (advantageous both for inventory and cost).

Chair design relates to function, intensity of use and appearance. While comfort is of first importance for task chairs and those for meetings, other factors may count more highly in reception areas and restaurants. With such chairs the specifier can be moderately adventurous; but the careful choice of task chair is critical to the well-ordered office.

Choosing a task chair

My relationship with my chair is as personal as that with my underclothes.

An office worker

Choosing a task chair takes time. A formal and thorough process involving staff is useful both practically and politically. A limited number of possible chairs can be tested by a group of user representatives, ending with a structured questionnaire.

The chair should allow each part of the body to be in its most comfortable position, but it should also encourage movement and be easily adjustable to different seating positions.

Its height should allow the feet to be squarely on the floor, without pressure on the underside of the thigh. The seat depth should provide 2–4 fingers between seat front and calf. This reduces pressure at the backs of knees or on buttocks, and permits good lumbar contact with the chair's backrest. To prevent the weight of the worker's raised forearms causing strain on their shoulders, armrests should be adjustable to not more than 1cm below relaxed elbow height. This is more helpful for upper limb support than palm or wrist rests.

Passive or active adjustment of the angle between seat and backrest encourages forward and backward movement of the torso (it is claimed that this helps the natural lubrication of the spine, and enhances the circulatory, respiratory and digestive processes).

Some chairs now respond automatically and helpfully to the body's movements; but manual controls remain. These too need to be ergonomic: easy to understand and operate, positive and secure in their action, and so placed that they are accessible without being in the way.

Chairs need to relate to the workplace around them: armrest heights that fit under worktops, casters that run smoothly over carpets without excessive wear or indentation, coverings that are non-slip, easy to clean and do not produce static. Materials need to be robust and easy to maintain or replace, and the chair's appearance should harmonize with the rest of the furniture.

Personal workstations

The more adjustment people are given, the more they are going to get things wrong.

A facilities manager

Workstations are now being tailored to specific activities, with people moving around between them, but there will always be workers who stay put at workstations designed to cater for a range of activities.

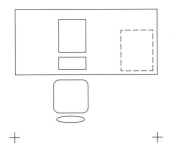

MINIMUM WORKSTATION – 180 × 180cm

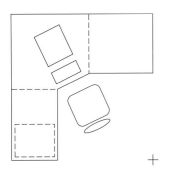

MAXIMUM GENERAL WORKSTATION – 180 × 180cm

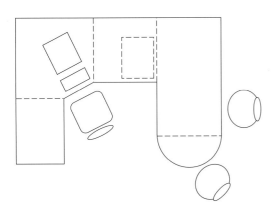

MANAGERIAL WORKSTATION – 180 × 360cm

Work surfaces

An ideal work surface has space within easy reach for documents, materials and equipment. As a result it may be L- or even U-shaped but, in these clean desk days, it will only have space for current papers. There may be pedestal storage underneath (although this should not prevent the user moving her legs around). The surface may have two or even three levels – for keyboard, VDT and general work. These should

adjust easily to suit the smallest or the largest person, and satisfy the senses: warm to the touch, with rounded edges and non-reflective.

The normal depth is about 80cm (within a range of 60–100cm). Large VDTs require greater depth; this may be achieved by placing them in the corner formed by right-angled surfaces.

Keyboard support should be level with the relaxed seated elbow height, with work surfaces for writing or hand tasks that involve close visual inspection being about 8cm higher.

Computers

With desk-top computers the top of the monitor should be level with the user's eyes, giving a comfortable viewing angle to the centre of the screen when the head is tilted forward. The distance from the screen depends on personal choice and screen size. The monitor should be angled upwards so that the screen surface remains perpendicular to the worker's line of sight. Reference documents should be positioned adjacent to, and at the same height as the screen.

Equipment and documents

Anything to which the worker needs constant access – telephones, files, stationery, calculators – should be within 40–60cm horizontal reach and positioned vertically between seat and shoulder heights. High-level storage is tending to be replaced by a limited amount of storage below the work surface, coupled with centralized storage areas.

Freestanding furniture

The ease with which the freestanding desk can be moved across the room (cabling permitting) looks attractive in these days of adaptability and change. Freestanding furniture also encourages reconfiguration by individuals and teams as the need arises – although this may drive the facilities manager wild!

Individual products – which may be items bought over some years – may lack a comprehensive and impressive image for the outsider, but certainly save money. However, they must comply with current regulations and have reasonable cable management if they are to remain useful.

Where the furniture is from one integrated range it provides a consistent environment and a simple inventory. Work and meeting surfaces, storage and screens fit together in a variety of ways, usually with linked cabling systems.

Figure 12.3 Typical workstation modules. Open plan layout with minimum furniture inventory.

■ When information came in weighty books and files it needed horizontal surfaces to support it. With weightless – electronic – data it is more natural to have it in the line of sight, and vertical. We are moving from having things to *put down*, to having things to *look at*. And voice-activated computers won't even need a shelf for the keyboard. Has the desk had its day?

Figure 12.4 An executive office with freestanding furniture from a unified range provides a variety of work settings.
Reproduced with the permission of Herman Miller Ltd

■ Screens can be used delicately to delineate space and dot-in privacy. Low ones can shield the seated worker from eye contact. High ones have their place, if they do not block the light. But are people so desperate to screen their legs that the visual sweep of a floor flowing under desks is lost?

System furniture

System furniture companies aim to be one-stop shops, providing work surfaces, storage, panels, task lighting and cable management, and maybe chairs and special furniture as well. Where this succeeds it provides all the obvious cost and organizational advantages. However, as some items may be much better

---

FURNITURE SYSTEMS: BASIC ELEMENTS

Screens. An integral part of most systems. They provide visual and acoustic privacy, often support work surfaces and storage, and may carry cabling and outlet positions. They may be load bearing, supported off the work surface or totally independent. Heights vary from about 30 to 180cm above the work surface.

Work surfaces. These have many configurations. They may be supported on legs or pedestals, or off panels, and can include cable ways and cable access. Although making up a workstation from different elements may be efficient, it may sometimes create unsightly and dirt-catching traps between each section.

Personal storage. This comes as floor pedestals – which may be mobile – or the more expensive high-level cupboards. These are often hung on the panels, but can be unstable if overloaded. The right choice of drawer size and fittings can greatly increase their usefulness.

Central storage. This is principally for filing and stationery storage, with lateral filing being more space effective than traditional filing cabinets (it is important that all filing should cater for different paper sizes). Units may have adjustable shelving and special fitments so that they can also contain other forms of general storage, such as electronic equipment, office consumables and jackets.

General storage. With free-address working, personal papers and possessions need either a 'garage' for mobile storage units, or lockers. Outdoor clothing storage requires good ventilation.

than others, it is advisable to look to other suppliers for elements in which the system is weak.

This furniture can be put together in numerous ways to suit different situations. Freestanding systems are supported on legs or pedestals; and fixed systems by panels, spines or legs – or a combination. To move systems furniture takes time and usually some skill or knowledge. However it does use space efficiently and provides a total environment: work and display surfaces, storage, enclosure and – of course – tidy wires.

Storage systems may be supplied along with the workstations or come from a specialist supplier.

Cable management

Despite forecasts to the contrary cables are here to stay, for quite a time anyway. Power and high-intensity data continues to need cabling. Within the office cordless telephones may be 'ether linked' (microwave or infrared beams) to local relay nodes; and computers can be battery operated (but recharging still requires plugging in).

Cabling inhibits flexibility. The computer is usually attached by horizontal cabling at worktop height to the main cabling in the floor, perimeter ducting or sometimes the ceiling. The neatness, flexibility, accessibility and safety of these worktop cable routes is a major design factor.

There is a counter argument for having fixed vertical elements – pods, bollards or poles – into which everything plugs. These may include lighting and air (or heating) as well as power, data and voice. They can be moved from one floor (or ceiling) outlet position to another without too much difficulty, but still limit flexibility, and can be obtrusive visual elements.

Wire management systems within furniture vary from the structured ducting within leg, desk or panel, to simply laying loose cables in a basket or trough. Room is needed for cable radii, junction boxes, connectors and plugs for 'threading through', and for future increases in cabling. Power is normally kept separate to avoid electromagnetic interference. Power, data, and voice outlet points should be within comfortable reach, and cableway access robust and easy to get at without serious disruption to the desk worker.

Furniture manufacturers meet these demands in different ways; but with untidy wires being unattractive, unsafe and possibly illegal, the efficient handling of cabling is a high priority in furniture choice. Even in the home office cabling needs careful consideration, especially if there are small children around.

Special furniture and equipment

Top managers increasingly have the same furniture as everyone else, so 'special furniture' now means items fulfilling needs other than those of the general office space. Reception areas, meeting and conference rooms, and restaurants may well need it. 'Special' can mean specially commissioned, or obtained from a different manufacturer from everything else, or just more up-market than the rest.

Reception areas

The two-tier extravaganza of a reception desk seems de rigeur; but how long will this last? Some firms are already accepting that different solutions are more appropriate – such as small consoles where receptionists and visitors stand side by side keying in information to produce individually printed badges. Whatever their form, reception desks are likely to remain prestigious objects, produced by a specialist designer.

Beyond its primary welcoming and control functions the reception desk has to accommodate other activities. It often incorporates a switchboard, security screens and a workstation. Providing a clear design brief is essential, and this must cover image as well as function.

Figure 12.5 Panel-based systems can create workstations with ample work surfaces and overhead storage. This one also provides a vision strip for the seated worker. *Reproduced with the permission of Herman Miller Ltd*

Text on image: Blairlogie

Figure 12.6 Blairlogie Capital Management, Edinburgh: This award-winning interior supports an open and non-hierarchical company structure. An upgraded 1960s building provides the latest technology, but with natural light and ventilation. Views towards the castle and a tartan carpet in the reception area emphasize its Scottishness.
Architects: Jestico +Whiles

If specific security is involved there may be need for a bag inspection counter. This should be table-top height, which allows security officers to work comfortably standing up, yet look down easily into deep bags.

Visitor seating may also make a statement, but should still be comfortable (though not too low or too soft). Tables are needed nearby for newspapers, for opening briefcases on, and for laying out papers if the meeting starts then and there. Panels, shelves and racks for literature and displays about the firm may be standards or specials, with lighting being an important element.

Executive offices

Office furnishings once denoted position within the hierarchy, and in places this continues. Other companies are more egalitarian: the executive's office may be larger, but its function is the same as everyone else's. There is also another way; where the executive uses his position to get something really good for his office – and the whole organization benefits from this statement of quality.

Some executives commission fine furniture and artworks from young craftsmen and artists, and put this together with style. Others shop around and buy the best-designed furniture available. But as with the reception desk, function is as important as appearance.

Meeting areas

Meeting areas varying from the space at the end of the desk or the room, to full-blown video-conference

and training rooms. Ordinary meeting rooms can be furnished with low-key standard furniture – if a large table is needed, several small ones can be put together.

Meeting rooms need plenty of vertical presentation surfaces: display panels, pinboards, whiteboards, flip-charts; projection screens, photocopying boards, visual planning systems: all either freestanding or wall hung. They also need shelves, projector stands and storage (for everything from equipment to extra chairs).

Conference rooms and boardrooms may be intended to impress visitors, with an elegant table and comfortable chairs. Food and drink may be served from a sideboard. But even in these rooms the gigantic single table – round, oval or oblong – is being superseded by modular ones.

The complexity of audio-visual equipment (with several monitors, slide and overhead projectors, and

Figure 12.7 Cable and Wireless, Mercury House, London: Communicating in the staff café.
Architects: Austin-Smith Lord

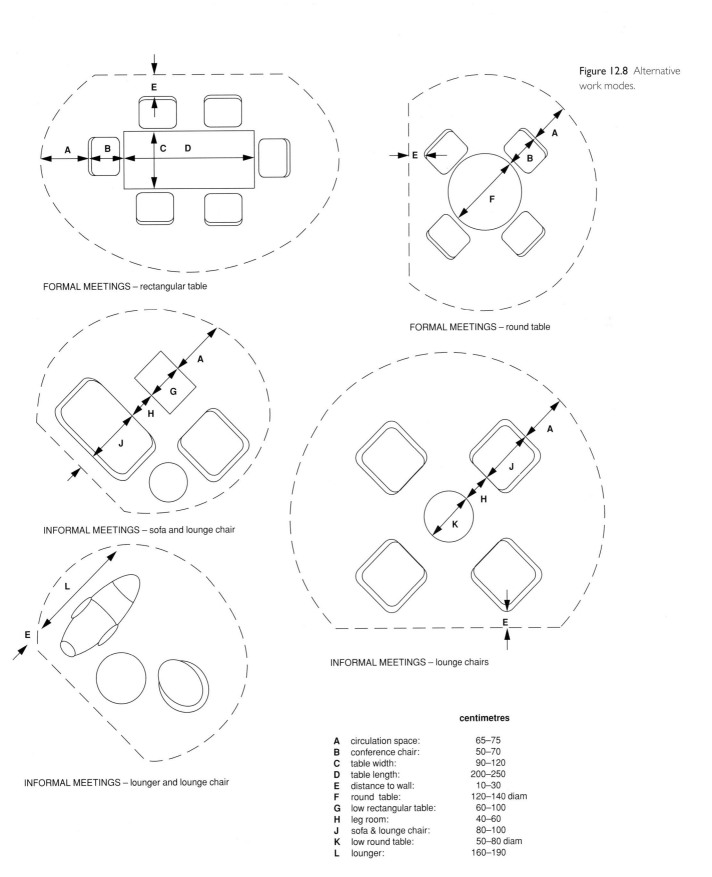

FORMAL MEETINGS – rectangular table

Figure 12.8 Alternative work modes.

FORMAL MEETINGS – round table

INFORMAL MEETINGS – sofa and lounge chair

INFORMAL MEETINGS – lounge chairs

INFORMAL MEETINGS – lounger and lounge chair

		centimetres
A	circulation space:	65–75
B	conference chair:	50–70
C	table width:	90–120
D	table length:	200–250
E	distance to wall:	10–30
F	round table:	120–140 diam
G	low rectangular table:	60–100
H	leg room:	40–60
J	sofa & lounge chair:	80–100
K	low round table:	50–80 diam
L	lounger:	160–190

Figure 12.9 Sony Music Entertainment, Soho, London: The café combines the trendiness of exposed services (and theatrical lighting after dark), with a civilized view into the courtyard during the day. The floor rises up to straddle the sill of the French windows, giving access to further seating outside.
Architects: Harper Mackay

fixed or retractable screens) may require special furniture, including a speaker's console. Audio-visual walls enable equipment to be shut away when not in use, for security and elegance.

Eating areas

The restaurant is somewhere special, a refreshing break from the office routine. So its furniture should tell a different story from that told elsewhere. Restaurant furniture may be café or garden furniture, bar furniture, lounge furniture or furniture from outer space: whatever it is, it is rarely supplied by the same manufacturer as supplies the desking.

Durability is essential, and the furniture must be easy to move for cleaning – unless it is built in. Now that restaurants are used as spaces for informal meetings out of eating hours, long-term comfort is important too. And chairs and tables need to be robust enough to lean back in, or to thump.

Serveries

Serving counters are specialist items. Heated elements and cupboards, chilled surfaces and refrigerators, hygiene combined with accessibility: all make for a complex technical brief. As a result, they are often purchased along with the kitchen equipment.

Figure 12.10 Wolff Olins, London: Servery consoles in the staff restaurant. Food is displayed on heated and chilled slabs, with a marble one for the cheese.
Interior Designers: Wolff Olins

Nevertheless, how they look can make or mar a restaurant. Restaurant and servery aesthetic (including clearing trolleys) should be one, with finishes, lighting and furniture design binding the two areas together.

Kitchens

Food preparation and production areas are often designed and equipped by specialist firms, with possibly some input from the caterer. The equipment is highly specific, with all aspects being precisely regulated. Type and complexity of menu affect what is required, though it is desirable to allow some flexibility for changes to the menu or caterer.

Refreshment points

Refreshment points may consist of a vending machine in an alcove, a vending lay-by or a full-blown tea kitchen complete with cupboards, fridge, microwave and a sitting area. Furniture and equipment may have a domestic feel, but should be durable.

Vending machines, providing various types of product are often supplied and serviced by the caterer. The quality of drinks from a vending machine varies as much as its cost and reliability, and thus choice of machine becomes a sophisticated process like choosing a task chair. However, there is less control over its appearance, and the designer is left with trying to absorb it into an attractive setting.

Toilets

Most of the 'furniture' in toilets consists either of sanitary fittings or of wall-mounted equipment – such as dispensers for paper, soap, towels and tampons; roller towels and hot-air dryers; and shaver sockets and sanitary disposers. This equipment is often serviced by a cleaning contractor, and may be supplied by it too. Nevertheless, the choice and positioning of these fittings needs to be part of the overall design.

Support spaces

Support spaces range from those with simple furniture needs – such as smoking and rest rooms – to complex ones: libraries, gyms, crèches and medical facilities. Furnishing the former can be part of the primary furniture contract. The latter need specialist advice and here, as with kitchens, the problem may be getting impartial guidance without disregarding the considerable expertise that the best suppliers have.

Home office furniture

Furniture for home working is becoming increasingly important as more people work at home – at least part of the time. Furniture is often domestic, with a dining chair and table forming the basis of the workstation. Simple DIY can produce adequate worktops and storage, but a specialist task chair is often essential.

HOME OFFICE FURNITURE: SELECTION CRITERIA

In addition to the normal selection criteria, the following aspects need to be considered.

Size. Whether it will fit – physically and visually – into relatively small rooms. Whether it can be got through narrow domestic doorways (especially bedrooms). Whether it can be closed up when not in use, so as to occupy less space.

Weight. Whether it can be easily moved by one – or at most – two people. Whether contents – or drawers – can be easily taken out to facilitate this.

Security. Whether office documents can be kept securely, and whether equipment can be child-proofed.

Appearance. Whether scale, materials and colours go well with the domestic surroundings.

■ The Georgian ladies' bureau, with drawers and drop-flap (for writing on and for concealing the mess within) was a precursor of today's home office furniture. Likewise, the Victorian cylinder bureau with its roll-down front, pull-out flap, and doors hiding compartments or drawers.

Figure 12.11 This home office furniture is domestic in character, yet provides the space and accommodates the technology like its commercial counterparts.
Reproduced with the permission of Herman Miller Ltd

Figure 12.12 A home office that flows into the garden. Depending on the task and the weather, work is done at the computer or in a hammock under the tree.

Home furniture is generally expected to be cheaper than that for general office use, and it gets less hard wear. Some of the most popular ranges are 'knock down', but there are manufacturers offering furniture reasonably high in both quality and price; and specialist contractors are providing built-in home offices with a sophistication akin to fitted kitchens.

Normally home office furniture is paid for by the user, and is his responsibility – though his company may contribute towards the cost. If, however, regulations and insurance requirements come to include the home workplace, then the employer may need to be more involved. Corporate responsibility – and the corporate inventory – will spread to cover workplace furniture wherever it may be.

Procuring furniture

Whether choosing a partition or furniture system, a task chair, special furniture for the boardroom or shelving for the home office, the process of selection is similar; even though the difference in scale may be immense. However, since selecting system furniture is so complex, we use it here as a model that may be adapted to simpler situations.

The primary criteria – function, image and budget – are established through considering activities and the spaces they are to occupy, the ambience that is desired and the money that is available. They interplay, so that whereas the budget may call for partial re-use of existing furniture, this may adversely affect the image or corporate culture the company is trying to achieve. How does the practical need to have new furniture for improved efficiency relate to the perceived need for new furniture as a sign of staff being appreciated?

An inventory of existing furniture and equipment (which must be drawn up if it does not exist) should list the quantity, size and – if known – supplier of each item, and describe its general condition: re-usable, refurbishable or past it. By checking this list against future requirements the amount of new furniture needed becomes clear.

User inputs

Involving users in the choice of furniture is even more important than their involvement in the project as a whole. For furniture is – literally – the worker's point of contact with the fit-out. A furniture committee representing users, facilities management and executive interests can consider all aspects of furniture procurement and efficiently reach decisions commanding general support.

However all parties need to understand clearly the criteria and their order of importance in the particular project: whether price takes precedence over comfort and image, or whether task needs must dominate.

Choosing suppliers

Choose furniture that has been around for at least two years. Ask around as to what other people in similar organizations use, and how they rate it.

Geoff Hollington: furniture designer

If an order is very small or specialized, and an existing supplier is considered wholly suitable, then the normal selection process can be bypassed. Otherwise it is desirable to draw up a long list of furniture manufacturers in the first instance. If there is a leap to a shortlist or one name, then an opportunity for significant improvement may be squandered.

The long list can be put together from existing suppliers, suppliers to friends and acquaintances, furniture seen in catalogues or at trade shows, well-known major manufacturers/suppliers and lesser known local firms.

Shortlist

The long list should be reduced to between three and six firms. This can be done by testing each firm against the following criteria:

– *Range.* What range of products the company provides, and for how long they will continue to carry parts and spares.
– *Design.* How functionally designed and robustly made the products are, and how the aesthetic fits the purchaser's company image.
– *Service.* How good the delivery and after sales service are. Whether the installation is carried out by the supplier, by a subcontractor, or in house.
– *Location.* If the firm is reasonably local, and able to be responsive.
– *Financial stability.* If the company is financially stable and likely to continue trading for the foreseeable future.
– *Pre-tender pricing.* Each firm should be asked to provide specifications and budget prices for a limited number of specific items (e.g. four-person workstation cluster, break-out table and a task chair).

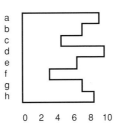

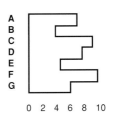

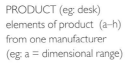

PRODUCT (eg: desk) elements of product (a–h) from one manufacturer (eg: a = dimensional range)

MANUFACTURER rating of manufacturers (A–G) from 0–10 against a single criterion (eg: after sales support)

Figure 12.13 Evaluation of performance criteria.

PRE-TENDER PRICING FOR A WORKSTATION

A medium-sized UK-based company moving to new offices sent out this typical enquiry to about a dozen suppliers in the south of England.

Information required
– specification
– plan of four person workstation cluster
– three-dimensional drawing of cluster
– price, itemized to show costs of: worktop and support, overhead storage, mobile pedestal, panels, electrical and cable management, task lighting, miscellaneous fittings, delivery charges, installation costs, discount
– unit price per workstation (excluding VAT) for an agreed quantity
– details of task chair, including unit price

Design criteria
– worktops to be laminate finish
– 2m run of lockable overhead storage
– one lockable mobile pedestal per unit (one box and one file drawer)
– panel segregation between workstations
– panels to be 1.7m or 1.3m high depending on overhead storage
– cable segregation, electric outlets and task lighting to each workstation

---

For a more detailed appraisal of the shortlisted firms and their products an assessment checklist is useful. Apart from details of the manufacturer and supplier, the list covers all the items in the furniture range. Appendix E shows such a checklist for system furniture; it can be adapted for other situations. Ratings can be shown numerically or as simple bar charts that can be used to compare items or suppliers.

Supplier services

Some suppliers just supply furniture – others provide a one-stop service. In addition to the supply of workstations, special furniture and seating, they may offer services such as:

– feasibility analysis
– space planning and design
– delivery and installation
– design and build
– removals and storage
– refurbishment
– inventory management
– planned maintenance
– leasing.

Design

Most furniture suppliers provide a space-planning service; but as it is based on using their product, design options are limited. The skilled independent designer, working with the user organization to develop a comprehensive design brief, and then using this to plan a specific environment, is likely to have a higher and broader degree of expertise, flair and impartiality. The designer inevitably has a more open judgement on when to select all items from one

■ Utopia: A place where all the workstations are the same, and where the furniture stays put and people get moved around.
A facilities manager

■ In Britain the Furniture Industry Research Association (FIRA) is the principal organization that carries out tests and provides guidelines on all aspects of furniture.

FURNITURE: COMPUTERIZED SERVICES

Computer packages enable the designer or supplier to provide services such as:

Space planning. Layout plans (with elements picked out in colour for clarity).
3D modelling. 'Wire framed' (which just shows the furniture in coloured outline, while leaving the whole space layout visible).
3D graphics. Which appear like colour photographs.
Virtual reality. A simulation of walking through an office, furnished with the selected range.
Tagging. Labelling and bar coding the furniture to provide ownership details.
Scheduling. Providing inventories and maintenance schedules.

'THE VDU DIRECTIVE'

EEC Directive 90/270 covers most aspects of workplace design associated with VDUs. It calls for:

– clear and controllable screen images
– movable base to the screen
– adjustable keyboard height and angle
– document holders
– adequate-sized work surfaces
– low-reflectance surfaces
– stable and adjustable chairs
– footrests
– avoidance of glare, and other environmental discomfort factors
– eye tests
– training in the use of the equipment.

---

range, when to mix suppliers, or when the right solution is built-in furniture.

The furniture designer can provide special pieces to blend with manufactured furniture, or to make a statement about the quality of the company. If such items come direct from a small manufacturer then prices are often competitive with standard items from the big firms; so although the sponsor may be involved to a greater degree, the tailor-made result repays that effort.

Regulations

In Europe regulations are in a stage of transition, with EU standards (CEN) taking over from national ones (for example, the furniture design standard EN 527 partially replaces BS 5940, and brings in common European requirements such as protection from sharp corners and from finger trapping). At times they co-exist, and even contradict.

Electrical regulations vary considerably between Europe and the USA, which means that American systems may not be fully compatible with European requirements (and some European regulations are also more stringent than those in Britain).

However, work surfaces which adjust to provide comfort for larger and smaller people is not a Directive recommendation.

Budget

What will it cost, what can the firm afford and how much did it cost last time? Should the budget alloca-

tion be divided equally between all staff members or should it be allocated according to function – or rank?

A preliminary calculation can be made using rules of thumb, based on a per person cost (high or low) for ordinary staff, double that for top executives, and other managers between these limits. A percentage is then added for special furniture – reception, meeting rooms, restaurant and so on.

For a typical open plan office of several hundred staff the overall cost breakdown might be:

	Per cent
Special furniture	25–30
Desks and worktops	20–25
Screens	20–25
Seating	15
Storage	10

Leasing may have tax advantages, as well as reducing immediate capital expenditure. Some built-in light fixtures may be regarded as furniture for tax assessment.

With furniture costs it is the size of the cheque at the end of the day that counts, not the size of the discount – which, in any event, is often no more than a sales technique. Genuine discounts relate to size of order and sometimes to ease of delivery, as well as to the supplier's desire for the contract.

Trials and mock-ups

Seeing furniture in the showroom provides a general feeling as to whether it is well made and looks right,

```
┌─────────────────────────────────────────┐
│ RULES OF THUMB: WORKSTATION COSTS        │
│                                           │
│ The cost of a workstation varies enor-   │
│ mously and, although as little as £200   │
│ may buy a basic desk, chair and pedestal,│
│ this may not be good value for money.    │
│ The following prices are useful          │
│ indicators.                               │
│                                           │
│                              £ (1995)     │
│ Basic desk, chair and storage      600   │
│                                           │
│ Simple workstation, with a sophisti-     │
│    cated desk, wire management, task     │
│    chair, low screens, floor-standing    │
│    storage                        1700   │
│                                           │
│ Adaptable, sophisticated workstation,    │
│    with complicated chair, screens,      │
│    overhead storage and task light 3750  │
│                                           │
└─────────────────────────────────────────┘
```

but for the shortlisted firms a more detailed evaluation is needed.

'Kicking tyres' is an important element in choosing furniture, with the user group not only representing different interests, but testing for usability. This is particularly necessary where new workstation configurations or space standards are being introduced. Sample furniture can be tested by users in the workplace for at least a week, and their experience then discussed by the group. They should also check that the instructions are clear.

A more thorough approach is to use mock-ups: complete work settings for small groups of people, in which they can carry out their day-to-day work. Mock-ups used for trials cost the supplier quite a lot – which the customer ultimately pays for one way or another. They may be quite simple: a four-person cluster – a standard product to an agreed specification; or complicated – a multisetting grouping in the user's specific finishes. The workstation should also be dismantled, relocated and reassembled by the facilities team to find out how long reconfiguration takes, and how easy it is. If all these tests are to be helpful, the evaluation criteria must be clearly agreed in advance.

The value of mock-ups is political and practical. Political – everyone knows what is going on and feels a part of the decision-making process; practical – the furniture can be checked to see how well it really works for the users, and how easy it is to reconfigure.

Tendering

Tendering should ideally take place against precise information, so that the prices can be squarely compared. Specifications require the smallest detail item-ized, such as lock type; and each fully described item has to be quantified. In 'fast-track' projects this is not always possible, and information may be only indicative. In such cases it is necessary to agree the key parameters – total budget and numbers of people to be accommodated – in order to establish fair price estimates. Detailed specifications and precise prices can then be settled as the contract proceeds (presuming that the manufacturer can supply from stock quickly enough).

Installation

Every furniture contract is different, ranging from a phased installation over weeks or even months as areas in the building are completed, to a single deadline with all 550 workstations up and running the Tuesday after Christmas.

When choosing the manufacturer, it is worth checking that it, and its supplier or installer do have the resources to meet the programme, including sufficient manpower for a swift installation. Where the installation is being carried out in house, the same criteria apply. Installation may comprise all the work, including all cable connections, or simply putting the components together. In the latter case the IT and electrical engineers have then to make their connections, with cost and programme implications.

Dilemmas

■ Under what circumstances is it more desirable for people to move than the furniture?

■ What is the future of loose furniture, as opposed to fixed system furniture? Will the use of basic built-in furniture spread?

■ What are the ergonomic implications of the laptop computer? What is the right furniture for it (seating and work surfaces)?

■ What impact is electronic storage having on the office now? What will it be in the future?

■ If restaurants become more used for other activities, how will their layout and furniture change?

■ What are the likely developments in home office furniture?

■ In what circumstances are the different approaches to selecting furniture valid:
  – a single furniture system, with as few components as possible;
  – combining the old with the new;
  – using domestic and other non-commercial furniture?

PowerGen
Coventry

PowerGen's headquarters near Coventry is an outstanding project. In 'fostering an innovative and entrepreneurial atmosphere', in environmental friendliness and in the elegant understatement of its aesthetic, it could be described as seminal. The sophistication of the whole building design, construction, fit-out and post-contract processes was exceptional, and the result is a pleasure to experience.

PowerGen, one of three major electricity-generating companies in England and Wales, was privatized in 1990. In 1992 a feasibility study recommended that the operations, split over two sites, should be brought together. Although a new building would cost marginally more than refurbishment, the end product and lack of disruption made it worthwhile.

'Working together – working better' as a mission statement or set of values was stated along with the design intent, the main element of which was to sup-

Figure 12.14 The reception area leads to a coffee bar in the first atrium. The stair tower at the end contains further refreshment points. Their slatted screens are more decorative than functional.

DESIGN INTENT

The 1992 feasibility study said that the new building should:

- promote and encourage team working
- encourage communications both within and between business units (BUs)
- provide flexible working space to meet requirements of varied work activities
- recognize the value of people to PowerGen's sustained success
- support the company's evolving culture
- provide a modern, efficient working environment
- allow individuals to influence their immediate environment
- be energy efficient with low running costs
- demonstrate environmental care
- provide a safe and healthy environment
- exploit the potential of new technologies

PETER COOK

Figure 12.15 First floor layout.
Key
1 main entrance at ground floor
2 entrance from 'wet lands' garden
3 service entrance at ground level
4 restaurant over reception
5 kitchen & servery
6 main staircase from reception
7 core
8 business centre tower;
9 cellular office/s
10 open office
11 atrium
12 computer area over facilities centre

Figure 12.16 The double-height reception area can be entered from the car park, or from the 'wetlands' down by a copse. At the opposite end of the building a security entrance doubles as the facility control centre.

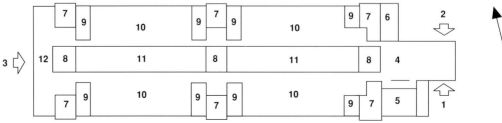

PETER COOK

■ 'I like the fact that I can find people' is a frequent comment.

■ The coffee machines are slow so people have time to talk; and because each node can serve 50 people, that brings members from different departments together.

Figure 12.17 A grand staircase leads up from reception to the restaurant and meeting rooms, allowing all these to be outside the security threshold.

port internal communications and team working. Alan Penn of the University of London carried out a communications analysis of the original Shirley site and of the Westwood project – as a result the building layout was adjusted in order to encourage interaction.

Bennetts Associates, architects for the shell and core and later, Fletcher Priest for the fit-out, were chosen after interviews with shortlists of architects known to have appropriate skills, experience and approach. Laing Midlands won tenders for both shell and fit-out contracts. PowerGen was delighted with the performance of them all.

A single person was central to the whole process, as with all successful projects. In this case it was Suzi Allison, first as facilities manager and later as project manager. She had the ear and confidence of the board, and exceptional relations with all those involved.

The new site, in Westwood Business Park, backs onto countryside. The building sits on it long and low – 85m × 20m and three storeys high. Each floor has two clear floorplates on either side of the full-length atrium. These are joined by staircases and activity centres. Main circulation runs along the edge of the atrium, providing clear routes and opportunities for casual interchange.

The staircase areas contain refreshment points, 'business centres' (for copiers, faxes, mail distribution and stationery), general filing, toilets and IT rooms. Cellular offices and meeting rooms lie alongside these cores, leaving the floorplates clear from front to back. External metal stairs provide the extra escape routes required because of the single internal volume.

The coffee bar is in the atrium, near to reception to encourage casual interaction. So is the library, with informal meeting spaces defined by banks of filing cabinets (topped with decorative asparagus). A grand staircase leads up from the main reception on the east side to the restaurant, and provides exquisite views over the 'wet-lands' landscaped pond to a meadow and copse beyond. The security entrance to the west is also elegant, and doubles as the facility control centre – with post room and monitors for the building management system.

Wood is an important element in the interior – timber staircases with neat black insets, timber slatted screens across the face of the staircase towers at either end of each atrium, and beech work surfaces with a dull lacquer to reduce glare. Colour is subtle – matte white ceilings and walls, grey desking and windows, carpet tiles speckled with beige and yellow and orange – but then a sudden riot of colour in the wall of the café, or the rug in reception by Kate Blee.

Other decoration includes artworks, which were supplied under a tendered contract, general taste parameters having been agreed with the board. In the atrium two 8m weeping figs stand, with their own watering system (and intense lighting which comes on after hours).

This is an environmentally intelligent and energy-conscious building, Naturally ventilated, it has high-level windows which on summer nights open automatically to cool the exposed ceiling slab and provide daytime passive cooling. Double-glazed windows have low-emissivity glass, and blinds and louvres protect the southern facade from summer sun penetration. Only areas that produce a lot of heat are air-conditioned. Heating is by perimeter electric radiators, with some ventilation through floor grilles in central areas. The floor void (generally 45cm) is deep enough to allow full air-conditioning should this prove necessary.

The coffered ceiling encourages daylight into the building, deflects sound, and supports light rafts. These contain both up- and downlighting, acoustic absorption and sprinklers. Artificial lighting operates only as needed (meters on the roof turn outer lights off at a certain threshold level), with users controlling the 'on' function through their telephones.

Such is its level of environmental friendliness that the building has won a 'Very Good' rating under the Building Research Establishment Environmental Assessment Method (BREEAM).

The way the furniture layout was designed was unusual. The users were given a 'space-planning pack' by the facilities department, so that individual and group input was encouraged but structured. Facilities management used software to apportion space, with the ' dead leg' positions by windows being allocated to the more stay-at-home teams (many of the staff work at home one day a week).

The furniture inventory is simple: a workplank; a shaped VDT corner; bubble, half-moon or ironing board extensions; pedestal and drawer units; and panels 110 or 130cm high (or 160cm if positioned at right angles to the windows). The range was chosen after extensive trials, investigation and tendering. Many of the chairs came from Shirley (refurbished over a period of eight months at a cost of about £20 each).

The move took place over Christmas, and though tough, was hitchless; all systems were up and running by 8am on 2 January. Apart from instructing staff carefully by means of interactive videos (now used for new recruits) the move was meticulously planned (Appendix F) and carried out by professionals. People packed and unpacked only the one personal crate they were allowed.

This is a most successful building. It scores highly right across the board, from its elegant landscaping (and discreet car parking), to the intelligence of its building management system. In organizational terms, it has allowed new working patterns to emerge (though the executives remain behind closed doors) and encourages trust and interaction between workers. As an outward statement of an inner intent it describes clearly a business determined to provide quality in a stylish but understated manner.

Interior Architects: Fletcher Priest
Architects (for the building): Bennetts Associates
Management Contractor: Laing Midlands
Project completed: 1994

■ Extra staff were employed to clear obsolete files, with management giving 50p to charity for each bag or box of rubbish.

■ The layout system was very like designing a kitchen on squared paper. Arrows were drawn to indicate movement of chairs and filing drawers, and the rule was 'no crossing of arrows'.

Appendix A
Procurement routes

There are four principal ways of procuring design and construction of buildings (and their interiors), though each has its variants. Two fundamentals are whether design and construction are separated or integrated; and whether prices are arrived at by competitive tendering or negotiation. There are also variations in the distribution of risk.

Traditional

All professional advisers contracted directly to the sponsor. Fees usually a percentage of construction cost, or may be lump sum. Main contractor selected by competitive tender, and subcontractors are contracted to it. Process is normally sequential, with design largely completed before tenders are invited. Process can be accelerated by selecting contractor earlier on (by tender on outline design and indicative descriptions of work, or by negotiation), drawing on its expertise to make the design easily buildable, and starting some work packages early.

- *Suitability*. Good when design solution may be complex and is important to effectiveness of users. Needs adequate preconstruction time for planning and design.
- *Flexibility*. Sponsor has good ability to make changes throughout process (but this freedom can be expensive).
- *Quality*. Possible to achieve very high standards, but needs proper arrangements for quality control during construction.
- *Time*. A potential weakness, but can be satisfactory if well planned. Prone to time overruns.
- *Cost*. Cost control should be an integral part of the process. Tendering produces certain, keen prices and a contract lump sum. Changes during (design and) construction can weaken cost control.
- *Responsibility and risk*. Responsibilities clear and well understood. Risks sensibly divided between the parties. Risks increase if production information is not complete before start of construction.

Fee construction

Design as the traditional method. Construction managed either by a construction manager (a consultant) or by a managing contractor. Each paid by fee, and can be involved during the design to ensure buildability. With construction management approach, separate contractors (usually selected by tender) contract direct with sponsor for individual work packages; with management contracting they contract with management contractor.

- *Suitability*. Good for fitting-out projects, because it combines design quality with project speed. Has advantage of bringing construction experience into design team, which can improve speed and economy of construction.
- *Flexibility*. Similar to traditional route, but cost control may be more difficult.
- *Quality*. Similar to traditional route, but designers have less involvement in quality control during construction.
- *Time*. Allows early start to construction and fast pace throughout project. Resulting operational benefits can outweigh construction cost disadvantages.
- *Cost*. Costs are based on preliminary information, so can be hard to control if design changes much during its later development. A weak aspect.
- *Responsibility and risk*. Responsibilities clear and sensibly divided between designers and constructors; but risk lies largely with sponsor.

Design and manage

Single firm selected (by tender or negotiation) to carry out whole project. It normally guarantees a maximum cost (often with arrangement for sharing any savings between sponsor and itself). It contracts with others to carry out design and construction.

- *Suitability*. Acceptable for projects where sponsor's brief is simple and sponsor has little in-house expertise. A 'one-stop shop'.
- *Flexibility*. Very limited, without uncontrollable changes to quality, time and cost.
- *Quality*. Sponsor has very little control over design, materials or workmanship / or over contractor's choice of designers and subcontractors. May be difficult to assess contractor's abilities in advance of appointing it. A weakness.
- *Time*. Can be fast. Normally includes a guaranteed completion date.

- *Cost*. Tenders may be hard to evaluate, but once agreed cost is guaranteed.
- *Responsibility and risk*. Responsibility lies largely with contractor. Quality risk is with sponsor; all other risks with contractor.

Design and build

Similar to design and manage, but selected contractor carries out at least part of construction itself. In 'develop and construct' variant sponsor appoints designers to produce a brief and outline design. At that point contractors tender on this, and may then be required by sponsor to contract with same designer to develop design ('novation').

- *Suitability*. Similar to design and manage, but sponsor can retain design control.
- *Flexibility*. Similar to design and manage.
- *Quality*. Sponsor has limited control during design, but designers are in position of 'serving two masters'.
- *Time*. Similar to design and manage. Design may take longer, but should bring benefits either in construction or in effectiveness and quality of result.
- *Cost*. Similar to design and manage.
- *Responsibility and risk*. Sponsor has some design responsibility; otherwise responsibilities and risks lie largely with the contractor.

Appendix B
Selection criteria for consultants

Business criteria

- *The firm*. Legal structure / age / size / professional standing.
- *Management*. Management structure (of firm and for project) / qualifications and experience of principals / qualifications and experience of senior managers / general appearance of staff and office.
- *Statutory policies*. Health and safety / quality management.
- *Training*. Programme for staff training (management and technical).
- *Finances*. Last three years' accounts / bank reference / credit references.
- *Insurances*. Professional indemnity cover / attitude to warranties.
- *Location*. Head office / proposed project office.

Project criteria

- *Experience*. Recent experience of similar projects / qualifications and experience of key project personnel / specialist skills (e.g. lighting design).
- *Past projects*. Nature / size / particular characteristics / results / client references.
- *Organization*. Method of work / use of CAD / other relevant technical facilities / liaison with sponsor / with other consultants / with contractors.

- *Understanding*. Knowledge of sponsor's type of business / empathy with sponsor's needs and aspirations.
- *Resources*. Adequate and appropriate staff to meet sponsor's timetable and other needs.
- *Regulations*. Thorough understanding of relevant regulations / efficient handling of regulatory process.

Performance criteria

- *Project results*. Achievements in terms of quality, budgets and timetables / awards.
- *Failures*. Claims history / litigation record.

GATHERING INFORMATION

It is easy to ask the wrong questions (or ask them in the wrong way), or simply to ask too many. Useful guidelines are listed below.

Decide on the project priorities (and thus the weighting to be given to the answers).
Give enough background information about the sponsor and the project so that answers can be made relevant.
Phrase the questions clearly and unambiguously.
Only asks questions that affect your decision.
Do not ask a question unless you can evaluate the answer.

Appendix C
Data collection

Initial data is historical, but as the briefs develop they require increasingly detailed and comprehensive information. The range is wide:

Objectives

- *Goals and targets*. Organizational / operational / financial / physical.
- *Aspirations*. Corporate / departmental / individual.

Context and issues

- *Operational data*. Departmental functions and structures / departmental sizes / growth (and shrinkage) estimates / linkages (internal and external) / support facilities required / environmental requirements / space, furniture and equipment standards / predicted process and technological developments.
- *Resources*. Finance / premises / staff availability / time.
- *Ownership data*. Title deeds, leases and covenants / warranties and guarantees / insurances / facili-

ties and maintenance contracts.
- *Statutory regulations*. Planning and building (including energy conservation) / health and safety / employer and employee / public liability (and the authorities which administer all these).
- *Utilities*. Drainage / water / gas / electricity / telecommunications.
- *Physical records*. Physical surveys / as-built drawings, specifications and schedules / furniture and other inventories / operating costs / maintenance schedules and costs.
- *Professional advisers*. Accountants, bankers, lawyers, insurance brokers / surveyors and quantity surveyors, architects, engineers, interior and industrial designers / specialists (e.g. catering, lighting, artworks).
- *Suppliers*. Construction materials and equipment – furniture and furnishings / office equipment.
- *Contractors*. General works, building services, landscape / specialists (e.g. lifts, IT) / operators (e.g. catering).
- *Representative bodies*. Staff clubs and trades unions / community groups / relevant professional or trade associations.

Appendix D
Space-planning benchmarks

Recent examples of space-planning standards

Type of space Open/enclosed		Area (m²)	Number of units	Capacity (people)	Usage ratio
Computer company					
General workspace					
Meetings office	E	6.8		10	1:1 (mainly)
Salesman's office	E	4.6	26	1	3:1
Workstation					
Secretarial/admin	O	9.3	3	2	1:1
Other	O	4.6	29	1	1:1
Cluster	O	30.0	4	4	25:1
Phonebooth	E	2.2	6	1	15:1
Break-out area	O	10.0		6	15:1
Personal storage		0.5	87		1:1

Total number of seats 137   Total staff 87 mobile
32 static

Type of space Open/enclosed		Area (m²)	Number of units	Capacity (people)	Usage ratio
Ancillary and support spaces					
Reception		28.0			
Customer ante room		70.0			
Kitchen/pantry		14.0			
Theatre		93.0		75–100	
Group room		35.0		25	
		23.0		10–12	
		14.0		6–8	
		9.3		2–4	
Demonstration room		14.0			
Storage/staging		14.0			

Management consultancy

Workstation/office:

Partners	E	13.9			
Principal managers	O	9.3			
Senior managers	O	7.8			
Other permanent staff	O	7.0			
Temporary staff	O	5.6			

Government office

Workstation/office:

Head of department	E	20.0			
Managerial	E	15.0			
Professional/secretarial	E/O	9.0			
Admin/clerical	O	6.0			

These figures include a desk area, local storage, a designated meeting table if appropriate, and secondary circulation.

Oil company

Workstation/office:

Director	E	28.0			
Manager	E	19.0–28.0			
Executive	E	9.3–14.0			
Professional	E/O	Up to 7.0			
Overall space allocation		16.0–21.0			

Mainly cellular, with 'activity centres' combining work, meeting and informal areas, with supplies, storage, reference, fax and printer.

Appendix E
Assessment checklist for system furniture

Based on criteria by Wes McGregor of the Cochrane
McGregor Group
The criteria should be weighted.

	Criteria
Company	Location of manufacturing base
	Ability/willingness to provide specials
	After sales support
	Speed of response
	Future product development
	Technical standards
	Ecological policies
	Financial stability
Supplier	Manuacturer, supplier, or agent
	Local distribution depot
	Local supplier – quality of support
	Availability of other services
	Directly employed installation team
	Reconditioning service
	Maintenance training programme
	Leasing facilities
Range	Includes all items required
	Dimensional range
	Adaptability
	Ready assembled, or 'knock down'
	Metal or timber based
	Integral task lighting
	Integral environmental controls
	Fire and water damage resistant
	Availability and suiteing of locks
	Image appropriate to organization
	Conformity to regulations (national, international)
	Specials at no extra cost
	Performance guarantee
	Good immediate (and continuing) delivery
	Continuity of supply
Finishes	Choice of worktop finish
	Anti-glare finishes
	Range of finishes
	Range of fabrics
	Continuity of finishes and fabrics

	Criteria
Maintenance	Ease of cleaning
	Wearing quality of soft surfaces
	Ease of replacement of fabrics
	Ease of floor cleaning underneath
	High interchangeability of components
	Low reconfiguration costs
	Ease of in-house reconfiguration
	Ease of storage
	Durability
Desking	Dimensional range
	Flexibility for planning
	Availability of handed work surfaces
	Panel hung work surfaces
	Desk-mounted overhead storage
	Height (and slope) adjustability
	Levelling adjustment (quality andease)
	Construction – frame, finishes and trim
Desk wire management	Lay-in
	Ease of access
	Two channel separation
	Junctions and radii
	Vertical ducting
	Power, data, voice outlets
	Ease of relocation and expansion
	Supplier installation
Desk pedestals	Range of pedestals
	Mobile pedestals
	Range of internal fittings and accessories
	Construction – frame, finishes and trim
	Drawer mechanism quality
Panels	Dimensional range
	Variable height availability
	Acoustic performance
	Curved or glazed options
	Ease of assembly
	Levelling adjustment (quality and ease)
	Construction – frame, finishes and trim
	Panel hung accessories
Panel wire management	Lay-in
	Ease of access

Criteria

	Two channel separation
	Ease of relocation and expansion
Panel hung storage	Dimensional range
	Range of internal fittings and accessories
	Filing systems (lateral/pull-out)
	Construction – frame, finishes and trim
	Fixings to panels
	Door mechanism quality
Other storage	Dimensional range
	Height range
	Range of internal fittings and accessories
	Filing systems (lateral/pull-out)
	Coat storage
	Wire management – yes/no
	Levelling adjustment (quality and ease)
	Capability of relocation while loaded
	Construction – frame, finishes and trim
	Fixing to panel
	Pitch of fixings
	Location of handle and lock
	Interchangeability of back panel

Criteria

Task chair	Five-star base
	Dual wheel casters
	Gas-lift seat height adjustment
	Lumbar support and back adjustment
	Reclining function
	Arm adjustability (height and width)
	Placing of controls
	Ease of adjustment
	Softness
	Quality – construction and finish
	Range of fabrics
Side chair	Size
	Softness
	Quality – construction and finish
	Range of fabrics
	Stackability
Lounge chair	Size
	Lumbar support
	Reclining function
	Softness
	Quality – construction and finish
	Range of fabrics
Special items	Consistency with system
	Quality of design
	Quality – construction and finish

Appendix F
PowerGen – Coventry Procedures for building occupation

The move from Shirley to Westwood Park took place from 23 December 1994 to 2 January 1995. The stated principles and guidelines were:

Objectives
- [ ] provide continuity
- [ ] minimize disruption
- [ ] vacate Shirley for disposal

Approach
- [ ] single phase
- [ ] reduction of business continuity risk
- [ ] use of business unit (BU) move co-ordinators
- [ ] selection of experienced commercial move contractor

Ground rules
Packing
- [ ] working files to be packed and unpacked by move contractor
- [ ] personal crates limited to one per person
- [ ] working files to be unpacked by 2 January 1995
- [ ] personal files to be unpacked by 6 January 1995

Information technology

- [ ] removal contractor to transfer IT equipment, including:
  - ○ virus check PCs
  - ○ full hardware testing
  - ○ check of system access
- [ ] BU supervision of testing must have executive director support

Vacation of Shirley

- [ ] only furniture and equipment planned into accommodation to be moved
- [ ] items for disposal to be dealt with prior to the move or handed to the facilities department for disposal

Access

- [ ] Shirley premises to be cleared by 1.30pm, 23 December 1994
- [ ] IT services withdrawn from 12.30pm
- [ ] prior authorization required from move manager for access to sites during move period
- [ ] Westwood open from 8.00am on 3 January 1995

Role of the business unit move co-ordinators

- [ ] empowered to make move decisions on behalf of their business unit
- [ ] single point of responsibility for move, planning and execution
- [ ] single point of contact between BU and move manager
- [ ] communication of all instructions to BU staff
- [ ] ensuring compliance with programmes, rules and procedure

Day one support

- [ ] 'help desk' and trouble-shooters
- [ ] provision of effective signage
- [ ] 'Day One Pack'
- [ ] building user services guide

Summary of day one successes

- [ ] unpacking complete (except personal crates)
- [ ] IT and telephone systems fully operational
- [ ] business centres stocked and operational
- [ ] all meeting facilities available
- [ ] support services available and services directory issued
- [ ] post distribution as normal

Project team responsibilities

Business continuity

- [ ] provide access to London for essential services
- [ ] manage early moves to Westwood
- [ ] plan for contingencies
- [ ] fully test PCs, printers, etc.

Staff disruption

- [ ] manage the packing/unpacking of working files
- [ ] establish an effective labelling system
- [ ] provide packing guidance and safety awareness

Vacation of Shirley

- [ ] manage the clearance of the site

Business unit responsibilities

Business continuity

- [ ] appoint move co-ordinator
- [ ] compliance with agreed rules, procedures and programmes

Staff disruption

- [ ] reduce amount of storage
- [ ] pack and unpack personal crates

Vacation of Shirley

- [ ] identify and dispose of surplus or redundant BU owned equipment prior to the move.

glossary

BMS	Building management system
BS	British Standard
CAD	Computer-aided design
Caddie	Mobile pedestal unit for personal storage (also: puppy)
CAFM	Computer-aided facilities management
Carrel	A screened booth for quiet study (America)
CCTV	Closed circuit television
CEN	European Committee for Standardization
Churn (rate)	(Frequency of) changes in staff, or in interior layouts
CIE	Commission Internationale de l' Eclairage (international body for lighting standards)
Construction manager	A consultant appointed to manage parallel construction contracts, see Chapter 8
dB	Decibel: the measure for sound – also dB(A)
DECT	Digital European Cordless Telecommunications
Developer standard	See Chapter 8
DIN	Deutsche Industrie Normal (German standard – cf: BS)
DTP	Desk-top publishing
Facilities manager	Person responsible for maintaining and operating (business) premises, and providing a range of associates services
Fitting-out	Designing and installing the internal parts of a building (especially a commercial one), often including the furnishing
Free address	First-come first-served workstations (also: Hot desking)
Fully fitted	See Chapter 8
GIA	Gross internal area, see Chapter 9
Hot desking	See: free address
Hoteling	Phoning in to reserve a workspace (also: JIT)
HVAC	Heating, ventilating and air-conditioning
ISDN	Integrated services digital network (special digital telephone line for fast data transmission)
ISO	International Standards Organization
IT	Information technology
JIT	Just in time – an industrial logistics concept (see: hoteling)

Lamp	An artificial light source (e.g. 'light bulb', fluorescent tube)
Luminaire	Light fitting
Lux	Lumens/m² – a measure of the amount of light falling on a plane (in offices, taken as the horizontal plane at desk-top height)
Management contractor	See Chapter 8
NIA	Net internal area, see Chapter 9
NLA	Net lettable area, see Chapter 9
Novation	Transferring the sponsor's contractual relationship with a designer to the contractor
NUA	Net usable area, see Chapter 9
PBX	Private branch exchange (telephone switchboard)
PCS	Personal communications services (telephone numbers allocated to people, not places)
Project manager	Person appointed to plan, organize and energize a project, see Chapter 8
Puppy	See caddie
RH	Relative humidity
RSI	Repetitive strain injury
SBS	Sick-building syndrome – 'an excess of work-related irritation of the skin and mucous membranes' (World Health Organization)
Shell and core	See Chapter 8
Smart card	Plastic card with embedded computer chip containing information/instructions (cf: swipe card)
SoHo	Small office–home office
SON	High pressure sodium discharge lamp
Swipe card	Magnetized plastic card encoded to act as a key or pass (cf: smart card)
Telecommuting	Working at a remote location, but linked to the main office by telematics (also: teleworking)
Telematics	All forms of telecommunications and information technology (often combined)
Teleworking	See: telecommuting
ULD	Upper limb disorder (a workplace injury)
VAV	Variable air volume (air-conditioning system)
VDT	Visual display terminal – computer viewing screen (also: monitor, VDU)
VDU	Visual display unit
Virtual	Community/office/team – in various locations, but unified by IT

references

Bailey, S (1990) *Offices: A Briefing and Design Guide*, Butterworth Architecture, London.

Barrett, P (ed) (1995) *Facilities Management: Towards Best Practice*, Blackwell Science, Oxford.

Bear, G (ed) (1994) *The Guide to Better Decisions in Facilities Management*, CML Data, Croydon.

Becker, F (1990) *The Total Workplace*, Van Nostrand Reinhold, New York.

Bion, W R (1961) *Experiences in Groups*, Tavistock Publications, London.

British Council for Offices (1994) *Specification for Urban Offices*, Publishing Business, London.

Clamp, H and Cox, S (1989) *Which Contract?* RIBA Publications, London.

Cleland, D I and King, W R (1975) *Systems Analysis and Project Management*, 2nd edn, McGraw-Hill Kogakusha, Tokyo.

Coles, K and Kiernan, T (1994) *Relocation and Managing Premises*, National Council for Voluntary Organizations, London.

Crane, R and Dixon, M (1991) *Office Spaces: Architects' Data Sheets*, Architecture, Design & Technology Press, London.

Duffy, F (Hannay, P ed) (1992) *The Changing Workplace*, Phaidon Press, London.

Duffy, F, Laing, A and Crisp, V (1993) *The Responsible Workplace*, Butterworth Architecture, Oxford.

Eley, J and Marmot, A (1995) *Understanding Offices*, Penguin Books, London.

Gardner, C and Hannaford, B (1993) *Lighting Design*, The Design Council, London.

Graf, J (1983) *The Office Book*, Frederick Muller, London.

Gray, C, Hughes, W and Bennett, J (1994) *The Successful Management of Design*, Centre for Strategic Studies in Construction, Reading.

Hall, E T (1966) *The Hidden Dimension*, Doubleday, New York.

Hampden-Turner, C (1994) *Corporate Culture*, Judy Piatkus, London.

Harper, D R (1978) *Building: The Process and the Product*, Construction Press, Lancaster.

Harris, D A, *et al.* (1991) *Planning and Designing the Office Environment*, Van Nostrand Reinhold, New York.

Hartkopf, V, *et al.* (1993) *Designing the Office of the Future – The Japanese Approach to Tomorrow's Workplace*, John Wiley, New York.

Hofstede, G (1984) *Culture's Consequences*, Sage Publications, Beverly Hills, CA.

Joedicke, J (1985) *Space, Form and Architecture*, Karl Kramer, Stuttgart.

Jones Lang Wootton (1994) *The City Research Project: Property Occupational Trends by the Financial Services Sector in London*, London Business School and the Corporation of London, London.

Kerr, P (1995) *Gridiron*, Chatto & Windus, London.

Kinsman, F (1990) *Millenium: Towards Tomorrow's Society*, W H Allen, London.

Kleeman, W B (1991) *Interior Design of the Electronic Office*, Van Nostrand Reinhold, New York.

Kurtich, J and Vodvarka, F (1992) *Interior Architecture*, Van Nostrand Reinhold, New York.

Lam, W M C (1977) *Perception and Lighting as Formgivers for Architecture*, McGraw-Hill, New York.

Malnar, J M and Vodvarka F (1992) *International Interior Design*, Van Nostrand Reinhold, New York.

Malnar, J M and Vodvarka F (1992) *The Interior Dimension*, Van Nostrand Reinhold, New York.

Maslow, A H (1954) *Motivation and Personality*, Harper & Brothers, New York.

Naisbitt, J (1994) *Global Paradox*, Nicholas Brearley Publishing, London.

Neufert, E (Jones, V ed) (1980) *Architects' Data*, 2nd edn, Blackwell Science, Oxford.

Olins, W (1990) *The Wolff Olins Guide to Corporate Identity*, Design Council, London.

O'Reilly, J J N (1987) *Better Briefing Means Better Buildings*, Building Research Establishment, Watford.

Palmer, M A (1981) *The Architect's Guide to Facilities Programming*, McGraw Hill, New York.

Panero, J and Zelnick, M (1979) *Human Dimension and Interior Space*, John Wiley, New York.

Prior, J J (ed) (1993) *BREEAM/New Offices – Version 1/93*, 2nd edn, Building Research Establishment, Watford.

Public Buildings and Works, Ministry of (1966) *Activity Data Method*, HMSO, London.

Pulgram, W L and Stone, R E (1984) *Designing the Automated Office*, Whitney Library of Design, New York.

Quinan, J (1987) *Frank Lloyd Wright's Larkin Building*, MIT Press, New York.

Rappoport, J E, Cushman, R F and Daroff, K (1992) *Office Planning and Design Desk Reference*, John Wiley, New York.

Rayfield, J K (1994) *The Office Interior Design Guide*, John Wiley, New York.

Raymond, S and Cunliffe, R (1994) *A Design Guide for the Provision of Company Restaurants*, Eclipse Group, London.

Ross, P (1995) *The Cordless Office*, Morgan Lovell, London.

Rossbach, S (1987) *Interior Design with Feng Shui*, Penguin Arkana, New York.

Rowbotham, P (1985) *Dealing Room Design*, IBC, London.

Russell, B (1983) *Designers' Workplaces*, Whitney Library of Design, New York.

Sampson, A (1995) *Company Man*, HarperCollins, London.

Saxon, R (1994) *The Atrium Comes of Age*, Longman, Harlow.

Scuzi, P (1995) *Design of Enclosed Spaces*, Chapman & Hall, London.

Sommer, R (1969) *Personal Space*, Prentice-Hall, Englewood Cliffs, NJ.

Stocker, P and Howarth, A (1992) *Office Design and Planning*, HMSO, London.

Sundstrom, E (1986) *Work Places*, Cambridge University Press, New York.

Tannen, D (1995) *Talking from 9 to 5*, Virago Press, London.

Tutt, P and Adler, D (1985) *New Metric Handbook*, Architectural Press, London.

Tweedy, D B (1986) *Office Space Planning and Management*, Quorum Books, New York.

Williams, A (ed) (1994) *Specification 94*, EMAP Business Publishing, London.

Williams, S (1989) *Hong Kong Bank*, Jonathan Cape, London.

Wilson, S (1985) *Premises of Excellence*, Business User Studies, London.

Wineman, J D (ed) (1986) *Behavioral Issues in Office Design*, Van Nostrand Reinhold, New York.

Women's Design Service (1993) *Accessible Offices*, Women's Design Service, London.

Worthington, J and Konya, A (1988) *Fitting Out The Workplace*, Architectural Press, London.

This list covers books only. Neither magazine articles nor unpublished material are included, although both provided valuable sources.

Page numbers appearing in bold indicate illustrations, together with their captions

Accessibility considerations 87, 88, 134, 158
Accessories 144
Accommodation planning committee/team 29, 105, 114
Acoustic design 38, 159–61
    examples 8, **95**, 116
Activities 33–43
    character of 33–4
    collective activities **34**, **41**
    congenial activities 36, **41**
    group activities 34, **41**
    operational needs 36, 37, 37–41
    physical needs 37–41
    psychosocial needs 41–3
    regulatory aspects 37
    social activities 36, **41**
    solo activities 34, **41**
    symbolic aspects 37
    types 34, **35**
Adjacency matrix **126**
Advising 26
Aeron chair **171**
Air conditioning, see HVAC
Air flows 157–8
Ambience 81–93
    aims 81–2
    corporate aspects 82–5
    physical aspects 87–93
    psychological aspects 85–7
Ambient messages **82**
Ancillary spaces 59, 65
Andersen Consulting [London] 114–17
Anthropometrics 39, 88
Apicella Associates **143**
Architectural lighting 146, 155
Archives 70
Area measurement 120
Aromatherapy 89
Artificial light 154–6
Artworks 85, **87**, 117, 144–5, 176, 187
Arup Associates **74**, **145**
Association of British Insurers [London] **49**
Atria **28**, **43**, 46–7, 56–7, 74, 80–1, **166–7**, 184
    effect on space planning 122
    plants in **43**, 144, 187
    and ventilation 7, **49**, 157
Auditoria 69, **70**
Aukett Associates viii, 1, 4–8, 46–7, 54–6, **57**, **73**
Austin-Smith Lord 65, 70, 84, 87, 92, 144, 145, 146, 176
Automobile Association [Basingstoke] **118–19**

Barr & Stroud·[Glasgow] 78–9

Behavioural science 21
Bennetts Associates **170–1**, 184–7
BHP Petroleum Ltd [London] **53**, **132–3**
Bissett Adams **17**
Blairlogie Capital Management [Edinburgh] **176**
Blinds 143
Boardrooms 63, **86**, 176
Bomb threats 52, 76, 144
Booths 61
Boxes, soundproof 63
Break-out areas/spaces **34**, **38**, 65, 78, **90**
British Airways Compass Centre [Heathrow] 46–7, 54–6, **57**, **73**
British Council offices **68**, **97**
British Council for Offices, Specification for Urban Offices 119
BT (British Telecom) Westside [Hemel Hempstead] viii–1, 4–8
Bubble diagram **126**
Building management systems 164–5
Building services 151–65
    acoustic control 159–61
    HVAC systems 156–9
    information technology requirements 164–5
    lifts and escalators 162
    lighting 152–6
    plumbing 161–2
    power distribution 161
Buildings
    depth of floorplate **123**
        characteristics resulting 123
    fabric and services 124
    factors affecting suitability 121, **122**
    life spans of constituents **123**
    plan form and dimensions 122, **125**
    refit/build choice 107
    selection criteria **121**
    structure 123–4
    types 121
    vertical dimensions **124**
Bürolandschaft 24
Business functions
    direct functions 26, **27**
    indirect functions 26–7
Business IT systems 164

Cable & Wireless [London] 65, **70**, 84, **87**, 92, **145**
Cabling and cable management 7, 45, 55, 123, 134–5, 164, 175
CAD workstations 63
Cafés/restaurants vii, 4, 5–6, 30, 71–2, **71**, 95, 166, 176, 178–9
Caring culture 12
Carpets 76, 131, 139, 140–1, 160
CDP (Collett Dickenson Pearce) [London] **25**, 62, **138**
Ceilings 138–9
    finishes 139, 141

heights 123–4
    light fittings 145–6
Cellnet [Slough] 68
Cellular offices 14, **42**, 58–9, 61, 85, 114, **115–16**
Centralized offices 23
Chadwick Group 114–17
Chairs 41, 60, **171**, 172
Change 11, **12**
Chemical Bank [London] 140
Chiat/Day [New York] iv–v, 94–6
Churn costs 14, 51, 130
Circulation routes/spaces 50–1, 59, 76–7, 127
    widths recommended 128
'Club' environment 18, **20–1**, 25
Clubrooms/bars 73
Collective activities **34**, **41**
    spaces for 61–2
Colour
    appearance 153
    schemes 91, 93
    specification **92–3**
    temperature 153
Communicating, different ways 47
Communications 26, 47–53
    executive **14**
    face-to-face 41–2, 53
    kinds 48–9
Completion levels [for office development] 101
Computer conferencing 64
Conference rooms **64**, **70**, 176
    see also Meeting areas/rooms
Confidentiality 42, 43
Congenial activities 36, **41**
Construction stages 111–12
Contract administration 111
Contractor selection 110–11, 169
Contracts 110
Controlling/regulating activities 26
Cooling and heating 158–9, **158**
Cordless systems 30, 135, 164, 165, 175
Cores [of buildings] 124, **125**
Corridors 51, **53**, 76, 127, **149**
Courtyards 74
Creating/creativity 26
Crèches 73–4
Crisis centre [Heathrow] **54–5**, 56
Curtains 143

Data transmission and storage 48–9
Davies Baron 46–7, 54–6, **57**, **73**
Daylight 153–4
    control methods **154**
De Beers [Ascot] **135**
Decentralized offices 23
Decorative lighting 156
Defence Research Agency Haslar [Gosport] **32–3**, 44–5
DEGW **16**, **136**, 140
Delicatessen shops 72–3

Delivery areas 52, 77
Design brief
    building 108–9, 125, 184
    furniture 181–2
Design Images 78–9
Design stages 109–10
    concept stage 109, 128, **129**
    construction/production
        information 110, 129
    development stage 110, 128
    scheme design 109–10
Developer standard [level of
    completion] 101
Digital Equipment Company
    [Stockholm] 29–30, 112, 163,
    165
Dining rooms 72, **136**
Disabled people, and office design 52,
    68, 76, 87, 88
Dispersed working 4, 21–2
Diversified Agency Services [London]
    9
Domestic/lounging furniture **20–1**, **29**,
    37, 66, **73**, 85, **95**
Door matting 141
Doors 137
Downlighters 7, 45, 145, 155, **155**, **156**
Drawing offices **23**, **24**, 63
    see also Studios

E-mail 15, 48
Eating areas 72, 78, 178–9
    see also Cafés/restaurants; Dining
        rooms; Refreshment areas;
        Venderettes
Electronic communications 48–9
Electronic filing, advantages
    /disadvantages 49
Electronic meetings, see Video
    conferencing
Electronic patching 51, 164
Emergency lighting 156
Encounters 53
Energis [Reading] **13**
Entrances/exits 52–3
Ergonomics 39–41, **40**
Ernst & Young [Chicago] **24**, **37**, **42**,
    49, **61**, 148, **149**
Ernst & Young [London] **144**
Escalators **46–7**, **75**, 76, 162
Executive communications 14
Executive office furniture 176
Eye contact 87–9

Face-to-face communications 14, 41–2,
    53
    distances 88, **89**
Facilities management 14–15
    IT systems used 165
    project involvement 100, 108
Feng-shui 87
Fibre-optic cables 164
Filing centres/units 45, 65, **118–19**

dimensions **137**
Finishes 139–41
FIRA (Furniture Industry Research
    Association) 182
Fire alarms 145, 162–3
Fire escape routes 78, 124, **128**, 163
Fire precautions 43, 52, 162–3
Fitness/health centres 73
Fitting-out 101, 102, 111–12
Fletcher Priest **20–1**, **38**, **58–9**, **75**,
    121, **170–1**, 184–7
Flexibility 2, 49
Floor loadings 124, 134
    measurement units used 120
Floors
    accessibility 134
    finishes 134, 139–41
    permeability 134
    raised floor systems 123, 124, 134
Flowers and plants 19, 144, **146**
Foster and Partners, Sir Norman
    10–11, **18–19**, 88
Free-address working **vi**, 39, 43, 66,
    94–6, 163
Freestanding furniture 173
Freestanding lights 147, 155
Furniture 171–83
    assessment criteria 180–1, **181**,
        192–3
    costs 182, 183
    freestanding 173
    installation 183
    mock-ups 131, 182–3
    procurement procedures 180–3
    requirements 38–9, 171–2
    selection procedures 45, 130–1,
        180–1, 187
    special 175–9
    supplier services 181, 182
    system 174–5, **192–3**
    types 172

Gardens 74
Glaxo Holdings [London] **51**, **62–3**
GMW Partnership **49**
Gold collar workers 2, 22, 45
Good manners 87
Goods lifts 77, 162
Graves, Robert **83**
Green issues 83, 84
Grids, office building 127–8, **129**
Grimshaw & Partners, Nicholas **46–7**,
    54–6, **57**, **73**, **150–1**, **166–9**
Group activities 34, **34**, 41
    size **35**
    spaces for 62–4, 125
Growth measures 12
Guild, Trisha **91**

Hairdressers 73
Harper Mackay **24**, **25**, **62**, **64**, **76**, **83**,
    90, **138**, **139**, **142**, **147**, **178**
Hearing 89–90, **89**

Heathrow Airports Ltd [London] 16
Heating systems 7–8, 45, 158–9, **158**,
    187
Herman Miller Ltd **174**, **175**, **179**
Herron Associates **28**
Hierarchy of [human] needs **21**, 22–3
Hillier, William 53
Historical models of the office 23–4
Home working 4, **23**, **35**, 77
    furniture selection 179–80
Hongkong & Shanghai Bank
    headquarters 88
Hopkins & Partners, Michael **vi–vii**, **52**
'Hot desks' 4, 85, 164
Hoteling approach [to office] 25, **42**,
    60, 115, 148, 164
Human aspirations **21**
HVAC (heating [and cooling]/
    ventilating/air conditioning)
    systems 55, 156–9
    comfort requirements 156–7
    controllability 130, 157
    economic considerations 157
    noise 158

IBM [London] **vi–vii**, **52**
Illuminance 152–3
Image 84–5
Images transmission 49
Imagination [London] **28**
Induction training 112, 187
Information, movement of 48–9
Information technology 48–9
    and building services 164–5
    effects 13–14, 21, 24
Inkinen, Jari 66–7
Intelligent building, meaning of term
    164, 187
Interaction, between individuals 41
Ironmongery 141–2

Jestico + Whiles **68**, **97**, **176**
Joronsen, Liisa 66, 67

Kelly Design, Ben **86**
Keyboard operators, ergonomics 39,
    41
Kinaesthetics 88
Kitchenettes 65, 179
Kitchens 72, 179
Knowledge resource centres 69

Laird Partnership, Michael **39**, **43**
Lamp types 154–5
    characteristics **155**
    colour temperatures listed 153
Landscaped offices 24, 144
Learning [as business function] 27
Learning organizations 25
Legibility 83, 117
Leo Burnett [London] **20–1**, **38**, **58–9**,
    75, 121, 162
Libraries 69

Lifts/lift lobbies 76, 124, 162
Light, characteristics 152–3
Light fittings
    architectural lighting 146, 155
    ceiling fittings 145–6, 155
    characteristics **155**
    freestanding lights 147, 155
    lamps suitable **156**
    task lights 147, 155
    wall fittings 146–7
Lighting levels
    age effects 153
    typical values 153
Lighting requirements 37, 64
Lighting systems 152–6
    controls 7, 55, 130, 156, 187
    examples 7, 45, 55, 79, 116, 130,
        140, 142, 147
    maintenance 156
Lighting track systems 156
Linkage ring **125**, 126
Lloyds Bank [Bristol] **74**, **145**
Location [of office] 23
Locationless working, see Free-address
    working
London Underground Limited [Canary
    Wharf] **31**
Loth, Dale **23**
Luminaires, see Light fittings
Lynne Franks PR Ltd **86**

Mail rooms 69–70, **131**
Maintenance, lighting systems 156
Management 26
Measurements 2
    metric–imperial conversions 120
    space planning 120–1
Medical centres 70
Meeting areas/rooms **9**, 37, **62–3**,
    63–4, **91**, 176–8
Meeting points 53, 62
Mercury Communications [London]
    146
Mobile offices 23, 24
Mobility 51–2, 82–3
Morgan Lovell **129**
Movement
    patterns 50, **50**, 127
    types 48-9
Moving in 112
    examples 8, 45, 130, 187, 193–4
Munsell Colour System **92**
    example of colour specifications **93**
Murray Symonds Associates **13**, **51**,
    53, **62–3**, **132–3**
Music, piped 30, 89, 160

Natural Office [DEC, Stockholm] 29,
    30
Natural ventilation 157, 187
    and daylight **154**
    heating/cooling modes 158
    and noise 158

Negotiating 26
Newsagents 73
Noise control strategies 160
Noises and sounds 38, 89–90, 158,
    159
    sources **159**
    transmission paths **160**

Objects, movement of 48
Off-site working 4, 114, 148
Office
    concepts 23–6, **23**
    meaning of term 21
    reasons for having 22–3
OFTN (office for the nineties) concept
    114, 115
Old buildings, underfloor wiring 123,
    134–5
Organizational scenarios **11**
Orientation, usage of signs 52
ORMS **50**, 80–1, **134**, **135**
Outsourcing [of facilities] 15

Paper movement 48
Paper-processing centres **8**, 65, 114
Partition systems 136, 137, **137**
    noise paths around **160**
Passages [in open plan space] **8**, 77
Peace and quiet 38, 43
Penn, Alan 53, 186
People
    movement of 48
    and organizations 11–12
Personal lockers, see Storage, mobile
Personalization [of workplace] 85–6
Pesce Ltd **iv–v**, 94–6
Plant [machinery] rooms 75
Plants and flowers 19, 144, **146**
Plumbing 161–2
Polarities of change **12**
Pool spaces 61–2
Power distribution 161
PowerGen [Coventry] **170–1**, 184–7,
    193–4
Predesign stage 101–9
Presentation rooms 64, 69, **70**, **134**
Primary spaces 59, 60–4
Pringle Brandon **9**, **31**, **140**
Privacy 43, 86–7
Private offices **42**, 61, 114, 130
Procurement routes [for building
    work] 103, 188–9
Project
    briefing process 107–9
    business plan 107
    causes 101
    closing down 113
    design brief 107, 108–9
    leadership 102–3
    management 102
    monitoring and control 106–7
    participants 100
    planning 103

process flow charts **99**, **104**
procurement routes 103, 188–9
promoting/selling 107
responses 101
review/feedback 113
scope 101
start-up 105–6
strategic brief 105, **106**, 107–8
task matrix **105**
team selection 103, 105, 169, 189
user involvement 29, 66, 82, 108
Property costs 14–15
Proximity 41–2
Prudential Assurance [London] **136**,
    140
Psychosocial considerations 41–3,
    85–7
Purposes [of offices] 21–3

Quiet rooms 73

Reception areas 52–3, 68–9, 176
    examples **20–1**, **37**, **56–7**, **62**, **84**,
        132–3, **146**, **147**, **184–5**
Reception desks/modules **49**, **52**, 68,
    79, **143**, **144**, 175–6
Refreshment areas/points **38**, 65, 179,
    184
    see also Cafés/restaurants
Refuges [from bomb/fire threats] 52,
    76, 163
Regulations 110, 143, 152, 156, 182
Reprographic units 70
Research and development 27
Resource use 27
Restaurants, see Cafés/restaurants
RSI (repetitive strain injury) 39
Rules of thumb
    accessibility 88
    anthropometrics 39
    circulation 128
    colour 91
    IT and telephone cabling networks
        164
    libraries 69
    lifts 162
    lighting levels 153
    measurement conversions 120
    power distribution 161
    sound reduction 160
    workstation costs 183
Running-in [of new offices] 112–13
Ryder Nicklin Partnership 78–9

Sawyer Architects 44–5
Security arrangements 43, 52, 68, 163
Senses and distance **89**
Sensory aspects [of design] 87–93
Serveries **5**, 72, **140**, 178–9
Service spaces 59, 74–5
Service terminals 133, 141
Settings 133–47
Shared desks/workstations 4, 18, 60–1,

66, 114
Shell-and-core development 101
Shops [in offices] 72–3
Signage 52, 145
Smart/swipe cards **49**, 53, 163
Smell 88–9
Smoking rooms 7, 115
Social activities 36, **41**
Social spaces 59, 71–4
Sol Cleaning Service [Helsinki] 66, **67**
Solar control 55, 143, 154
Solicitors' offices 24, **80–1**
Solo activities 34, **41**
    spaces for 60–1
Sony Music Entertainment [London]
    139, **178**
Sound
    compared with noise 38, 89–90,
        159, **159**
    enhancement 160
    levels in office 161
    nature of 159–60
    reduction 160, 161
Soundproof rooms 63
Space planning 119–29
    additive and subtractive
        approaches 127
    aims 119–20
    area measurement **120**
    building shell 121–5
    examples of benchmarks 190–1
    fitting needs to building shell
        126–9
    floorplate characteristics **123**
    grid modules 127–8
    measurement units used 120
    organization's needs 125–6
    relationships between
        departments/functions 125–6
Space requirements 37, 128, 190–1
    eating areas 72
    libraries 69
    work modes **177**
    workstations 4, 45, 63, 114, 130,
        148, **173**, 191
Spaces 59–77
    ancillary spaces 59, 65
    circulation spaces 59, 76–7
    jargon names used 60
    primary spaces 59, 60–4
    service spaces 59, 74–5
    social spaces 59, 71–4
    support spaces 59, 68–70
    types 59, **59**
Spatial integration 53
Spencer Fung Architects **91**
Spotlights **6**, **142**, 146, 155, **155**, **156**
Stacking 126–7
Staff rooms 74–5
Staircases **46**, **74**, 76, **76**, 78, 124

Standard Life Assurance [Edinburgh]
    39, **43**, 76, 163
Stanton Williams **20–1**, **38**, **58–9**, **75**
Status symbols 43, 85
Stimulation vs distraction 42
Storage areas 66, 75, **94**, 137–8, 163
Storage, mobile 18, 19, 61, 66, 96,
    149
    storage space for 65
Strategic brief [for project] 105,
    107–8
    data inputs **106**, 108, 190
'Street' approach 26, 78
Studios **23**, **24**, **35**, 63
    see also Drawing offices
Study cells 61, **63**
Support spaces 59, 68–70
    furniture needs 179
Sustainability 83–4
Sverdrup Facilities Inc. **24**, **37**, **42**, **49**,
    61, 148–9
System furniture 174–5
    assessment criteria 192–3

Talk Radio [London] **64**, **83**, **142**, **147**
Task lights 147, 155, **155**, **156**
Task matrix **105**
Taste
    and image/style 84
    sense 89
Taylor Joynson Garrett [London] **80–1**
Team working 34, **35**
    spaces for **16**, **17**, 62, 125
Technics 97–187
Technology, effect on change 13–14
Ted Baker Ltd **83**, **90**
Telekurs [London] **50**, **134**
Tendering 110, 183
Terraces **18**, 74
Territoriality 43
Thomas Partnership, Percy **32–3**,
    44–5
Time 13
    activity settings **63**
    executive communications **14**
    workspace occupancy **13**
Toilets 65, 124, 162, 179
Touch [sense] 89
Touch-down desks 4, 24, 60
Trading activities 26
Training suites 69
Transient space 60–1
Travel agents 73
Tye, Alan **35**

Unisex toilets 65, 162
Unitel mobile work centre **129**
Uplighters **39**, 145, 146, 147, 155,
    155, **156**

User involvement/collaboration 29,
    66, 131, 169, 180

VDTs/ VDUs (visual display
    terminals/units)
    EC/EU Directive 182
    ergonomics **39**, **40**
    lighting recommended 145
Venderettes **38**, 65, 179
Ventilation
    examples 7, 55
    modes 157
    natural **154**
    requirements 38, 157–8
    see also HVAC
VIA (Vision Into Action) International
    [London] **10–11**, 18–19
Video conferencing 48, 64
Views 38
'Virtual' concepts 15, 17
'Virtual' walkthroughs 121, 182
Vision [sense] 90, 93

Walls and partitions 135–7
    finishes 141, **142**
Waterfalls/fountains **84**, 90, 160
Waterside/riverside/canalside areas
    18, **71**
Watkins Gray International **118–19**,
    130–1
Ways of working, changing 1–2
WC cubicles 65
Western Morning News [Plymouth]
    150–1, 166–9
White noise 90, 160
Wickens Tutt Southgate [London]
    143
Windows 142–4
    openable 82, 83, 157
Wolff Olins **71**, **178**
Wood surfaces 30, 45, 140, 187
Work surfaces 173, 174
Workplace
    changing 2–3
    dynamics **16**
    pressures and threats 16–17
Workshops 74
Workstations **13**, 39, 41, **44**, **58**, 59,
    60, **66**
    ergonomics **40**
    personal 39, 51, 85, 172–3
    pricing 181, 183
    space requirements 4, 45, 63, 114,
        130, 148, **173**, 191
    time use **13**
Workstyle 2000 [BT] survey 4, 7, 8

Zoning 126–7